A Comprehensive Study

ON THE BOOK OF REVELATION

Exploring Prophecy Concerning
The Son of God ~ Yeshua

Editor:
This book was self-edited by the author.

Book Project Management:
Raindrop Creative, Inc. | StartWrite Publish Team

First paperback edition July 2024.

ISBN (paperback): 979-8-9885933-2-4

TABLE OF CONTENTS

AUTHOR NOTE

It has been decades since I first opened the Bible to the Book of Revelation. Then, as a mere babe in Christ, I knew that this bookend of the Bible was important. However, I understood very little of its content. I did at that time and even later as a young, licensed preacher of the Good News of Jesus, as many have and continue to do...eisegete *The Word of God* or attempt to make sense of what I read based upon my reasoning, even so, tremendous lack of understanding on how Biblical study should be prayerfully and carefully interpreted from the information provided therein – this is called Biblical exegesis. During my infantile approach to reading and trying to understand the Bible, I did not know about Biblical Hermeneutics, which simply means how one is to read the Bible and understand its content based upon the information God has provided for us in the sixty-six Canonical Books of the Bible widely accepted by Protestant Churches. The takeaway from what I have said should be this: *the Bible interprets itself.*

In order for the Bible to make sense, its readers must give careful attention and seek an understanding of its content broadly and collectively. Like a complex and intricate puzzle, the varied themes of the Bible need to be carefully sorted and fitted together to reveal the complete picture that God has presented; the various elements of the Bible must be understood and connected to grasp its full meaning. Each book, chapter, and verse plays a crucial role, much like individual puzzle pieces. Without the context and interplay of these parts, the grand narrative and deeper message of the Bible remain incomplete and perhaps confusing to its reader.

It has been in recent years – since the turn of the 21st Century, that my interest in Biblical Prophecy was stirred, resulting from these increasingly chaotic and uncertain times, with there being no end in sight, that I have given much time and effort to attempt to know the mind of God or to hear from Him according to His Word – the Holy Bible, as to what in the world is going on and the solution He offers to our global woes and problems. The Book of Revelation serves as a concluding book of the Bible that reflects and synthesizes the Bible's major themes and messages, not the least of which this world's woes and problems and why they are so prevalent and increasing. And ultimately, God's fix for our suffering and global crisis, even so, His restoration of all things through His Unique – eternally existing Son ~ Jesus, the promised and prophesied *Messianic King*.

With confidence, I assure you, all readers of this well-put-together and easy-to-understand book, that this piece of the puzzle – *A Comprehensive Study of The Book of Revelation* will provide you a more thorough understanding of *The Word of God* from the Book of Genesis concluding here in the Book of Revelation. Closing out this book, I share with you the *Prophetic Word of God* as found in Scripture. These scriptures, for those who have a heart to hear, thus say Yahweh ~ God, your faith in Him will be strengthened, and prayerfully others will be led to *the saving grace of Jesus!*

DEDICATION AND PREFACE

As I give thought to my grandson Harrison, my granddaughter, Rumi, and potential offspring to be granted to me by my God and Father. Having matured as a child of God and now a grandfather, I recognize all the more the increasingly godless world that each of you are growing up and living in. Therefore, I pray that you are raised by your parents to know my God, the God of the Holy Bible, who alone offers salvation through His Unique Son ~ Jesus. And that you will embrace Jesus as your Lord and Savior. My writings and preparing this study or book are motivated primarily by my concern and love for you, including the Love I have for God and, not the least of which, all of His people, *Saved and Unsaved* alike.

My adult sons and daughters, I write with you in mind, also praying for each of you with such earnest and continuous prayer that I had not engaged in before until I began to see the possibility of becoming a grandfather. Then, the reality of being blessed by God to reach this honored station in life – a grandfather has caused me to pray for my family all the more.

For those who read the Book of Revelation and grow to understand it, God, who inspired this writing (and the entirety of the Holy Bible), says, in Revelation Chapter 1:3, ESV. *"Blessed is the one who reads aloud the words of this prophecy, and blessed are those who hear, and who keep what is written in it, for the time is near:"* meaning the Second Coming of Jesus and the end and judgment of those belonging to this present evil world and Satan, and the rebellious angels.

To be blessed is for one to have a personal relationship with God, their heavenly Father and Creator. And to know the eternal future that He has prepared for all who are united as one with Him through His Unique or eternally existing Son ~ Jesus, who gave Himself as a sacrifice for the payment of our sins. Even so, for those who belong to Him to know His plans regarding dealing with the rebellions of the fallen heavenly host and those of this world who, yet, choose to remain in sinful rebellion against God and are, therefore, one with Satan and this corrupt and fallen world...such ones according to the Bible, which includes and concludes with the Book of Revelation will be cast into the Lake of Fire – the Second Death.

The Book of Revelation is undoubtedly the most challenging book of the Bible to understand for reasons you will come to see as you begin reading this book. Therefore, I have undertaken to write this study so that you may come to better understand this amazing apocalyptic work and the wisdom of God discovered herein. Nevertheless, presently, no one may perfectly explain with exactness or perfection the unfolding mysteries of this *End-Time* book of God. All the same, what I have provided in this study will give you sufficient Biblical footing or foundational understanding to stand on and thereby mature in your understanding of the mind, ways, and will of God for your sojourn on this earth and the eternal destiny that awaits you through Jesus the Messianic King. As you prayerfully seek the counsel of God for understanding, your knowledge and wisdom will permit you to comprehend the grander picture or understanding of the Bible provided by our heavenly Father. And so, for all who has an ear to hear, *"Study to shew thyself approved unto God, a workman that needeth not to be ashamed, rightly dividing the word of truth."* (2 Timothy 2:15, KJV).

Lastly, to my Bride, Lisa, and treasure from God our Father, thank you for your unceasing care, love, unwavering patience, and prayers for me!

CHAPTER 1

INTRODUCTION TO THE BOOK OF REVELATION

This book's title, Revelation (Apocalypto or Apocalypse), means uncovering or unveiling. In this Book of Revelation, Jesus is Uncovering His mysteries or hidden things to mankind, which is to be understood as a summary of the other 65 books of the Protestant Bible or Holy Writ. Where I quote Scripture in this study or book, I primarily utilize the New International Version of the Bible (NIV) and occasionally use the translations of the English Standard Version (ESV) and King James Version (KJV). The Book of Revelation is written in code, but not some deep mystical or secret coding. It's simply this, without understanding the Old Testament (O.T.) Scriptures, the book of Revelation, cannot be understood or decoded.

The understanding or interpretation of these codes or writings are provided within the manuscripts of the O.T. The O.T. is also to be understood as containing patterns or written guides pointing toward what is to occur in the future – or the *End of Days*, as provided here in the Book of Revelation. Essentially, this book of Revelation is about the Bridegroom ~ Jesus, receiving His Bride, the Church or regenerated mankind, as well as His judgment upon all who have rebelled against Him. Ultimately, what was lost in the Garden of Eden and its effects upon mankind historically is shown restored, and how Jesus is going to bring about the restoration of things as provided in this book of

Revelation. And so, the essential theme of The Book of Revelation unveils this restored union with Christ and his people – the redeemed of the Lord, the Church – Christ's Bride.

There are only 22 chapters of the book of Revelation and about 400 verses. However, 800 references to the Old Testament are contained within this book. Understanding these various texts of the O.T. is paramount to making sense of the Book of Revelation. We must keep in mind the Bible interprets or explains itself. The book of Revelation pulls or pieces together all of the O.T. prophetic writings or eschatological information, beginning from Genesis to what Jesus and other New Testament (N.T.) writers had to say when they walked this earth.

King Solomon, in the Book of Ecclesiastes 1:9, has this to say, "What has been is what will be, and what has been done is what will be done, and there is nothing new under the sun." In these Old and New Testament writings, cyclical prophetic patterns are provided that reach their consummation or ultimate fulfillment in the Book of Revelation.

Another look at understanding what I've stated regarding the O.T. and N.T. and their prophetic writings.: The New Testament is in the Old Testament contained; the Old Testament and its prophecies by the New Testament are explained; or an alternative way to consider the matter, the future is hidden in the past. It is, therefore, necessary for all Christians to be able to see or understand the Bible comprehensively in light of both the O.T. and N.T. to truly understand this extraordinary heavenly book and for one to get to know the Triune God, who inspired or breathed forth into His appointed authors this infallible account of the God of Creation and His dealing with the people of His making through what the Church calls the Holy Bible – God's Word.

This will require a lifetime of Biblical study, which is essential to understanding the Book of Revelation and developing an in-depth knowledge of our loving Creator and God and who we become in Him. With the Bible's narratives likened to pieces of a puzzle, when put together, the grand scheme or the intended view of the puzzle or Biblical landscape begins to come into view more broadly and clearly, as the narratives, like pieces of a puzzle are understood and fitted together that the picture may be seen fully or comprehended better.

God inspired the Biblical authors to write so that the Bible is understood from its greater content...in other words, the Bible's interpretation or understanding is found within itself. However, second temple writings – i.e., the Dead Sea Scrolls, the Book of Enoch, and other ancient and Rabbinical material allow the Church age to better understand the ancient Biblical culture and their thinking contextually.

These sources can assist us with better understanding the Bible, as it would also be greatly beneficial if we, students of the Bible, at times, would seek to understand our English translation of the Bible in light of its original Hebrew and Greek writings.

That said, and yet again, without referencing or having an understanding of Old Testament books such as Genesis, Exodus, Isaiah, Jeremiah, Daniel, Ezekiel, Joel, Zachariah, and others, we cannot begin to make sense of the Book of Revelation. Even so, with these sources and resources helping one understand the Book of Revelation, there are differing views regarding this End of The Age Book and the study of Eschatology or End of Days events with added and varied perspectives from what I offer in this study. As you read this book, I ask that you do not become bent out of shape or be too dogmatic about your views or the perspectives of others regarding this complex book. But rather, bear this fact in mind if you hold fast to your belief in Jesus...In the end, you win! We will reign with Him for all eternity!

Common Eschatological Views:

1. **Dispensational Premillennialism**: This view holds that human history is divided into distinct periods or dispensations, each characterized by a different way in which God interacts with humanity and reveals His will. Dispensationalists believe in a future

and yet imminent rapture of the church, where Believers are caught up or raptured to meet Christ in the air before the seven-year period known as the *Great Tribulation – God's wrath or Judgment* unleashed on earth. They maintain that after God judges the earth's inhabitants, Jesus – The Christ, will return visibly and bodily to the earth, after which He establishes His kingdom and its literal thousand-year reign on earth (the millennium), a period of peace and righteousness. This view distinguishes between God's plan for Israel and the church, seeing them as separate entities with distinct roles in God's redemptive plan. And not the belief in Replacement or Covenant Theology or Supersessionism; the universal Church belonging to Jesus does not supersede or take the place of Israel. God has not broken His covenant with His chosen people. Israel will return to Jesus, theirs, and the Church's Messiah during the Great Tribulation.

2. **Pre-Tribulation Rapture:** This belief is closely associated with dispensational premillennialism but is not a proponent of dispensationalism. It teaches that Christ will rapture Believers before the period of The Great Tribulation, sparing them from the worst of the end-time judgments. The tribulation period is typically seen as a time of unprecedented suffering and chaos on earth, culminating in the 2nd Coming or Parousia of Christ and the establishment of his millennial kingdom.

Other views of Eschatology include:

1. **Post-Tribulation Rapture**: This view holds that the rapture will occur after the tribulation period, just before Christ's visible return to earth. This position maintains that Believers will experience the tribulation alongside unbelievers but will be caught up to meet Christ as he descends to establish his kingdom.

2. **Historic Premillennialism:** Unlike dispensational premillennialism, historic premillennialism does not emphasize a sharp distinction

between Israel and the church but largely is a proponent of Replacement Theology – meaning the Church has taken the place of Israel. This view, which in varying measures is also held by proponents of the last two views, intersects with or is one with Nationalism. They believe Christ will return before a literal thousand-year period of peace but do not necessarily hold to a pre-tribulation rapture. Historic premillennialists believe that the church will undergo persecution during the tribulation but will ultimately be vindicated and reign with Christ in the millennium.

3. **Amillennialism:** This view interprets the millennium symbolically rather than literally, seeing it as the present reign of Christ in the hearts of Believers. Amillennialists do not expect a future earthly kingdom but believe Christ's return will coincide with the final judgment and the establishment of the new heaven and earth.

4. **Postmillennialism:** This position believes that the world will gradually be transformed by the spread of the gospel and the influence of Christianity, leading to a golden age of peace and righteousness. Christ will return after this spiritual and social renewal period to inaugurate the final state. Also, with these last three views, one can readily justify the false doctrine or theology of the so-called Prosperity Gospel.

Regarding Replacement Theology: It intersecting or Being One with Nationalism and both intersecting or being inseparable from American Politics:

- *In light of our highly charged and politically and racially divided nation, I believe the following insight will greatly illuminate why this nation is at such an uncertain, and I will add dangerous crossroads.*

Nationalism among white and a few "black" evangelicals in America often intersects with their religious identity and political beliefs. For the record, regarding political parties, my household is registered as

"Unaffiliated." Although I can see some good things that our two major political parties hold, both of them give me great concern regarding the direction in which they desire to take this country.

Before moving forward, I will now plainly state that America is not a Theocratic nation. Donald Trump can not be compared to King Cyrus in any sense! Lastly, it is God's desire in this dispensation of His *Grace and Mercy* to rule in and over the heart or soul of every being in particular and, without exception, those who have embraced Jesus as their Lord and Savior.

An explanation of the View regarding Nationalism:

1. **Religious Identity:** Many white and a few "black" evangelicals in America see their faith as intertwined with their national identity. They wrongly view the United States as a Christian nation, although founded on Judeo-Christian principles, and believe, yet again, wrongly that this country has a unique relationship with God – hence called Replacement theology. Jesus, at His 1st Advent to the earth, did not come to establish a Christian nation anywhere territorially but rather within the hearts of mankind. However, at His 2nd advent, Jesus will establish His Kingdom in the land or territory that He allotted or gave to Abraham and his Jewish descendants, this being Jerusalem, with the actual ancient boundaries being from the Euphrates River to the Nile River. *This land is God's sacred and cosmic territory; God has and will ultimately defend His people – the Jews and the land that is rightfully theirs. We will see this in this concluding book of the Bible.*

2. **Cultural and Social Values:** White and some "black" evangelicals often prioritize certain cultural and social values, such as traditional family structures, morality, and conservative beliefs. They may view the preservation of these values as essential to maintaining the strength and integrity of the nation. With this, I am in agreement.

3. **Political Engagement:** White and some" black" evangelicals have been actively engaged in politics, often aligning themselves with conservative political parties and candidates who promote policies that align with their religious and moral convictions. They may support politicians advocating for religious freedom, pro-life policies, and traditional marriage. With this, too, I am in agreement with regard to conservative views of Biblical moral correctness and pro-life.

4. **Nationalism and Patriotism**: Many white and some "black" evangelicals exhibit strong feelings of nationalism and patriotism, expressing pride in their country and its history. They may display symbols of patriotism, such as American flags, and participate in nationalistic events and celebrations.

5. **Concerns about Change**: Some white and "black" evangelicals perceive societal changes, such as increasing secularization, cultural diversity, and shifting social norms, as threats to their way of life and to the nation as a whole. This can lead to a defensive posture and a desire to protect what they see as traditional American values. I, too, hold common ground with the concern of secularization and shifting norms. But instead of such things being a threat to this nation, I won't necessarily argue against this position. However, I would rather put emphasis on these matters: they are rebellion against God and a threat and danger to Believers of Christ who may not be strong in their faith. Or such immoral conduct leading others away from God.

6. **Perceived Threats:** In some cases, white and some "black" evangelical nationalists may manifest as a response to perceived threats, both external (such as terrorism or foreign influence) and internal (such as liberal policies or cultural shifts). This can foster a sense of "us versus them" mentality and a desire to defend against perceived enemies. This right here is a reason for concern, and again, lending to our "Highly charged and politically divided nation.

Ultimately, this is Satan and spiritual wickedness working behind the scenes in the unseen realm, bringing chaos and division amongst mankind. What we must keep in mind is that because Satan uses mankind to do his bidding, we, therefore, are not to see our conflict as being against one another. Rather, this battle we are engaged in is spiritual. Therefore, we who are Christians must be praying people; our weaponry is spiritual, and this realm is the place of our warfare.

It's important to note that not all white and "black" evangelicals hold nationalist views, and there is a diversity of opinion within these demographics.

My current position toward eschatology or end-time events is Dispensational Premillennialism. I don't see my view changing. I believe that God has not appointed His Church to wrath: see 1 Thessalonians 1:10 and chap. 5:9. More evidence or Scriptural references will allow you to understand my positioning as you read through this study. On the other hand, there will be trouble or persecution in this world, and from this world that we – the Church will experience and have to endure even unto death John 16:33. But not such trouble of the Great Tribulation of Matthew 24:21, where God's wrath will be unleashed upon this rebellious and unrepentant world.

As we go through this rather comprehensive but not exhaustive study of the Book of Revelation, it is not my position as we study this otherworldly and prophetic Scripture found in this book to convince you to necessarily see things as I do or think as I think. Instead, it is for me to inform your thinking as we see God bringing about some critical, supernatural, and astonishing events to bring judgment upon this world and salvation to all who have ears to hear, those who will receive His Word, even Jesus Himself – the Lord of lords and King of Kings.

It is important to note that the Triune God, as revealed in Scripture, reigns Supreme! Therefore, absolutely nothing that occurs on this earth or in heaven catches Him off guard. He alone causes whatever it may be to happen to bring about His ultimate plan and greater purpose for His creation. Or He permits the heavenly host along with mankind to exercise their free will but yet to ultimately bring about His plan to deal with the rebellion of mankind and the rebellious host in heaven, the unseen or transcendental realm.

Our future for all who belong to God is in *Great Hands.* He declares in Isaiah 46:9,10: "Remember the former things of old; for I am God, and there is no other; I am God, and there is none like me, **10** declaring the end from the beginning and from ancient times things not yet done, saying, 'My counsel shall stand, and I will accomplish all my purpose,'

Therefore, regardless of what is going on or taking shape in this fallen world, regardless of God's judgment, that is soon to come upon this world. If we have been washed of our sins by the blood of Jesus – the Lamb slain before this world was created. Then, with Him, we reign as victors over death and God's final judgment. And, therefore, because of Him, we win in the end!

CHAPTER 2

FOUR INTERPRETATIVE METHODOLOGIES FOR EXAMINING THE BOOK OF REVELATION AND CHAPTERS SUMMARY

Brief Description of The Four Methodologies:

1. **Historicists:** They view the Book of Revelation as a general overview of types and patterns occurring throughout history.
2. **Preterist:** They view this book as true prophecy, but it has already been fulfilled.
3. **Futurists:** They view the Book of Revelation as if it is all still to come, literally.
4. **Polemicists:** They view this book as mere allegories, metaphors, and parables.

I believe each view holds merit, but one position doesn't make the other views invalid. Instead, together, these views give us a better understanding of the Book of Revelation.

Summary

The Book of Revelation, also known as the Apocalypse of John, is the final book of the New Testament and is considered one of the most enigmatic and complex books in the Bible. As stated, this book is attributed to the apostle John, who was shown what to write according to Jesus' instructions. This book is believed to have been written during a time of intense persecution of Christians, likely in the late first century, around AD 90.

A brief overview of the Book of Revelation, from chapters 1 through 22:

Chapters 1-3: Introduction and Letters to the Seven Churches:

- **Chapter 1:** The book begins with an introduction in which John describes his vision of Jesus Christ, who instructs him to write down what he sees and send it to the seven churches in Asia Minor (modern-day Turkey).

- **Chapters 2-3:** Seven letters are addressed to the churches in Ephesus, Smyrna, Pergamum, Thyatira, Sardis, Philadelphia, and Laodicea, containing messages of encouragement, warnings, and exhortations to repentance.

  Chapters 4-5: Vision of Heaven and the Lamb:

- **Chapter 4:** John sees a vision of the heavenly throne room, with God (the Father) seated on the throne, surrounded by elders and living creatures - Cherubs worshiping Him.

- **Chapter 5:** A scroll – God's deed to the earth, sealed with seven seals, is introduced, and only the Lamb (Jesus, the Son of God, who is the Christ) is found worthy to open it, initiating a series of God's judgments upon this rebellious world.

Chapters 6-7: Opening of the Seven Seals and Sealing of the 144,000, an appointed or completed number literally of those from the tribe of Israel to include the Saints of this era

- **Chapter 6:** The Lamb begins to open the seals, unleashing a series of judgments upon the earth, including the Four Horsemen – fallen spirit beings or Elohim and even gods of the Apocalypse, who will be used as God's agents of wrath.

- **Chapter 7:** Before the final judgment, 144,000 servants of God are sealed for protection, representing the faithful remnant of Israel and others who come to Christ.

Chapters 8-11: Trumpet Judgments and Two Witnesses:

- **Chapters 8-9:** Seven angels sound trumpets, each heralding a new judgment upon the earth, including plagues, natural disasters, and demonic locusts.

- **Chapter 10:** The mighty angel delivers a message of judgment and restoration.

- **Chapter 11:** Two witnesses prophecy in Jerusalem, performing miracles and preaching repentance before being killed by the beast – the ultimate Antichrist, who is also called the Assyrian in the Old Testament.

Chapters 12-14: The Woman, the Dragon, and The Lamb:

- **Chapter 12:** John sees a vision of a woman (representing Israel) giving birth to a male child (Jesus), who will be pursued by the dragon (Satan). The dragon is defeated by Michael, the archangel who casts Satan out of heaven.

- **Chapter 13:** Two beasts emerge, one from the sea (representing political power, with the Antichrist as its ruler and one from the earth (representing religious deception – Babylon, the revived Roman Catholic Church, the world's false religious system with the false prophet as its leader, who deceives the people and persecute and kills its antagonist.

- **Chapter 14:** The Lamb (Jesus) stands victorious with His followers, and three angels proclaim messages of judgment and salvation.

Chapters 15-16: Seven Bowl Judgments, the Worst of God's Wrath:

- **Chapter 15:** John sees a vision of seven angels with seven golden bowls containing the wrath of God, preparing to pour them out upon the earth.

- **Chapter 16:** The angels pour out the bowls, bringing devastating plagues upon the earth, culminating in the final judgment.

Chapters 17-19: The Fall of Babylon the Great – The Consolidated One World Government with the Counterfeit and False Church and The Victory of Jesus Over this System of Satan and mankind:

- **Chapter 17:** John sees a vision of a great prostitute (the false church representing spiritual adultery and worldly corruption permitted and celebrated by this Antichrist religious system) riding on a beast (representing political power and its unity and authority given it by this united government and its dictator – the Antichrist), which is revealed as the systems of Babylon, together, Babylon the Great with Satan as their God.

- **Chapter 18:** The systems of Babylon are judged and destroyed, lamented by kings, merchants, and sailors – the wealthy oligarchs and those who worship commerce, materialism, and self-achievements.

- **Chapter 19:** The heavenly hosts rejoice over the fall of Babylon the Great and the triumph of Christ, who returns as a conquering warrior to defeat His enemies.

Chapters 20-22: The Millennium, God's Final Judgment upon all who are rebellious, and The New Jerusalem:

- **Chapter 20:** Satan is bound, and Christ reigns with His saints for a thousand years (the Millennium). Afterward, Satan is released and defeated, and the final judgment takes place.

- **Chapter 21:** John sees a vision of a new heaven and a new earth, and the New Jerusalem descends from heaven, symbolizing the eternal dwelling place of God with His people.

- **Chapter 22:** The book concludes with an invitation for all who are alive to partake in the water of life – Jesus Himself, and warnings against altering this book's contents and a final prayer for the Lord's return.

Overall, the Book of Revelation is filled with vivid imagery, symbolism, and prophecy, conveying messages of judgment, redemption, and hope for Believers in the midst of persecution and tribulation. It offers encouragement to Believers to remain faithful to Christ and His teachings, even in the face of trials and great opposition, with the assurance of His ultimate victory and the promise of eternal life in His presence if we hold fast to our faith in Jesus.

In the End, We – the Bride of Jesus, His Church Win Through Christ alone, The Unique – Eternally Existing Son of God!

You have been presented with six Eschatological views on the study of the Book of Revelation and four different methodologies that are utilized to try to understand or interpret this extraordinary book.

Additionally, I mentioned that with these varying approaches to studying this book and with extra-biblical resources outside of the Bible to help one understand it contextually. That there are yet varying understandings or interpretations of the Book of Revelation. This should not cause one to be overly concerned because of the often difficult passages of Scripture contained within this book. That said, the prophetic material provided is essential reading for one's complete understanding of the Bible and knowing God's ultimate plan for His creation as He brings an end to this world as we know it.

Just the same, the Book of Revelation is not necessarily considered a book that establishes the core tenets of the Protestant Christian faith, although it brings many of them to the forefront. Therefore, where students or readers of this book may not maintain or take the same position with their interpretation of certain eschatological aspects contained therein, it is perfectly okay to agree to disagree. In order for one to know where they should stand firm on Biblical interpretation or a particular Church's doctrine or where one can be flexible or vary with concluding views, I've provided the following guide.

1. Primary Doctrines: These are the foundational beliefs that are considered essential to the Christian faith. They include doctrines such as the Trinity, the deity of Jesus Christ, salvation by grace through faith, the authority of Scripture, and the resurrection of Jesus Christ. Primary doctrines are non-negotiable and form the core of Christian belief.

2. Secondary Doctrines: These are doctrines that are important but not essential to salvation or core Christian identity. They may include beliefs about church practice, modes of baptism, views on spiritual gifts, and eschatological perspectives. While secondary doctrines may vary among different Christian traditions, they are not considered primary or foundational to the faith.

3. Tertiary Doctrines: Also known as "disputable matters" or "minor doctrines," these are beliefs that are less central to the Christian faith and are often subject to interpretation or disagreement among believers. Tertiary doctrines may include issues such as dietary practices, observance of certain holidays, or specific interpretations of prophetic passages. While these doctrines may still be important within certain contexts or traditions, they are generally considered less significant than primary and secondary doctrines.

Depending on the context and focus of theological inquiry, some theological frameworks may further categorize doctrines into additional levels or subcategories. However, primary, secondary, and tertiary doctrines provide a general framework for understanding the relative importance and centrality of different beliefs within the Christian faith.

__Note:__ I have attempted to write this book expounding line upon line to bring clarity or understanding to specific Scriptures as provided in the Book of Revelation. In so doing, and in an attempt to keep your reading or study fluid, my sharing or commentary is either expressed in italics within brackets or apart from Biblical text. I will also add that any grammatical errors you encounter in this book, these errors are mine alone. Nevertheless, this should not prevent you from greatly benefitting from the content contained within this book...not in the slightest. Let's get started!

CHAPTER 3

OUTLINE AND REVELATION CHAPTER 1

Introduction and Vision of the Son of Man:

1. **Verse 1-3:** Introduction
   - The revelation of Jesus Christ, which God gave Him to show His servants what must soon take place. John bears witness to the word of God and to the testimony of Jesus Christ, and he blesses those who read and hear the words of the prophecy and keep what is written in it, for the time is near.
2. **Verse 4-8:** Greetings to the Seven Churches
   - John addresses the seven churches in Asia: Grace and peace are extended from the Father, the seven spirits before His throne, and Jesus Christ, the faithful witness, the firstborn of the dead, and the ruler of kings on earth. He is the one who loves us and has freed us from our sins by His blood and made us a kingdom, priests to His God and Father. He is coming with the clouds, and every eye will see Him, even those who pierced Him, and all tribes of the earth will wail on account of Him.
3. **Verse 9-20:** Vision of the Son of Man
   - John identifies himself as a fellow partaker in the tribulation, kingdom, and patient endurance in Jesus. He was on the island called Patmos because of the word of God and the testimony of

Jesus. On the Lord's Day, He was in the Spirit, and He heard behind him a loud voice like a trumpet. He turned to see the voice that was speaking to him, and he saw seven golden lampstands, and in the midst of the lampstands, one like a son of man, clothed with a long robe and with a golden sash around His chest. His hair was white like wool, as white as snow, and His eyes were like a flame of fire. His feet were like burnished bronze, refined in a furnace, and His voice was like the roar of many waters. In His right hand, He held seven stars, and from His mouth came a sharp two-edged sword, and His face was like the sun shining in full strength.

As we now move into our study of the Book of Revelation, we will have revealed to us the Person of Jesus, the Power of Jesus, and the Plan or Program of Jesus. Jesus is the Author of this seemingly strangely written book, as considered by our era. John, Jesus' beloved and friend, is merely His entrusted and reliable Scribe as it was for other Biblical prophets of God.

Revelation Chapter 1

1 The revelation (*or unveiling of hidden mysteries*) from Jesus Christ, which God gave him to show his servants what must soon take place. He made it known by sending his angel (or messenger) to his servant John, **2,** who testifies to everything he saw—that is, the word of God – *the Father,* and the testimony of Jesus Christ – *His Unique Son, who in His deity also exists eternally).*

When God refers to an individual in the Bible as a friend or His beloved, as was the case for John and all born again Believers, He does not withhold His future plans from them or us, the Church – His children, or the assembly of God.

Gen. 18:17 reads, "Then the LORD said, Shall I hide from Abraham what I am about to do." In James 2:23, Abraham was called God's friend.

John 15:15 has this to say regarding Christ's Apostles and disciples,

"I no longer call you servants because a servant does not know his Master's business. Instead, I have called you friend." Abraham was informed by the angels regarding the destruction of Sodom and Gomorrah. Additionally, Daniel was provided insight into the rise and fall of great nations and the ultimate establishment of God's kingdom. We see God's prophetic proclamation throughout the Old and New Testaments.

In the New Testament, God entrusted John, whom Jesus loved, with His prophetic mysteries and End Time message to conclude the Bible. Even so, Jesus entrusted his mother to John. Therefore, John's writings can be trusted as Jesus' Word to mankind – we who are friends and, more prominently, are the children of God our Father; therefore, John's writings are certainly reliable.

3 Blessed is the one who reads aloud the words of this prophecy, and blessed are those who hear it and take to heart what is written in it because the time is near (or at hand; the doctrine of imminence, this being the resurrection of the dead and rapture of the Church and ultimately, Jesus' 2nd Coming – The End of Days. This blessing, as recorded here, is the first of seven benedictions in the Book of Revelation).

Greetings and Doxology:

4 John,

To the seven churches, (Jesus' Bride to whom He is about to provide intimate details regarding their character. *They were located* in the province of Asia (currently, Turkey, not Asia as known today). *John addresses these churches by saying,* Grace and peace to you from him who is, and who was, and who is to come (this is Jesus Himself and His eternal existence, and although was dead, He is yet alive), and from the seven spirits (or sevenfold Spirit or aspects of the Holy Spirit as provided in Isaiah 11:1,2: which are **#1** the Spirit of the Lord, **#2** of Wisdom, **#3** the Spirit of Understanding, **#4** of Counsel, **#5** the Spirit of Might. **#6** of *Knowledge*, and **#7** of the *Fear* of Yahweh. However, others view these seven spirits as Angelic beings who are seen as guardians over these churches).

Repeating verse 4: Grace and peace to you from him who is, and who was, and who is to come, and from the seven spirits before his throne (the throne of God the Father. In this greeting, the Triune God is in view – God the Father, God the Son and God the Holy Spirit), **5** and from Jesus Christ, who is the faithful witness, (of God His Father: see John 8:18 and Yeshua or Jesus – the Son of God a martyr for the cause of His Father), the firstborn from the dead, and the ruler of the kings of the earth. (Jesus, having conquered the Devil, Death, and the grave or Hades, is now held as Ruler and King over all things: see Col. 1:18; Matt. 28:18 and Eph. 1:20-22).

It is important that we understand that throughout Scripture, God speaks utilizing numbers, signs, and symbols, which John's Jewish readers and audiences would have understood. As students of the Bible, we must, therefore, perform our due diligence to understand and rightly apply these military-like codes or hidden mysteries of God that served to protect His people by keeping their enemies and His enemies in the dark.

Also, throughout the Bible, God utilizes the pattern of seven (or His Heptadic structure), which is akin to God's signature, as He unfolds His completed or perfected meanings, their significance, or mysteries of what He is providing in this usage of seven as well as other numbers and symbols containing and conveying His hidden truths. God does everything in sevens, establishing his governmental work on earth and signing off on it, indicating completion or perfection. In the Book of Revelation, fifty explicit groups of sevens are mentioned; I'll list a few: seven churches, seven stars, seven candle sticks, seven seals, seven bowls, and seven trumpets; also see Daniel 9:24-27.

Now ending verse 5, To him - *Jesus* who loves us and has freed us from our sins by his blood, **6** and has made us to be a kingdom and priests (or better translated who are kings and priests) to serve his God and Father—to him be glory and power forever and ever! Amen. ***Verse 7 John***

says, "Look, he is coming with the clouds," and "every eye will see him (this occurs during Jesus' 2nd advent, unlike His coming as a thief in the night was mentioned in 1 Thess. 5:2, this view encompassing the resurrection of the dead and rapture of the Church); *and so, everyone will see him at His 2nd Coming* even those who pierced him," and all peoples on earth "will mourn because of him." So shall it be! Amen. **8** "I am the Alpha and the Omega," says the Lord God, "who is, and who was, and who is to come, the Almighty." (God the Father is speaking; He speaks only once more in Rev. 21:5,6. Here and there, He is representing His Supremacy and triune existence with God the Son and God the Holy Spirit; together, they are One. Even as man is one, therein possessing our triunity of mind, body, and spirit – hence, we are living souls).

John's Vision of Christ:

9 I, John, your brother and companion in the suffering and kingdom and patient endurance that are ours in Jesus, was on the island of Patmos because of the word of God and the testimony (or John's faith and witness) of Jesus (John was therefore, subsequently imprisoned on this island because of government-sponsored persecution: see John 15:20; Matt. 5:10-12 and 1 Thes. 3:4). **10** On the Lord's Day (understood by some as the Day of the Lord – the end of days or this era's looming final judgment: see Joel 2:1,2. However, many believe this day meant Sunday). I was in the Spirit *(says John, this being his heightened sensory awareness resulting from God allowing him to see into the spiritual realm),* and I heard behind me a loud voice like a trumpet (the sound of a trumpet is a signal for what was to unfold or come next. The Jews had different trumpets that indicated different intentions by their leaders, i.e., the trumpet blown before the rapture, a trumpet blast before Israel went to war, and the trumpet sounding before God's coming judgment). *And so, John stated, I heard behind me a loud voice like a trumpet* **11** which said: "Write on a scroll what you see and send it to the seven churches: to

Ephesus, Smyrna, Pergamum, Thyatira, Sardis, Philadelphia and Laodicea." (John's writing comprises the entire Book of Revelation).

12 I turned around to see the voice that was speaking to me. And when I turned, I saw seven golden lampstands, **13,** and among the lampstands (representing the seven churches as seen in heaven) was someone like a son of man – *Jesus Himself.* (See Daniel Chapter 7:13,14 and John 5:26,27. Seven revelations or pictures are now to be given regarding the character or nature of Jesus). He – *the Son of Man* was dressed in a robe reaching down to his feet and with a golden sash around his chest (a picture of Jesus being both King and the Great High Priest).

14 The hair on his head was white like wool, as white as snow (representing His purity and wisdom), and his eyes were like blazing fire (His divine judgment and omniscience are in view). **15** His feet were like bronze glowing in a furnace (representing His strength and soundness and His readiness to Judge), and his voice was like the sound of rushing waters (a picture of Jesus' Supreme Authority and power). **16** In his right hand, he held seven stars (which are the angels or the messengers to these pastors, or as some believe, the stars are the pastors of these churches), and coming out of his mouth – *the mouth of Jesus* was a sharp, double-edged sword (a picture of Jesus' absolute power and justice that His word wields is presented here). His face was like the sun shining in all its brilliance (a depiction of Jesus' divine glory and majesty, also a pointing back to His transfiguration: see Matt. Chap. 17).

John's Reaction:

17 When I saw him, I fell at his feet as though dead. (As it was for John, our encounter with Jesus should be life-transforming towards awe and reverence of Him. And His Word as provided in Scripture, not simply knowledge to be acquired by reading it. But rather Jesus' Word leading to our transformation unto eternal life). ***Continuing with verse 17,*** Then he – *Jesus* placed his right hand (to display comfort and blessings) on me and said: "Do not be afraid. I am the First and the Last. **18** I am the Living One; I was dead, and now look, I am alive forever and ever! And I hold the keys of death and Hades. (Death has been mankind's dread. However, Jesus has defeated both death and Hades – the place for the dead and, currently, all who die or sleep in the Lord. Of these things, true Believers in Christ are no longer to fear)!

John's Commission to Write a Table of Content of Sorts:

19 "Write, therefore, what you have seen (that is, John's walk with Jesus during His ministry on earth and perhaps his gospel writing and three epistles depending upon their actual dating), *and* what is now (the Church being under great persecution and their challenges), and what will take place later (*the End of Days or End Times,* we are currently in this final era. However, God's wrath is yet to come. Beginning in chapter 4, and from that point on, there is no mention of the Church. Revelation 7:14 gives us a picture of a specific multitude of people in heaven, but they are identified as coming out from the Great Tribulation; therefore, this can't be the Church. Much later, in Rev. 19:6-10, we are shown that the universal Church is observed worshipping in heaven. However, it is not until Rev. Chapters 21 and 22 that the Church or the Bride of Christ is seen descending from heaven with Jesus, their Bridegroom.

This indicates to me and others that the Church is not on earth during the outpouring of God's wrath, which John will shortly begin to describe in chapter 6; what dread will begin to befall those who remain on earth. After God's judgments are completed, then the Church will return with Jesus. Reason and Scripture suggest that Christ's Bride, those of His kingdom, will not suffer with those who are on the earth at this time – those who will become Saints of God and the wicked and rebellious ones of this fallen world).

20 The mystery of the seven stars that you saw in my right hand and of the seven golden lampstands is this: The seven stars are the angels (or messengers, whether actual angels or pastors is debated) of the seven churches, and the seven lampstands are the seven churches.

CHAPTER 4

OUTLINE AND REVELATION CHAPTER 2

Messages to the Seven Churches - Part 1:

1. **Verse 1-7:** Message to the Church in Ephesus
   - Introduction: Jesus speaks to the angel of the church in Ephesus, commending their hard work, perseverance, and discernment in testing false apostles.
   - The Rebuke: Nevertheless, Jesus rebukes them for losing their first love.
   - The Warning: Jesus warns them to repent and do the works they did at first, or else He will remove their lampstand from its place.
   - The Promise: To the one who conquers, Jesus promises the right to eat of the tree of life in the paradise of God.
2. **Verse 8-11:** Message to the Church in Smyrna
   - Introduction: Jesus speaks to the angel of the church in Smyrna, acknowledging their tribulation and poverty.
   - The Encouragement: Jesus encourages them not to fear the suffering they will endure but to remain faithful, even to the point of death.
   - The Promise: To the one who conquers, Jesus promises the crown of life and exemption from the second death.

3. **Verse 12-17:** Message to the Church in Pergamum
   - Introduction: Jesus speaks to the angel of the church in Pergamum, acknowledging their faithful witness, even in the face of persecution.
   - The Rebuke: Jesus rebukes them for tolerating false teachings and practices, such as the teachings of Balaam and the Nicolaitans.
   - The Warning: Jesus warns them to repent, or else He will come and war against them with the sword of His mouth.
   - The Promise: To the one who conquers, Jesus promises hidden manna and a white stone with a new name written on it.
4. **Verse 18-29:** Message to the Church in Thyatira
   - Introduction: Jesus speaks to the angel of the church in Thyatira, commending their love, faith, service, and patient endurance.
   - The Rebuke: Jesus rebukes them for tolerating the false prophetess Jezebel, who leads His servants into sexual immorality and idolatry.
   - The Warning: Jesus warns them to repent and turn away from these practices, or else He will come and throw Jezebel and her followers into great tribulation.
   - The Promise: To the one who conquers and keeps Jesus' works until the end, He promises authority over the nations and the morning star.

This chapter contains messages from Jesus to four of the seven churches in Asia Minor, highlighting their commendable actions, rebuking their shortcomings, offering warnings, and promising rewards for those who overcome.

Revelation Chapter 2

We are now to look at the condition of seven literal churches, which were house churches and Christians in general. Jesus, like a Doctor, is going to examine and diagnose the ills and spiritual health challenges of each church. The spiritual shortcomings of these churches can be found in today's churches and in us individually. Interestingly, the order in which these churches are presented to us. Many dispensationalists understand them as a pattern of sorts of historical unfolding or seven dispensations or stages of the Christian church's history.

Provided in the letters to each of these seven churches, Jesus employed seven elements or outlines for addressing them: **#1** The meaning of the Church's name. **#2** Revelation of Jesus regarding the churches. **#3** What is good about the churches. And **#4** What is bad about the churches. **#5** Jesus offers Encouragement or exhortation toward the churches. **#6** His promises or rewards for the churches. And **#7** Jesus commands for each church – to hear His Words. However, the church of Smyrna had only six elements. Nothing bad was said about this church.

There are 4 applications to each church: **1**. Local – there are currently churches just like them. **2**. General – there are aspects of these churches in today's churches. **3**. There are things about these Churches that speak to us personally. And **4**. These churches are used by Jesus to provide us with a prophetic end-time history. The interpretation of the seven churches in the Book of Revelation as a prophetic timeline or a representation of historical epochs.

Overview Of This Interpretation:

1. Ephesus (Revelation 2:1-7): Often seen as representing the apostolic age of the early church, characterized by fervent love for Christ but also warned about losing their first love. This church is in grave peril.

2. Smyrna (Revelation 2:8-11): Considered to symbolize the period of intense persecution against the church, particularly during the Roman Empire's persecution of Christians.

3. Pergamum (Revelation 2:12-17): Interpreted as reflecting the era when the church compromised with pagan practices and doctrines,

corresponding to the time of Constantine and the merging of Christianity with the ancient Roman state.

4. Thyatira (Revelation 2:18-29): Often associated with the medieval church, characterized by corruption, compromise, and the rise of false teachings from religious authority.

5. Sardis (Revelation 3:1-6): Viewed as representing the period of the Reformation, where the church experienced a revival of true faith but also faced spiritual deadness and nominal Christianity.

6. Philadelphia (Revelation 3:7-13): Considered to symbolize the era of evangelical missions and revival movements, marked by a faithful remnant spreading the Gospel despite opposition.

7. Laodicea (Revelation 3:14-22): Interpreted as representing the end times or the modern church era characterized by lukewarmness, materialism, and spiritual complacency. This church is also facing grave peril. That said, any church or either of us can be identified with each of these churches at any given time.

This interpretation sees the letters to the seven churches not only as specific messages to the historical churches in Asia Minor but also as symbolic representations of broader spiritual conditions and trends throughout church history. However, it's essential to note that this view is just one of many interpretations of the Book of Revelation, and different scholars and theologians may have varying perspectives on its meaning and significance.

Church in Ephesus:

The Apostolic Church.

1 "To the angel (perhaps a member of the heavenly host charged with revealing Jesus' truth. Or a letter written directly to the Church's Overseer. Whomever it may be or both, John is instructed to write), **To the angel a of the church in Ephesus write:**

These are the words of him who holds the seven stars in his right hand and walks among the seven golden lampstands. **2** I know your deeds, your hard work, and your perseverance. I know that you cannot tolerate wicked people, that you have tested those who claim to be apostles but are not and have found them false. **3** You have persevered and have endured hardships for my name and have not grown weary.

4 Yet I hold this against you: You have forsaken the love you had at first (love for Jesus Himself and, perhaps specifically, the difficult lost souls of this world they had lost love for). **5** Consider how far you have fallen! Repent and do the things you did at first. If you do not repent, I will come to you and remove your lampstand from its place. **6** But you have this in your favor: You hate the practices of the Nicolaitans, which I also hate. (Their sin, some are inclined to believe, was in abusing the grace of God in order to excuse immoral behavior, in particular, sexual sin: see Rom. 6:1,2).

7 Whoever has ears, let them hear what the Spirit (indicating that these are love letters from God and even the Doctor's written spiritual examination of their condition) says to the churches (these letters were to be shared and read throughout the churches). To the one (this also includes each of us) who is victorious (by remaining faithful to Jesus), I will give the right to eat from the Tree of Life, which is in the paradise of God (whereby the faithful and or victors being in the presence of Jesus for all eternity).

Church in Smyrna:

The Persecuted Church. Jesus had no rebuke of this church.

8 *"To the angel of the church in Smyrna write:*

These are the words of him who is the First and the Last, who died and came to life again. **9** I know your afflictions and your poverty (these churches were being denied civil liberties by townsmen or those belonging to the trade guilds if not by the State to earn wages that they may function normally within what was to be free-enterprise; therefore, they experience abject poverty because they were Christians) —yet you are rich – *Jesus says* (because they were one with Him, possessing already and yet to come their eternal hope and great reward)! I know about the slander of those who say they are Jews and are not but are a synagogue of Satan. (Not every person who calls themselves a Christian is a child of God. But rather, they do the evil work of Satan, and they even belong to him – their father; such people God will judge! On the other hand, the child of God will be known by their love for others, their obedience to God, and such ones possessing the Fruit of the Spirit).

10 Do not be afraid of what you are about to suffer. I tell you, the devil will put some of you in prison to test you, and you will suffer persecution for ten days. (Something worth noting: 10 specific Roman Emperors persecuted the church over a period of 2 hundred years. Under their rule, it is believed that around 5 million Christians were martyred for their faith in Jesus. I remind you Biblical prophecies are cyclical. Children of the Living God, are you prepared to face such persecution... It is coming)! ***Continuing with verse* 10,** be faithful, even to the point of death, and I will give you life as your victor's crown. **11** Whoever has ears, let them hear what the Spirit says to the churches. The one who is victorious will not be hurt at all by the second death.

Church in Pergamum:

The Worldly Church is a mixed marriage of sorts, as some suggest, as found in the meaning of the name of this church. Any church with extreme pagan practices with the extreme of this marriage is a church that has strong governmental ties and influence on or control of people through its laws, like that of the Ancient Roman Catholic Church, beginning with the rule of Constantine in the 4th century and evolving into the institution of Papal authority. Listen! This, now loosely speaking, regarding this so-called United States of America, and those on the "Right" and certainly the "Far-Right," seems to be advocating for such church and State marriage, which is spiritual adultery; more on this later.

This church in Pergamum may have also embraced Gnosticism: Gnosticism is a religious and philosophical movement that emerged in the early Christian era, particularly in the first few centuries AD. Gnosticism emphasizes the pursuit of secret or hidden knowledge (gnosis) to be discovered within man or apart from God as the means to achieve some alternative methods to salvation as they define salvation and spiritual enlightenment. Gnostics claimed to possess special insights into the divine realm and the nature of reality, often through mystical experiences or esoteric teachings. The embrace of Yoga, in its essence, involves such practices; additionally, a range of New Age teachings holds such views. Are you committing spiritual adultery?

Gnosticism is, therefore, to be characterized by dualistic beliefs, the idea of a divine spark within humanity trapped in a material world, and the belief that salvation comes through knowledge of one's true spiritual nature and liberation from the material realm. Gnosticism also often rejected the physical world as inherently evil or inferior to the spiritual realm. Along with this ideology, what the Bible calls sexual sin, they permitted; they even taught that Jesus did not bear the image of man – in other words, Jesus did not take on a body of flesh. Gnosticism was considered heretical by early Christian leaders and was condemned by many church fathers for its rejection of orthodox Christian teachings and its emphasis on secret knowledge over faith in Jesus Christ alone. Despite this, Gnostic ideas and texts have had a lasting influence on Christian theology and spirituality. I will now ask again. Are you committing spiritual whoredom)?

12 *"To the angel of the church in Pergamum, write:*

These are the words of him who has the sharp, double-edged sword. (Jesus' Word brings judgment and division; it surgically probes or pierces to the depth of mankind's soul, whereby exposing our innermost self: see Heb. 4:12). **13** *Jesus says*, I know where you live—where Satan has his throne. Yet you remain true to my name. You did not renounce your faith in me, not even in the days of Antipas, my faithful witness, who was put to death in your city—where Satan lives.

14 Nevertheless, I have a few things against you: There are some among you who hold to the teaching of Balaam, who taught Balak to entice the Israelites to sin so that they ate food sacrificed to idols and committed sexual immorality. **15** Likewise, you also have those who hold to the teaching of the Nicolaitans. **16** Repent, therefore! Otherwise, I will soon come to you and will fight against them with the sword of my mouth.

17 Whoever has ears, let them hear what the Spirit says to the churches. To the one who is victorious, I will give some of the hidden manna. I will also give that person a white stone with a new name written on it, known only to the one who receives it (as transformed individuals indicated by our new name. And an invitation of sorts given as represented by this white stone, we are, therefore, granted access to God's banquet).

Church in Thyatira:

Meaning daughter, and this name Thyatira is believed to be associated with Semiramis, the alleged wife of Nimrod; moreover, Thyatira means continuing sacrifice. Such churches are present today, and they represent a sacramental church – hence, a church that embraces pagan rituals and beliefs instead of Salvation through Christ alone and early Church orthodoxy. Within this Church of Thyatira, their practices or teachings were akin to practices held by the ancient and current so-called "Roman Catholic Church." A church, also operating as an arm of government with political influence and inherent power and authority – namely, Popes. Or other appointed or self-appointed heads over such questionable churches that will ultimately be established by this world's end-time system – Babylon the Great. Wherein leadership was often accompanied by gross immorality, as seen during the Middle Ages under the Vatican, where murder, infanticide, gross sexual immorality, bribery, etc., was prevalent within this system and, according to the Book of Revelation, will reemerge. And of which is present but has yet to reach maturity, but it will according to the Book of Revelation. This church may have also embraced Gnosticism.

18 *"To the angel of the church in Thyatira, write:*

These are the words of the Son of God, whose eyes are like blazing fire and whose feet are like burnished bronze (these are symbols of Jesus's readiness to administer His righteous judgment. Here only was this emphasis made on Jesus' identification as being the Son of God to this church because of the city's idol worship of foreign gods, wherein Apollo and the Emperor were acclaimed as the sons of Zeus). *Verse 19, Jesus says,* I know your deeds, your love and faith, your service *or ministry* and perseverance, and that you are now doing more than you did at first.

20 Nevertheless, I have this against you: You tolerate that woman Jezebel, who calls herself a prophet. (Jezebel was the wicked and rebellious woman of the Old Testament who killed God's prophets in order to silence His "Word," she instead taught and welcomed false doctrines and rejected true prophecy from God. Moreover, she was married to the minor Antichrist, Ahab, one of many Antichrists, the evil king of Israel. There were many minor Antichrists seen throughout the Bible; Jesus, additionally, warns His Church that many are among them/us and many more will come before the arrival of the last and ultimate Antichrist. What the spirit of Jezebel teaches is that the church can compromise and be one with this world, whereby dancing with the Devil. For any church or person partnering with the Devil, this is a deadly two-step!

John has this to say to the churches in his epistle, **1 John 2:18:** "Dear children, this is the last hour; and as you have heard that the antichrist is coming, even now many antichrists have come. This is how we know it is

41

the last hour. **19** They went out from us, but they did not really belong to us. For if they had belonged to us, they would have remained with us, but their going showed that none of them belonged to us. Also, see Matt. 24:4,5; Mark 13:5,6; and Luke 21:8.

These individuals or antichrists are and will be akin to Judas, whereby associating themselves closely with the Church, nevertheless, who was never nor will be one with Jesus in heart, but rather are of the same spirit as Judas. We will learn more about Judas and the like when we get to chapter 13 of this Book of Revelation. On the other hand, there have been and will be those who forsake Christ, not such ones who have the spirit of Judas, but rather those souls who, from fear and persecution, abandon their faith in Jesus. And so, we clearly see there are false representatives of or within the church who never belonged to God, like Judas, who is called the son of perdition.

And yet, there are other well-intended, although being babes or weak followers of Christ, who, as free-willed children of God and fearful individuals, have and will commit apostasy for the sake of self-preservation or for whatever the reason; this leading to their forfeiture of Salvation and God's grace. The subject of Once Saved Always Saved and the idea, now broadly speaking, on the Doctrine of Election in light of Scripture evidence doesn't hold up. God has given mankind free will virtues unto good or evil, allowing individuals to choose their actions and shape their destinies according to their own moral agency or conscience. We must, therefore, choose whom we will serve or partner with unto life eternal or unto death and eternal suffering. For those of you who find it hard to believe in Jesus and the contents of the Bible. With a sincere heart, offer this simple prayer: "Jesus, I'm struggling to believe in you; help me!" Then start reading your Bible, beginning with the New Testament and the gospel of Matthew, and also find a true Believer in Christ to talk to.

Concluding verse 20, *By her – Jezebel's* teaching, she misleads my servants – *says Jesus* into sexual immorality and the eating of food sacrificed to idols (or false gods that they may gain this world; instead of

Jesus who gave Himself a sacrifice for all who will believe in Him). **21** I have given her time to repent of her immorality, but she is unwilling. **22** So I will cast her (this person is mentioned as an actual woman who has wrongly assumed some form of authority over this church). *Because of her unwillingness to repent from her evil teaching and practices, Jesus declares* I will cast her on a bed of suffering, and I will make those who commit adultery with her suffer intensely unless they repent of her ways. **23** I will strike her children dead (because they will also embrace her and Satan's lies). Then all the churches will know that I am he who searches hearts and minds, and I will repay each of you according to your deeds.

24 Now I say to the rest of you in Thyatira, to you who do not hold to her teaching and have not learned Satan's so-called deep secrets, 'I will not impose any other burden on you, **25** except to hold on to what you have until I come.' (We are being sharply reminded to remain faithful to Jesus. Or there will be dire consequences for the unrepentant, and to the far extreme, one's name being removed from the Lamb's Book of Life such ones who remain in or practice the sinful ways of this world: see Rev. 3:5).

26 To the one who is victorious and does my will to the end, I will give authority over the nations— **27** that one 'will rule them with an iron scepter and will dash them to pieces like pottery —just as I have received authority from my Father (this will occur when Jesus returns and establishes His millennial reign on earth). **28** I will also give that one the morning star. (The faithful ones of Christ will behold Him – our Bright and Morning Star, the Light of The World: see Rev. 22:16 and John 8:12). **29** Whoever has ears, let them hear what the Spirit says to the churches.

Outline and Revelation Chapter 3

Letters to the Churches (Continued):

1. **Verse 1-6:** Letter to the Church in Sardis
   - The letter is addressed to the angel of the church in Sardis. Jesus identifies Himself as the one who has the seven spirits of God and the seven stars. He acknowledges their reputation for being alive, but He warns them that they are dead spiritually. He urges them to wake up and strengthen what remains, for their works are not complete in the sight of God. He reminds them to remember what they have received and heard and to repent. Otherwise, He will come like a thief (this could be a reference to one's death, Christ's rapture of the Church, which is the commonly held view, or perhaps even Christ's His Second Coming), and they will not know at what hour He will come. Yet, there are a few in Sardis who have not soiled their garments (through unfaithfulness or spiritual whoredom), and they will walk with Him in white, for they are worthy.
2. **Verse 7-13:** Letter to the Church in Philadelphia
   - The letter is addressed to the angel of the church in Philadelphia. Jesus identifies Himself as the holy one, the true one, who has the key of David, who opens and no one will shut, who shuts and no

one opens. He commends them for their works and acknowledges their patient endurance. He promises to keep them from the hour of trial that is coming on the whole world, to try those who dwell on the earth. He encourages them to hold fast to what they have so that no one may seize their crown. He promises that He will make those of the synagogue of Satan bow down before their feet and know that He has loved them. He urges them to hold fast to what they have so that no one may seize their crown.

3. **Verse 14-22:** Letter to the Church in Laodicea
   - The letter is addressed to the angel of the church in Laodicea. Jesus identifies Himself as the Amen, the faithful and true witness, the beginning of God's creation. He rebukes the Laodiceans for being lukewarm, neither hot nor cold. He warns them that because they are neither hot nor cold but lukewarm, He will spit them out of His mouth. He advises them to buy from Him gold refined by fire so that they may be rich and white garments to clothe themselves and to cover their shame. He counsels them to anoint their eyes with eye salve so that they may see. He declares that He reproves and disciplines those whom He loves, so they should be zealous and repent. He stands at the door and knocks; if anyone hears His voice and opens the door, He will come in and eat with him, and he with Him. He promises that to the one who conquers, He will grant him to sit with Him on His throne, as He also conquered and sat down with His Father on His throne.

This chapter continues the letters to the churches, addressing the churches in Sardis, Philadelphia, and Laodicea. Each letter contains commendations, rebukes, and exhortations specific to the spiritual condition and challenges facing each church.

Revelation Chapter 3

Church in Sardis:

Such churches are now in existence, protestant or denominational churches that broke away from the self-proclaimed, pagan, and heretical "ancient Roman Catholic Church" during the period of the Renaissance and Protestant Reformation. As for what Sardis means, it is not known. How does this church relate to some Protestant churches today? Well... they don't know what they stand for; they are operating in the flesh. Even so, the world has begun to infiltrate many of these churches because they are spiritually sleepwalking or spiritually dead.

1 "To the angel a of the church in Sardis write:

These are the words of him who holds the seven spirits of God and the seven stars. I know your deeds; you have a reputation of being alive, but you are dead – *Jesus said*. (Works without Christ are dead! There are many who call themselves Christians; however, they are nominal or Christians by name only. These folks are, in fact, dead; the Holy Spirit and obedience to Jesus are not evidenced in their lives. This is a church or an individual that has whitewashed tombs, which look beautiful on the outside but on the inside are full of bones of the dead and everything unclean. In the same way, on the outside, *they* appear to people as righteous, but on the inside, *they* are full of hypocrisy and wickedness: see Matt. 23:27,28).

Therefore, Jesus says, 2 Wake up! (This church was no longer attentive or faithful to Jesus from whom they received life and spiritual vitality). *Jesus warns them,* Strengthen what remains and is about to die, for I have found your deeds unfinished in the sight of my God. 3 Remember, therefore, what you have received and heard; hold it fast, and repent. But if you do not wake up, I will come like a thief, and you will not know at what time I will come to you. (Everyone has a time that is appointed to death: see Job, 14:5 and Hebrews 9:27, which can be likened to a thief in the night when one chooses to live after the course of this world. The question is...Are you ready to meet with death; thereafter, either judgment unto eternal life, or will your sentence be to perdition, which will be awaiting your entrance)?

4 Yet you have a few people in Sardis who have not soiled their clothes (or returned to the ways or sustenance of this lifeless world). They will walk with me, dressed in white, for they are worthy. **5** The one who is victorious will, like them, be dressed in white (such ones are no longer stained by sin or the filthiness of this world). I will never blot out the name of that person from the Book of life, but will acknowledge that name before my Father and his angels. (See Ex. 32:32; Ps. 69:28 and Dan. 12:1. However, for those who have chosen to be reunited with death or soil themselves with this wicked and adulterous world, their name will be removed from the Book of Life). **6** Whoever has ears, let them hear what the Spirit says to the churches.

Church in Philadelphia:

It is considered a Missionary church; its name means brotherly love.

7 *"To the angel of the church in Philadelphia, write:*

These are the words of him who is holy and true (such was this church), who holds the key of David (Jesus is the promised Messianic King who is to reign on David's throne forever. He alone grants admittance to His kingdom: see Isa. 9:6,7). What he – *Jesus* opens, no one can shut, and what he shuts, no one can open. (If we remain one with Jesus, we are kept safe and secure in Him. However, until we are called or brought to our eternal and perfected state, we must remain a submitted and faithful Bride to Jesus' Lordship; in this way, we are kept secure in Him. Nevertheless, Jesus dares not, but more importantly, neither can He force His will upon us nor force one to remain one with

Him or faithful to Him; this would not be love. Jesus will not hold us against our will; He will, nevertheless, give us over to our desires, as it was for Adam and Eve, as well as all others who have rebelled against Him or His Truth. One's liberty to choose to remain faithful to God or to reject Him is seen throughout the Bible and remains the case for the Saved and unsaved alike. Yes, it is Jesus who draws sinful mankind to His saving grace. Just the same, mankind can decide to go their own way as they reject their Bridegroom – the One who loves them beyond measure).

8 *Jesus says,* I know your deeds. See, I have placed before you an open door that no one can shut. I know that you have little strength, yet you have kept my word and have not denied my name. **9** I will make those who are of the synagogue of Satan, who claim to be Jews (a true Jew exercises faith in Jesus alone) though they are not – *true Jews, but rather who belong to Satan,* but are liars—I will make them come and fall down at your feet (the feet of the Bride of Christ or His Church) and acknowledge that I have loved you (all true Believers in Jesus both Jews and Gentiles, who have become children of God). **10** Since you have kept my command to endure patiently, I will also keep you from the hour of trial that is going to come on the whole world to test the inhabitants of the earth. (And so here we have it. God's loving and faithful Bride – His Church will not experience His hour of wrath – the Great Tribulation that is to come upon the rebellious people of this world).

11 I am coming soon. **Hold on** to what you have so that no one will take your crown (There is a spiritual war occurring! Satan, the enemy of our soul and God's enemy, wants our crown, our very Salvation. This is the only way that he can target God – that is, by coming after us, God's Bride or his beloved children, in an attempt to turn us from our Faith in God our Father or to keep others from faith in God their Creator). **12** The one **who is victorious** I will make a pillar in the temple of my God. Never again will they leave it. I will write on them the name of my God and the name of the city of my God, the new Jerusalem, which is coming down out of heaven from my God; and I will also write on them my new name. (As a wife carries her spouse's name, so will we carry the new name Jesus assigns to us. Yes, we will belong to Him forever and ever; there will be no death to do us part; Death and the Devil will have been eradicated)! **13** Whoever has ears, let them hear what the Spirit says to the churches.

Church in Laodicea:

Laodicea means people's own opinions; this church was doing its own thing; there was no godly accountability within its ranks. This church was indifferent, a church in name only, and greatly deceived because of what they had acquired and had going on – a mere form of godliness; they were a theater with everyone being actors, and everyone was being entertained. There is no accommodation for this church.

Bear in mind, as we advance in this study of the Book of Revelation, the word church is not mentioned again until Revelation 22:16. This suggests to me that the church has indeed been raptured).

14 "To the angel of the church in Laodicea, write:

These are the words of the Amen, the faithful and true witness (unlike this church); *however*, the ruler of God's creation – *Jesus, He is faithful. Jesus says,* **15** I know your deeds that you are neither cold nor hot. I wish you were either one or the other! **16** So, because you are lukewarm—neither hot nor cold—I am about to spit – or vomit you out of my mouth (which is a better rendering because they held no spiritual benefit at all; they merely had a form of godliness, but no spiritual fire, not even a little bit). *Jesus continues,* **17** You say, 'I am rich; I have acquired wealth and do not need a thing.' But you do not realize that you are wretched, pitiful, poor, blind, and naked. **18** I counsel you to buy from me gold refined in the fire, so you can become rich; white clothes to wear, so you can cover your shameful nakedness; and salve to put on your eyes, so you can see.

This church had become one with the world, self-sufficient, and facing peril. However, Jesus is offering them Salvation as seen by Him offering them refined gold or they becoming refined by Him, and thereby receiving white garments and spiritual healing for their blindness caused by this world or Satan's deception regarding spiritual truth or Jesus' Truth that Satan wanted to keep them and us in darkness or blindness to.

19 Those whom I love I rebuke and discipline. So be earnest and repent. **20** Here I am! I stand at the door and knock. If anyone hears my voice and opens the door, I will come in and eat with that person, and they with me. (People, Jesus wants us to dine with Him! Listen. He is knocking on the door of our hearts. However, He must be welcomed to indwell within our hearts and to be completely embraced in the church and by each of us individually as Lord and Savior that we may be with Him at His Father's Great Banquet. Jesus being our Lord, we must be committed to following His will for our lives in sacrificial service, worship, and praise of Him. When a church or a person becomes complacent and comfortable because of what they have accomplished and, therefore, forgetting about God, they become indifferent to spiritual matters and concerns. This church was in dire need of spiritual conversion)!

21 To the one who is victorious (indeed, we must contend for our faith; Satan wants to keep us in bondage and spiritual blindness: see Jude 1:3. 1 Tim. 6:12 reminds us that we must fight the good fight of faith; this life that we live is actively and constantly engaged in spiritual warfare; therefore, we must prayerfully fight the good fight of faith). To the victors, *Jesus proclaims that* He will give them the right to sit with *Him* on *His* throne, just as *He* was victorious and sat down with *His* Father on his throne. (Indeed, we must remain faithful). Lastly, Jesus proclaims, **22** Whoever has ears, let them hear what the Spirit says to the churches."

A Look at This Word Rapture:

In Greek, rapture is rendered as the word Harpazo. The Greek word "ἁρπάζω" (harpazó) primarily means "to seize," "to snatch away," or "caught up." It can imply a sudden, forceful action of taking something or someone away. This word is used in various contexts in the New Testament, including descriptions of sudden actions or events, such as the catching away of Believers in passages like 1 Thessalonians 4:17. Additionally, it can convey the idea of seizing or taking hold of something with urgency or decisiveness. I've provided a few usages of this word from the New Testament.

Rapture or Harpazo usage found in Scripture:

Matt. 11:12 - Grab violently.   **Matt. 13:19** - Seed Snatched away.
Mark 3:27 - Plunder, the strong man. **John 10:12** - Attack or Carry off.
John 10:28, 29 - Father's hand.   **Acts 8:39** - Vanish or disappear.
Acts 23:10 - Soldiers rescue.   **2 Cor. 12:2-4** - Paul's visit to heaven.
Jude 1:22-23 - Saved from fire.   **Rev. 12:5** - Caught up to heaven.

7 Literal Raptures or Translations in the Bible according to the meaning of Harpazo:

Enoch –   Gen. 5:24; Jude 1:14 and Heb. 11:5
Elijah –   2 Kings 2: 5 &11
Paul –   2 Cor. 12:2 and Acts 14:19,20
Phillip –   Acts 8:39
Jesus –   Acts 1:9
John –   Rev. 4:1
The two Witnesses – Rev. 11:11

Pictures of Rescues or Raptures:

Lot's Family –	Gen. 19:15,16
Noah's Family –	Gen. 7:9,10
Joash –	2 Chron. 22:11,12 and 2 Kings 11:3,4
Rehab's Family –	Josh 6:22
The Shunammite –	2 Kings 8:1
The Son –	Rev. 12:5
Isaiah –	Isa. 26: 19-21

Distinctions between the Rapture and Jesus' Return and Millennial Reign:

Rapture:	**Return of Jesus:**
Up	He Comes Down
To Heaven	To the Earth
Imminent - No Signs	Set Signs As Provided In Scripture
Old Test. Hidden	N.T. Mystery Unveiled and Clearly Prophesied

Rapture:	**Return – Jesus's Millennial Reign:**
Church	All nations/ethnicities return with Jesus – The Universal Church.
Occurring as a Night-thief	Day of the Lord – all will see Jesus at His return.
Satan Loosed – no restraints	Satan will be Bound
Coming for His Bride	Returning with His Bride/Church
Caught up in the air	Reign on the Earth
Throne room in heaven	Throne setup in Jerusalem
Seven-year tribulation	Jesus' 1000-year Reign with Peace on Earth
Only the Bride Sees	Every Eye shall See

The Church Will Escape the Great Tribulation:

Luke 21:36 reads, "Be always on the watch and pray that you may be able to escape all that is about to happen and that you may be able to stand before the Son of Man." Consider this fact: Jesus tells us that "trials and tribulations will come." Our response to such times: the short answer is we are to remain faithful so that we do not fall away or turn from Jesus. And if you find yourself here on earth after the rapture. I prayerfully encourage you to faithfully endure the hour of trouble.

That said, as we continue with this study, we will see nowhere in the Bible Jesus telling His Church or His Bride how to survive during the Great Tribulation – the time of the outpouring of His wrath. Why not?... The Church will have been raptured. Look. Does it make any sense that all who are redeemed by the blood of Jesus – His Bride would have to endure their Bridegroom's wrath? Of course not! If this was the case, I submit that this could rightfully be called spousal abuse; I just don't see Jesus doing this. Why would He allow His Bride to experience His wrath that He will be bringing upon the wicked of this world? Besides, we, the Church, are made righteous by His blood and sealed with the Holy Spirit.

However, until that time before the rapture, the church or God's people are admonished and encouraged to remain faithful by being watchful of Satan's trickery or deception by being prayerful. Furthermore, Jesus states that the gates of hell will not prevail against His Church, Matthew 16:18. Nowhere in the Book of Revelation after the seven letters were written to the seven churches is the Church mentioned as being overcome by Satan. Or any church, for that matter, having an encounter with Satan, the Antichrist, or the false prophet during the seven years of tribulation.

1 Thes. 1:10: Hear this promise of Jesus as recorded by Paul... "And wait for His Son from heaven, whom He raised from the dead – Jesus, who rescues us from the coming wrath.".

Rev. 3:10: "Since you have kept my command to endure patiently, I will also keep you from the hour of trial that is going to come on the whole world to test the inhabitants of the earth."

1 Corinthians 15:51-52 (ESV): "Behold! I tell you a mystery. We shall not all sleep, but we shall all be changed in a moment, in the twinkling of an eye, at the last trumpet. For the trumpet will sound, and the dead will be raised imperishable, and we shall be changed."

1 Thessalonians 4:16-17 (ESV): "For the Lord himself will descend from heaven with a cry of command, with the voice of an archangel, and with the sound of the trumpet of God. And the dead in Christ will rise first. Then we who are alive, who are left, will be caught up together with them in the clouds to meet the Lord in the air, and so we will always be with the Lord."

And in **Matthew's** writing, he has this to say in **chapter 20:16,** regarding Jesus' teaching on the parable of The Workers In The Vinyard: "So the last will be first, and the first will be last." This was said after Jesus explained to His Jewish audience that regardless of when someone comes to work in the Master's vineyard, He alone determines who is first and who is last in importance and what their reward or payment will be. In the **previous chapter, verse 30,** Jesus also says, "But many who are first will be last, and many who are last will be first." Jesus gave this response when Peter asked the question, "Who would be permitted into the kingdom of God." Apart from the generally accepted understanding of these scriptures, Jesus is also pointing to His Jewish family that will reject Him. As a result of their rejection of Him, although the Jews were chosen first by God, they will be entering Jesus' kingdom after the Gentiles or Christ's Bride; hence, the first will be last and the last first. The Church will be raptured into God's kingdom before the hour of trouble. However, the Jews will have to go through this most troubling of times before they call on Jesus as their Savior, after which they, too, are restored to the kingdom of our God.

As for the Day of the Lord or Wrath of God:

1 Thes. 5:1 "Now, brothers and sisters, about times and dates we do not need to write to you, **2** for you know very well that the day of the Lord will come like a thief in the night. **3** While people are saying "Peace and safety," destruction will come on them suddenly, as labor pains on a pregnant woman, and they will not escape. **4** But you, brothers and sisters, are not in darkness so that this day should surprise you like a thief. **5** You are all children of the light and children of the day. We do not belong to the night or to the darkness.

6 So then, let us not be like others, who are asleep, but let us be awake and sober. **7** For those who sleep, sleep at night, and those who get drunk, get drunk at night. **8** But since we belong to the day, let us be sober, putting on faith and love as a breastplate and the hope of salvation as a helmet. **9** For God **did not appoint us to suffer wrath** but to receive salvation through our Lord Jesus Christ. **10** He died for us so that, whether we are awake or asleep, we may live together with him. **11** Therefore, encourage one another and build each other up, just as, in fact, you are doing.

CHAPTER 6

OUTLINE AND REVELATION CHAPTER 4

The Heavenly Throne Room:

1. **Verse 1-2:** Invitation to See - John sees a door standing open in heaven and hears a voice like a trumpet calling him to come up and see what must take place after this.

2. **Verse 3-6:** Description of the Throne and Surroundings - John describes what he sees: a throne in heaven with someone seated on it who had the appearance of Jasper and Ruby. Around the throne was a rainbow that looked like an emerald. Surrounding the throne were twenty-four other thrones, and seated on them were twenty-four elders dressed in white with crowns of gold on their heads. From the throne came flashes of lightning, rumblings, and peals of thunder. Before the throne were seven lamps blazing, which are the seven spirits of God.

3. **Verse 7-8:** Four Living Creatures - In the center, around the throne, were four living creatures covered with eyes in front and behind. The first creature was like a lion, the second like an ox, the third had a face like a man, and the fourth was like a flying eagle.

4. **Verse 9-11:** Worship of the Creator - The living creatures and the twenty-four elders fall down before the one seated on the throne and

worship him who lives forever and ever. They cast their crowns before the throne, saying, "You are worthy, our Lord and God, to receive glory and honor and power, for you created all things, and by your will, they were created and have their being."

This chapter provides a vivid description of the heavenly throne room, emphasizing the majesty and sovereignty of God, who is worshipped by heavenly beings.

Revelation Chapter 4

As we begin chapter Four, bear in mind that the message and the language become Jewish-centered. Why...Because the Church has been raptured! Additionally, John's vision and messages, as provided to his readers or audience, alternate between heaven and earth.

In Revelation 1:19, John is told to write to the seven churches about "What was," "What is," and "What was to come. Chapter 4 begins with "What is to come," leading to the conclusion of history as we know it and its final days.

1 After this (everything John had written previously, with the emphasis being upon the seven churches, which is not to be mentioned again, nor the name Church, until later in the Book of Revelation. Nonetheless, the term Saints will be mentioned, but these individuals do not make up the universal Church, which at this period in history will not be seen on earth until it returns with Jesus at His 2nd Coming or Parousia). *John now says*, I looked, and there before me was a door standing open in heaven. And the voice I had first heard speaking to me like a trumpet (this being none other than Jesus) said, "Come up here, and I will show you what must take place after this" (meaning the seven letters John had written to address the seven churches).

2 At once, I was in the Spirit (this seems to suggest that John experienced a rapture of sorts, or translation in the likes of Enoch, Elijah, and the Apostle Paul), and there before me – *John continues* was a throne in heaven with someone sitting on it (this would be Yahweh God the Father). **3** And the one who sat there had the appearance of Jasper and Ruby. A rainbow that shone like an emerald encircled the throne. (The radiant glory and splendor of Yahweh was revealed. The rainbow also served as a reminder of God's covenant with Noah and the New Covenant established in Christ. From this point on, everything evolves around the throne).

4 Surrounding the throne were twenty-four other thrones, and seated on them were twenty-four elders (who are believed to be the 12 Patriots of the Tribes of Israel and the 12 Apostles of the New Testament and Apostolic Churches. However, others believe these are angels). They were dressed in white and had crowns of gold on their heads. **5** From the throne came flashes of lightning, rumblings, and peals of thunder (representing the majesty and power of God). In front of the throne, seven lamps were blazing. These are the seven spirits of God (translated or understood by many as the seven-fold Spirit or the Perfect and Complete – Holy Spirit. See notes in Rev. 1:4, where the seven-fold Spirit is with the churches and are believed to be pastors or angels. However, if you hold to the view that the seven-fold Spirit represents the Holy Spirit, He and the Church of this age are now in heaven. It should go without saying this is the view I maintain.

6 Also, in front of the throne, there was what looked like a sea of glass, clear as crystal (a picture of beautiful calm, peace, and harmony in the presence of Yahweh). In the center, around the throne, were four living creatures, *believed to be superior angels – Cherubim,* and they were covered with eyes, in front, and in back. (The multitude of these eyes represents their omniscience, vigilance, spiritual insight, and God's providence operating throughout the created order. The number four represents creation; additionally, this number points toward events occurring within or affecting our earthly realm).

7 The first living creature was like a **lion** — *which is associated with Matthew's Gospel and reveals Jesus as King*; the second was like an **ox** —

akin to Mark's gospel, revealing Jesus as a Servant; the third had a face like a **man** — *which is associated with Luke's Gospel, revealing Jesus as the Son of Man,* the fourth was like a flying **eagle** — *which is akin to John's Gospel, revealing Jesus as the Most High and the Son of God.* **8** Each of the four living creatures had six wings and was covered with eyes all around, even under its wings. Day and night, they never stop saying:

" 'Holy, holy, holy is the Lord God Almighty,' who was, and is, and is to come." *See Ezek. Chapters 1&10 and Isa. 6:2,3.*

9 Whenever the living creatures give glory, honor, and thanks to him who sits on the throne and who lives forever and ever (this being a picture of Jesus having taken His seat at the right hand of His Father and our Father: see Mark 16:19 and Eph. 1:20). *After the living creatures gave praise to Jesus, their praise should serve as an example to us, verse* **10** the twenty-four elders fall down before him who sits on the throne and worship him who lives forever and ever. They lay their crowns before the throne and say:

11 "You are worthy, our Lord and God, to receive glory and honor and power, for you created all things, and by your will, they were created and have their being."

When we grasp the Majesty, Supremacy, Awesomeness, and Wonder of our Living God, this should also move us to the praise and reverence of God, our Everything, and All In All!

CHAPTER 7

OUTLINE AND REVELATION CHAPTER 5

The Scroll and the Lamb:

1. **Verse 1-4:** The Search for One Worthy to Open the Scroll
   - Introduction: John sees a scroll sealed with seven seals in the right hand of the one seated on the throne.
   - The Angel's Proclamation: An angel proclaims with a loud voice, asking who is worthy to open the scroll and break its seals.
   - The Search: John observes that no one in heaven, on earth, or under the earth is found worthy to open the scroll or look into it. This causes him to weep bitterly.

2. **Verse 5-7:** The Worthy One Revealed
   - The Lion of the Tribe of Judah: One of the elders comforts John, saying that the Lion of the tribe of Judah, the Root of David, has conquered and can open the scroll and its seven seals.
   - The Lamb Standing as Though Slain: John sees a Lamb standing, as though it had been slain, with seven horns and seven eyes, which are the seven spirits of God sent out into all the earth.
   - The Lamb Takes the Scroll: The Lamb comes and takes the scroll from the right hand of the one seated on the throne.

3. **Verse 8-10:** Worship of the Lamb
   - Introduction: The four living creatures and the twenty-four elders fall down before the Lamb, each holding a harp and golden bowls full of incense, which are the prayers of the saints.
   - The New Song: They sing a new song, saying, "Worthy are you to take the scroll and to open its seals, for you were slain, and by your blood, you ransomed people for God from every tribe and language and people and nation, and you have made them a kingdom and priests to our God, and they shall reign on the earth."
   - The Lamb's Worthiness: The living creatures and elders declare that the Lamb is worthy to receive power, wealth, wisdom, might, honor, glory, and blessing.
4. **Verse 11-14:** Worship of the Lamb by All Creation
   - Introduction: John sees myriads of angels around the throne and the living creatures and elders, their number countless, praising the Lamb with a loud voice.
   - The Extent of Worship: They declare, "Worthy is the Lamb who was slain, to receive power and wealth and wisdom and might and honor and glory and blessing!"
   - Universal Worship: John hears every creature in heaven and on earth and under the earth and in the sea, and all that is in them, saying, "To him who sits on the throne and to the Lamb be blessing and honor and glory and might forever and ever!"
   - The Final Amen: The four living creatures respond with "Amen," and the elders fall down and worship.

This chapter depicts the scene in heaven where the Lamb, Jesus, the Christ, is revealed as the only one worthy to open the scroll containing the future events of God's judgment and redemption. It culminates in universal worship and praise to the Lamb for His sacrificial work.

Revelation Chapter 5

The Scroll and the Lamb:

Be mindful that everything read from Revelation Chapters 6 through 19 comes from this scroll. This scroll ushers in *The Day of the Lord* or 7 years of Great Tribulation: see Isa. 8:16-18; 29:10-13; Dan. 8:23-26; 12:1-4; and verses 8-13. The scroll or book in Dan. 12:4-9 is believed to be this scroll that's before us.

1 Then I saw in the right hand of him who sat on the throne a scroll (this scroll is often described as the title deed to the earth, otherwise a legal document and also likened to a Will) with writing on both sides and sealed with seven seals. **2** And I saw a mighty angel (perhaps Gabriel) proclaiming in a loud voice, "Who is worthy to break the seals and open the scroll" (or this book of destiny and a Will for those who will inherit the earth)?

3 But no one (no mere man nor angelic being for that matter had earned the right to this title deed to the earth) in heaven or on earth or under the earth could open the scroll or even look inside it. **4** *John then says*, I wept and wept because no one was found who was worthy to open the scroll or look inside (the fact that no man was found worthy to open the scroll deeply grieved John). **5** Then one of the elders said to me – *John* (this elder was not likely an angel because angels did not understand the mystery of redemption, but rather an Elder, the Church's' representative: see Rev. 4:4), *and so the elder said to me* "Do not weep! See, the Lion of the tribe of Judah, the Root of David, has triumphed: see Gen. 49:8-10). He – *the Lion* is able to open the scroll and its seven seals."

This Elder knew Jesus as the Lion; John had only known Jesus as the Lamb. Now, John has been given a new revelation of Jesus and is encouraged not to weep because Jesus is the prophesied Lion King and Conqueror! All of the titles describing Jesus in the Book of Revelation are Jewish titles; this book primarily focuses on bringing the Jews back to

Him so that they may become one with the kingdom of God and one with Jesus' Church or Bride.

During the last 3 ½ years of the Great Tribulation, unrepentant mankind, along with Satan, are seeking the destruction of the Jewish people and others who have embraced faith in Jesus. However, the Jewish people must see Jesus as the Lamb slain – their Passover Lamb, for their sins before they can have Him or see Him as the Lion from the tribe of Judah and their King. When John was first introduced to Jesus by John the Baptist, Jesus was identified as the Lamb, who takes away the sins of the world: see John 1:29-30. But now Jesus is beheld by John as the King of kings and Lord of lords!

As the seals are broken, God will then begin addressing the three rebellions that took place against Him. **#1** Mankind's along with Lucifer or the Devil's rebellion as provided in Gen. 3:1 and Rev. 12:9; **#2** The Fallen Angels rebellion: see Gen. 6:1 and Rev. 9:11; and **#3** Man's rebellion at Babylon: see Gen. 10:8-10 and 11:1-5. Babylon is to be recognized as this world's governmental and religious systems – secular humanism, or man's ordering himself apart from God: see Rev. chap. 13.

Jesus has already dealt with sin on the cross; the matters being addressed in the book of Revelation from chapter 4 to the end of this book don't pertain to the universal Church; rather, these rebellions and the restoration of the Jews are in view: see Romans Chapter 11. The world's sin has been dealt with by Jesus' atoning blood. For this reason, the Church or born-again Believers will not experience the wrath of God; Jesus has borne our deserved punishment for our sins upon Himself at Calvary's Cross.

6 Then I saw a Lamb – *says John*, looking as if it had been slain – *its throat cut and blood-stained,* standing *beside Jehovah, His Father, and our Father* at the center of the throne, encircled by the four living creatures and the elders. The Lamb had seven horns (thereby representing perfection and completion with all power and authority given to Him –

Jesus the Lamb) and seven eyes, *which the Lamb had* which are the seven spirits of God sent out into all the earth (is a picture of Jesus' omniscience and He and the Holy Spirit having been poured or sent out upon the earth: see Joel 2:28,29. Here, we see a pattern of Seven, Seven, Seven, the perfection of the Triune God. And not six, six, six, the mark of fallen man or the identification of Antichrist – the seed of Satan and their wicked and rebellious system).

What is now to occur in heaven verse: **7** He - *Jesus* went and took the scroll from the right hand of him – *God the Father* who sat on the throne. **8** And when he had taken it, the four living creatures and the twenty-four elders fell down before the Lamb. Each one had a harp, and they were holding golden bowls full of incense, which are the prayers of God's people. (The prayers of the resurrected Church and, in particular, the martyred Saints of the Great Tribulation, who were killed for their faith in Jesus, were heard by God; now He is ready to respond with His judgment upon the wicked of the earth).

9 And they sang a new song (a redemption song, the first of its kind. Before the scroll was read, there was a time of worship; there was an explosive proclamation, of praise and worship in heaven to honor the Lamb ~ Jesus)! *And the people were,* Saying: "You are worthy to take the scroll and to open its seals because you were slain, and with your blood, you purchased for God persons from every tribe and language and people and nation.

10 You have made them to be a kingdom and priests; (otherwise translated, You have made them kings and priests) to serve our God, and they will reign on the earth." (Already, the Church's members reign as kings, but also not yet, in that, during Christ's millennial reign, followers of Christ will be perfected in these roles. The church had been raptured; however, at the return of Jesus' 2nd Coming to reign on earth for a millennium, His Bride, the Church, or His kingdom of priests will be with Him). **11** Then I looked and heard the voice of (**#1**) many angels, numbering thousands upon thousands, and ten thousand times ten thousand. They encircled the throne and, **#2,** the living creatures, and **#3)** the elders.

12 In a loud voice, they were saying: "Worthy is the Lamb, who was slain, to receive power and wealth and wisdom and strength and honor and glory and praise!" (This three-fold number of created beings, in verse 11, stands in place and counters the three rebellions on earth: the Edenic rebellion involving the fallen Cherub ~ Satan; the rebellion of the fallen angels/watchers and they marrying women in Genesis Chapter 6. And the rebellion of Babylon – mankind establishing their own kingdom apart from God.

The book of Revelation is about God making all things new. And His original plan for Eden, heaven with earth, this being Jesus reigning on earth for a millennium with His restored family and kingdom; heaven and earth or heaven with earth once again united. And then, in its finality, there is the creation of a new heaven and new earth. And so, we will see God's will being done on earth as it is in heaven: see Mathew Chapter 6:10.

13 Then I heard every creature in heaven and on earth and under the earth and on the sea, and all that is in them, saying: "To him who sits on the throne and to the Lamb be praise and honor and glory and power, forever and ever!" **14** The four living creatures said, "Amen," and the elders fell down and worshiped. (For a moment, just before the climactic end of this era, God will draw back the curtain into eternity so that all who awaited the return of Christ the King will see that Earth's title Deed and Will has been given over to Jesus. And that He is soon to return to establish His kingdom and millennial rule on earth).

CHAPTER 8

OUTLINE AND REVELATION CHAPTER 6

The Seven Seals and the Four Horsemen:

1. **Verse 1-2:** The First Seal: The White Horse
   - Introduction: John sees the Lamb open the first of the seven seals.
   - The White Horse and Its Rider: A white horse appears, and its rider holds a bow and is given a crown. He goes out conquering and to conquer.
2. **Verse 3-4:** The Second Seal: The Red Horse
   - The Red Horse and Its Rider: The Lamb opens the second seal, and a red horse appears. Its rider is given a great sword, and he takes peace from the earth, causing people to slay one another.
3. **Verse 5-6:** The Third Seal: The Black Horse
   - The Black Horse and Its Rider: The Lamb opens the third seal, and a black horse appears. Its rider holds a pair of scales in his hand, symbolizing scarcity and famine. A voice among the four living creatures declares the prices of food.
4. **Verse 7-8:** The Fourth Seal: The Pale Horse
   - The Pale Horse and Its Rider: The Lamb opens the fourth seal, and a pale horse appears. Its rider is Death, and Hades follows

him. They are given authority over a fourth of the earth to kill with sword, famine, pestilence, and wild beasts.

5. **Verse 9-11:** The Fifth Seal: The Martyrs Under the Altar
   - Introduction: When the Lamb opens the fifth seal, John sees under the altar the souls of those who had been slain for the word of God and for the witness they had borne.
   - Their Cry for Justice: They cry out with a loud voice, asking how long until God will avenge their blood on those who dwell on the earth.
   - Assurance and Patience: They are each given a white robe and told to rest a little longer until the number of their fellow servants and their brothers is complete, who were to be killed as they themselves had been.

6. **Verse 12-17:** The Sixth Seal: Cosmic Disturbances
   - Introduction: When the Lamb opens the sixth seal, there is a great earthquake, the sun becomes black as sackcloth, the moon turns red like blood, the stars fall from the sky, and the sky is split apart like a scroll being rolled up.
   - Reaction of People: The kings of the earth, the great ones, the generals, the rich, the powerful, and everyone, slave and free, hide in caves and among the rocks of the mountains, calling on the mountains and rocks to fall on them and hide them from the wrath of the Lamb.
   - The Question: They ask, "Who can stand before the wrath of the Lamb?"

This chapter introduces the opening of the first six seals, which unleash various events symbolizing conquest, conflict, famine, death, martyrdom, and cosmic disturbances, leading up to the question of who can stand before the wrath of the Lamb.

Revelation Chapter 6

The opening of the seals is the start of the Tribulation period, the last 3 1/2 years of the seven-year period described in the Book of Daniel Chapter 7, with Daniel Chapter 12:1-4 mentioning the scroll that had been sealed regarding the arrival of the Antichrist – this one who seeks to reign in place of Jesus upon the earth; the very seed of Satan. It's important to note that 1/3 of the Bible talks about the unfolding of God's wrath upon the earth, as we are about to see as the seals are opened – the beginning of Israel's birth pains or Jacob's trouble is in view in: see Jeremiah 30:7.

The following seven events will precede this time of trouble on earth and crescendo during the Great Tribulation:

1. Cataclysmic Wars – Matt. 24:6
2. Israel's Rebirth – Ezek. 20:33-38. This rebirth of Israel occurred on May 14, 1948
3. Gentile Occupation of Jerusalem – Luke 21:24
4. Gog's Alliance or Nations Aligning Against Israel – Ezek. Chapters 38-39
5. Global Peace and Unity under Babylon's rule – Rev. 13:7-8
6. 10 Kingdom Government Rule Over The Earth – Dan. 7:24
7. Temple Rebuilding With the Antichrist, with he establishing himself as god – the Abomination that causes desolation – 2 Thess. 2:1-3

Review of Eschatology or End-time positions:

Polemicist – The Book of Revelation is viewed as merely allegorical signs and symbols with accompanying stories to help understand Biblical truth. *Nevertheless, these allegories do not cancel out the relevance of the* *other views. Furthermore, they bring insight and clarity to the Biblical narrative. The same holds true for the other positions as well.*

Historicist – An overview of human history. *However, Biblical prophecy is cyclical as it builds to a climatic end or with repeated patterns until it reaches its ultimate fulfillment. The unfolding patterns: This is Biblical prophecy, a particular event that has happened or is happening and will happen again, thereby achieving its greater and or perfected end.*

Ecclesiastes 1:9-10 provides these words: "What has been will be again, what has been done will be done again; there is nothing new under the sun. **10** Is there anything of which one can say, "Look! This is something new"? It was here already, long ago; it was here before our time.

Jesus has this to say: *His or* "My Words will never pass away:" see Matt. 24:35. In other words, Jesus' words will remain true to every generation while addressing the same issues concerning mankind's present age, the age in past, and that which is to come.

Patterns of Prophecy:

Malachi 4:5 says: "See, I will send the prophet Elijah to you before that great and dreadful day of the Lord comes." Elijah lived some 400 to 500 years before this prophecy was fulfilled in the ministry, life, and spirit of John the Baptist. In Elijah's time, looking into the future, John will represent Elijah as the final prophet of his age as it was for Elijah. Jesus had this to say, "John the Baptist was the Elijah to come, but the people did not listen to him." Elijah showed up with Jesus on the Mountain of Transfiguration. And he will come again as one of the two witnesses in the Book of Revelation: see Chapter 11:3-12. For Scripture regarding John the Baptist: see Matt. 11:14; Matt. 17:11-12 and Luke:1:17.

In Matthew 2:14-15, God says, "Out of Egypt I called my son." Hosea was given this prophecy in Hosea 11:1; he says, "When Israel (the Jewish people) was a child (not yet established as a nation), I loved him, and out of Egypt I called my son." This occurred in the past. The account given in Matthew's gospel spoke regarding the present. We also see this prophecy fulfilled in Revelation Chapter 12, with the woman fleeing to the desert and coming out from the dragon – a picture of Egypt or Babylon. Egypt is synonymous with Satanic rule or this world from which God's people are called out and are being called out from.

Lastly, Jesus the Lamb was slain before time. In ancient Biblical times, there were types or symbolic sacrifices of Him; finally, Jesus was slain once and for all time. And so, Jesus' kingdom is already here on earth, represented by the universal Church resulting from the indwelling Holy Spirit within all Believers, but it is also yet to come. These occurrences are patterns of circular prophecies that will reach their intended end or ultimate fulfillment. They have already happened, and yet, some are still to come to pass for our age and the final stage of mankind's history.

Preterist – This view holds that everything in the Book of Revelation has been fulfilled, in part or in literal ways; however, not in the likes of the view I presented regarding further fulfillment.

Futurist – This view holds that everything from chap. 4 onwards are prophecies yet to come to pass.

There is some truth to each of these views as they represent the history of mankind and God's dealing with His creation. Therefore, the various views don't cancel the others out completely. However, I maintain the position I subscribed to earlier. Here, I line up with the Futurist view as a Pre-millennialist. But not to exclude relevant thoughts from the other views.

Brief Review of Eschatological Understandings:

1. **Amillennial** – There is not a 1000-year reign of Jesus; He is not returning but to judge the wicked. The church will change the world. Here, we have Replacement Theology in view; Israel is subsequently spiritualized as the church, her replacement on earth.

2. **Post-Millennial** – Because Jesus has come, things are getting better through the church. Then He returns. Replacement theology is also seen in operation under this view as well.

3. **Pre-Millennial** – Jesus returns after the Great Tribulation to establish His kingdom on earth for a millennial reign.

Views On the Seals Opening:

1. They are concurrent and run parallel to each other

2. They are successive, following a chronological and overlapping sequence; however, ending at the same point

3. The 6th seal is designated as the wrath of God: see Rev. chap 6:16,17, with the Trumpet and Bowl Judgments elaborating on the events of the 6th seal. Again, each of the judgments ends at the same point, the triumph of the kingdom of God. Trumpets 1 through 6 expand on the 6th seal, and the Bowls 1 through 6 cover the same ground, occurring near the end of the 6th Seal's opening and before Jesus' return. The unfolding events are here to be seen as sequential as well.

The horrific events – war, famine, diseases, and other cataclysmic terrifying phenomena occurring during the opening of the Seals point back to Jesus' Olivet Discourse in the synoptic gospels of Matthew Chapter 24, Mark Chapter 13, and Luke Chapter 21. These events are described as the beginning of birth pains that the world will experience leading up to Jesus' 2nd Coming, and yet ultimately the pattern or order of God's wrath that will come upon this world during the short span of the seven-year tribulation period, and specifically the last 3 ½ years.

Chapter 6

Verse 1: I watched as the Lamb opened the **first of the seven seals**. Then I heard one of the four living creatures – *a Cherub*, say in a voice like thunder (this Cherub or high-ranking angel had been given the authority to speak on God's behalf), *as he tells John,* "Come!" **2** I looked – *says John*, and there before me was a **white horse!** Its rider held a bow, and he was given a crown and rode out as a conqueror bent on conquest. (Regarding the horsemen and the impending events, see Zach. 1:7-17 and 6:1-8; Jer. 15:2,3 and Ezek. 14:21, they lend insight to this period of judgment.

Additionally, see Matt. 24:4-5 and verses 11&24 regarding this great deceiver riding on the white horse. This is the appearance of the ultimate Antichrist or the counterfeit Messiah – the Man of sin, the Lawless one, that Daniel Chap. 6 mentions. This rider is not the same rider on the white horse as seen in Rev. 19:11-16; here, this rider is pictured as Jesus, who has a sharp sword. The Antichrist, however, is pictured with a bow, a negative image, depicting a hunter, also a sign of war and destruction: see Jer. 6:23; 46:9 and 49:35.

Furthermore, this rider is pictured as arrowless as he arrives, an image of him bringing a false or temporary peace during his short reign as the world's emerging tyrant ruler. Note: Many false Antichrists and Messiahs will appear on earth before Jesus' 2nd Coming: see Luke 21:8. In Revelation Chapter 13, we will take a closer look at this matter of deception that will come from such deceivers, who will beguile many – the unsaved and Saved alike as previously mentioned.

Verse 11 of Rev. Chapter 19 reads, "I saw heaven standing open, and there before me was a **white horse,** whose rider is called Faithful and True. With justice, he judges and wages war. **12** His eyes are like blazing fire, and on his head are many crowns. He has a name written on him that no one knows but he himself. **13** He is dressed in a robe dipped in blood, and his name is the Word of God. **14** The armies of heaven were following him, riding on white horses and dressed in fine linen, white and clean. **15** Coming out of his mouth is a sharp sword – *Jesus' mere Word* with which to strike down the nations. "He will rule them with an iron scepter." He treads the winepress of the fury of the wrath of God

Almighty. **16** On his robe and on his thigh, he has this name written: KING OF KINGS AND LORD OF LORDS.

Difference Between the Antichrist and *The Christ:*

Antichrist	The Christ
Brings War	Brings Peace
Bow Without Arrows, A Hunter	Has The Sword Of A King
1 Crown – Self-Imposed Ruler	Many Crowns Cast Before Him – That are Rightfully His
Riding With Death & Hades, etc.	Riding With Him, The Host Of Heaven & His Redeemed
False Covenant To Be Broken	Covenant That Will Not Be Broken
Claim To Be A King	Is King of Kings

In the Bible, after Jesus, more is said about the Antichrist than anyone else. This Deceiver and son or seed of the Devil is described as imitating Jesus, even in his speech. Later on in Revelation, it is said of him therein as being described as a Beast, that he speaks like a lamb but is full of deceit. His religious vernacular will be persuasive; many will follow and bow to him. As a hunter, we see him and/or his influence at work through Nimrod, a mighty hunter – a type of Antichrist who rebelled against God in the account of the building of the city Babylon: see Gen. 10: 8-10. The name Nimrod means we will rebel.

Revelation verse 3: "When the Lamb opened the **second seal**, I heard the second living creature say, "Come!" **4** Then another horse came out, a **fiery red** one. Its rider was given power to take peace from the earth and to make people kill each other. To him was given a large sword: see Matt. 24:6. Reading from Ezekiel Chapters 38 and 39, these prophesied events may be telegraphing World War III, the battle of Gog and Magog, understood by some as occurring during the second half of the seven years of the Great Tribulation, with others seeing this event as occurring before the *Time of Trouble* or seven-year tribulation period. However, there are still those who see this war as being the last battle on earth, which will not be a battle in the conventional sense. Rather, this will be when Jesus destroys all the nations with an earthquake and His mere Word, those who will come against Him and Jerusalem, led by the demon Gog. During the first half of the seven years or 3 ½ year period, this is believed to be when the Antichrist comes onto the scene as a lamb making peace with Israel. But after 1,260 days or 3 ½ years, he unleashes his fury upon the Jews.

The following may be the nations that come against Israel. Their Biblical names: Psalm 83 has them listed as Edom, Ishmaelites, Moab, Hagorites, Byblos, Ammon and Amalek, Philistia, Tyre, and Assyria. Ezek. Chapters 38-39 name them: Gog, Magog, Meshek/Rosh, Tubal, Persia, Cush, Put, Gomer, and Beth Togarmah. Their modern names are Libya, Sudan, Iran, Iraq, Syria, Palestine, Jordan, Egypt, and Saudi Arabia. These are Islamic nations who hate Israel or tolerate them at best. Interestingly enough, their national flags have the same colors: Red, White, Green, and Black. These countries utilize war as a part of their false religion.

Whereas Christ came to bring peace on earth through love and Self-sacrifice, contrariwise, those who are enemies of Jesus, the nations mentioned, along with the Demonic realm, will be met with His wrath and eternal destruction. During the final battle of Armageddon, Israel is told to flee to the wilderness: see Rev. 12:6. This is believed to be a reference to Israel's flight to Jordan for refuge: see Matt. 24:15,16 and Luke 21:20,21. Isaiah 63:1-4 and Jer. 49:22 speak to Israel fleeing to Bozrah or modern-day Jordan, perhaps specifically to Petra.

Revelation verse 5: When the Lamb opened the **third seal**, I heard the third living creature say, "Come!" I looked, and there before me was a **black horse!** Its rider was holding a pair of scales in his hand. **6** Then I heard what sounded like a voice among the four living creatures, saying, "Two pounds of wheat for a day's wages, and six pounds of barley for a day's wages, and do not damage the oil and the wine." Matt. 24:7 speaks of a great famine at the *End of Days,* as does Luke 21:11.

7 When the Lamb opened the **fourth seal**, I heard the voice of the fourth living creature say, "Come!" **8** I looked, and there before me was a **pale** (chloros or pale green) **horse!** (A picture of the rotting dead is in view.) Its rider was named Death, and Hades (the abode of disembodied spirits following physical death) was following close behind him. They were given power over a fourth of the earth to kill by sword, famine, and plague and by the wild beasts of the earth. (Horses, according to the Bible, are symbols of God's judgment. It's a symbol that a conqueror is coming...Jesus is pictured as riding in on a white horse. He is coming to reclaim or take back that which was His; He will arrive or return as the Conquering King and Lion of Judah: see Gen. 49:9,10.

Bear in mind these end-time events unfolding here in the Book of Revelation. They are events that were prophesied in both the Old and New Testaments; therein, God deals with Israel, His chosen people who are now considered the enemy of the state by the Antichrist's new world order and or rebellious mankind who has chosen to be one with spiritual wickedness – Satan and the other rebellious angelic host; they also will be dealt with.

9 When he – Jesus, opened the **fifth seal**, I saw under the altar the souls of those who had been slain because of the word of God and the testimony they had maintained (because of the great persecution and martyrdom occurring at the hand of the rider on the white horse – the Antichrist). From the grave verse **10:** They called out in a loud voice, "How long, Sovereign Lord, holy and true until you judge the inhabitants of the earth and avenge our blood?"... *See Matt. 24: 9-13.* My brothers and sisters in Christ, since the time of Jesus' ascension, countless Christians have died for their faith are dying because of their faith in Christ, and I am convinced before Jesus returns, Christian persecution will only intensify; this includes martyrdom!

11 Then, each of them was given a white robe (their garments of salvation), and they were told to wait a little longer until the full number of their fellow servants, their brothers and sisters, were killed just as they had been. (These other slain Jews, including Gentile Believers, will be those who do not make a covenant with the Antichrist – that is, by taking the mark of the Beast, "666" a registration of sorts: see Rev. 13:15-17 and chap. 20:4).

12 I watched as he - *Jesus* opened the **sixth seal**. There was a great earthquake. The sun turned black like sackcloth made of goat hair, the whole moon turned blood red, **13** and the stars in the sky fell to earth, as figs drop from a fig tree when shaken by a strong wind. **14** The heavens receded like a scroll being rolled up, and every mountain and island was removed from its place. (There will be global cataclysm – drastic atmospheric changes. Does war bring this about? Or are such things caused directly by God? See Luke 21:25,26 and verses 35,36. Isaiah prophesied concerning this time: see chap. 34:2-4. Regardless of how this calamity unfolds, the earth will return to chaos before Jesus restores it for a third time: see Genesis Chapter 1 and chapters 7 through 9.

Revelation verse 15: Then the kings of the earth, the princes, the generals, the rich, the mighty, and everyone else, both slave and free, hid in caves and among the rocks of the mountains. **16** They called to the mountains and the rocks, "Fall on us and hide us from the face of him who sits on the throne and from the wrath of the Lamb! **17** For the great day of their wrath has come, and who can withstand it?" **Isa. 2:19 reads,** "People will flee to caves in the rocks and to holes in the ground from the fearful presence of the LORD and the splendor of his majesty when he rises to shake the earth.

In **chapter 13, verses 9-13,** Isaiah continues, "See, the day of the Lord is coming—a cruel day, with wrath and fierce anger—to make the land desolate and destroy the sinners within it. **10** The stars of heaven and their constellations will not show their light. The rising sun will be darkened, and the moon will not give its light. **11** I will punish the world for its evil, the wicked for their sins. I will put an end to the arrogance of the haughty and will humble the pride of the ruthless. **12** I will make people scarcer than pure gold, more rare than the gold of Ophir. **13** Therefore I will make the heavens tremble; and the earth will shake from its place at the wrath of the Lord Almighty, in the day of his burning anger. Also, see Isaiah 34:4.

Astonishingly, the people recognized that the hand of God was against them, yet they ran and hid instead of repenting. Nevertheless, we see this kind of behavior throughout the O.T. Read Joshua Chapter 10:16,17. Remember, Biblical prophecy is to be understood as a recapitulation of historical events, concluding when it reaches its ultimate fulfillment, as contained in this Book of Revelation. Or Biblical prophecy being viewed as a series of dress rehearsals for the final stage of mankind's unfolding history and climatic end.

Just as Joshua led God's chosen people – the Israelites, to claim the territory promised to Abraham and his descendants. Jesus, at His Second Coming or Parousia, is returning to reclaim this same land specifically and all the earth for a millennium. He will reign as King of kings and Lord of lords over that of man's futile making and the opposing Demonic realm!

CHAPTER 9

OUTLINE AND REVELATION CHAPTER 7

The Sealing of the 144,000 and the Great Multitude:

1. **Verse 1-8:** The Sealing of the 144,000 from the Twelve Tribes of Israel
   - Introduction: John sees four angels standing at the four corners of the earth, holding back the four winds of the earth.
   - The First Angel: Another angel ascends from the rising of the sun, having the seal of the living God, and he calls out with a loud voice to the four angels, instructing them not to harm the earth or the sea until the servants of God are sealed on their foreheads.
   - The Servants of God: John hears that 144,000 were sealed, 12,000 from each of the twelve tribes of Israel: Judah, Reuben, Gad, Asher, Naphtali, Manasseh, Simeon, Levi, Issachar, Zebulun, Joseph, and Benjamin.
2. **Verse 9-17:** The Great Multitude Before the Throne
   - Introduction: After this, John sees a great multitude that no one could number, from every nation, tribe, people, and language, standing before the throne and before the Lamb, clothed in white robes and holding palm branches in their hands.

- Worship and Blessing: The multitude cries out with a loud voice, saying, "Salvation belongs to our God who sits on the throne and to the Lamb!" All the angels, elders, and four living creatures fall on their faces before the throne and worship God, saying, "Amen! Blessing and glory and wisdom and thanksgiving and honor and power and might be to our God forever and ever! Amen."

- Identity and Blessing: One of the elders asks John who these clothed in white robes are and where they come from. John replies that the elder knows, and the elder tells him that these are the ones coming out of the great tribulation. They have washed their robes and made them white in the blood of the Lamb. Therefore, they are before the throne of God, serving Him day and night in His temple. He who sits on the throne will shelter them with His presence. They shall hunger no more, neither thirst anymore; the sun shall not strike them, nor any scorching heat. For the Lamb in the midst of the throne will be their shepherd, and He will guide them to springs of living water, and God will wipe away every tear from their eyes.

This chapter depicts the sealing of the 144,000 from the twelve tribes of Israel and the vision of a great multitude from every nation standing before the throne of God, indicating the salvation and inclusion of people from all backgrounds into God's kingdom.

Revelation Chapter 7

This chapter is just before God's continuing wrath or judgments, which are to be poured out on the earth, with the first of the seven Trumpet Judgments and concluding with the seven Bowl Judgments! The seventh seal, as will be seen in Chapter 8, inaugurates the blowing of this 1st trumpet and the remaining 6 trumpets, leading up to God finally ridding the world of evil!

However, before this actually happens, continuing with the breaking of the seventh seal and the blowing of the first trumpet in Revelation Chapter 8, here in Chapter 7, John is provided a view of what is or will be occurring in heaven. There is a pause, transition, or intermission in verses 1-17 where John responds to what will happen to those who die in the Lord, beginning from what had or will befall the earth with the horsemen and the first six seals. After the opening of this sixth seal, in chapter 6, John is permitted to see what was or would soon be occurring in heaven; this is the intermission or pause and his response regarding those persecuted for their faith in Christ leading up to the sixth seal, as pertaining to the question presented in Chapter 6:17.

There are other such pauses in the Bible; I'll share one, **Luke 4:18-20.** Jesus, opening the scroll, quotes Isaiah 61:1 and 2 in part. From Luke's Gospel, we have the following text, verse **18:** "The Spirit of the Lord is on me because he has anointed me to proclaim good news to the poor. He has sent me to proclaim freedom for the prisoners and recovery of sight for the blind, to set the oppressed free, **19** to proclaim the year of the Lord's favor." **20** Then Jesus rolls up the scroll and sits down.

However, in **Isaiah's rendering chapter 61:1-4** and beyond these verses, we have a *pause* before that which is later to come or fulfill Isaiah's prophecy about the coming Messiah – Jesus the Christ: **Verse 1** of Isaiah 61 reads, "The Spirit of the Sovereign Lord is on me because the Lord has anointed me to proclaim good news to the poor. He has sent me to bind up the brokenhearted, to proclaim freedom for the captives and release from darkness for the prisoners, **2a** to proclaim the year of the Lord's favor. (This is where Jesus stopped His reading in Luke's gospel).

The following is the pause, here meaning other historical events occurring until the latter fulfillment of this prophecy by Jesus at the end of this age, which reads as follows: **verse 2b** and the day of vengeance of our God, to comfort all who mourn, **3** and provide for those who grieve in Zion— to bestow on them a crown of beauty instead of ashes, the oil of joy instead of mourning, and a garment of praise instead of a spirit of despair. They will be called oaks of righteousness, a planting of the Lord for the display of his splendor. **4** They will rebuild the ancient ruins and restore the places long devastated; they will renew the ruined cities that have been devastated for generations.

John the Baptist and others thought Jesus would accomplish these things at His First Advent. The people were confused to include Jesus' chosen disciples when they didn't occur, although He made it clear to them that He had not come at that time to establish His earthly kingdom or to rule as their King at His 1st Advent or Parousia, but instead, there would be a ***pause or intermission;*** therefore, Isaiah's prophecy being fulfilled later, as explained here and seen being fulfilled or completed in the Book of Revelation.

Other Pauses:		**It's been:**
Luke 4:18	Isa. 61:2	2,000 years
Dan. 9:26	" 9:27	2,000 years
Acts 1:6	" 1:7	2,000 years
Hosea 5:5	" 6:1	2 days (2,000 years)
Malachi 4:4	" 4:5	400 years (2,000 years)
Micah 5:2	" 5:3	2,000 years (Israel has been restored, May 14, 1948)
Luke 1:31	" 1:32,33	2,000 years

Warnings and Encouragement regarding God's Wrath, Judgment, or Day of The Lord:

Mattew 3:7 Warns us to flee the coming wrath that is to overtake the world.

John 3:36 Warns whoever rejects Jesus that God's wrath remains on them.

Romans 2:5 Warns the unrepentant of sin is storing up wrath for when God judges them.

Romans 5:9 Encourages all who are justified by the blood of Jesus that they will not experience God's wrath! God's Bride, His Church, will experience persecution. However, God will not pour out His wrath upon His Redeemed – His children.

Ephesians 5:6 Warns us not to be deceived by liars. God's wrath will come on all who are disobedient.

1 Thessalonians 1:10 Encourages Believers to wait for Jesus, who rescues them from the coming wrath.

1 Thess. 5:9 Encourages Believers that God has not appointed those who have received salvation through Jesus to suffer His wrath.

What we must remember: although God is longsuffering and loving. However, because He is Holy and a Righteous Judge, sinful rebellion or rejection of Him or Jesus cannot go unpunished.

144,000 Sealed:

Regarding this number, there is the belief by some that this is the actual or total number of Jewish people who will be sealed by God. On the other hand, others are proponents of this being God's perfected or completed numbering of all who will come to faith during the Great Tribulation, this numbering being the multiples of the number 7, if you recall from early in our study, which is likened to God's signature indicating perfection or completion, this, therefore, suggest that rather than an actual number, this numbering of 144,000 will be God's appointed or completed numbering of all – the dead in Christ and from the twelve tribes of the Jews who will be preserved or kept safe by God sealing and Gentiles alike who will come to faith in Him. I lean towards this latter belief: see Rev. 6:9-11.

Revelation Chapter 7, verse 1: After this (that which succeeded the opening of the sixth seal), I saw four angels standing at the four corners of the earth, holding back the four winds of the earth to prevent any wind from blowing on the land or on the sea or on any tree **2** Then I saw another angel coming up from the east. (East is the direction from which God is described as coming from), *this fifth angel has* the seal of the living God, *to seal and claim the Lord's faithful ones.* He called out in a loud voice to the four angels who had been given power to harm the land and the sea: **3** "Do not harm the land or the sea or the trees until we put a seal on the foreheads of the servants of our God." (The intensifying wrath of God was imminent; however, He is going to protect those who turned to Jesus in faith).

These servants do not represent the Church, which was sealed by the indwelling Holy Spirit: see Eph. 1:13. One can, therefore, reason according to Scripture that these people who are representatives of those from the 12 tribes of Israel and possibly all others – here Gentile Saints coming to faith in Jesus are sealed differently by this angel from that of the sealing of the Church, which had been raptured. Subsequently, the Holy Spirit's operation or function ceased at the universal Church's rapture. He – the Holy Spirit, therefore, will depart from the earth because the dispensation of God's grace or the Holy Spirit's ministry will end with the rapture of the Church.

Jesus had told His disciples that He had to leave the earth so that the Holy Spirit may come and dwell within them. Even so, the Holy Spirit will have to leave the earth so that Jesus may return for His Second Coming and judgment of the world: see John 16:7 and 2 Thess. 2:6. The Jewish people will come to faith during the Great Tribulation. And as it had been purposed for them by Jehovah to be His beacon of hope to the nations in the Old Testament, they will now serve as a beacon of Christ for the unsaved of the world during the Great Tribulation for which they will be persecuted because of their belief in Jesus as their Messianic, King, and God.

But what does it mean to be sealed, as mentioned in the context of the universal Church? Again, Believers in Christ or the Church are sealed and indwelt with the Holy Spirit; also see 2 Cor. 1:21,22 and Eph.

1:13,14. However, in this context of these servants, the Scripture suggests to me that there will be a visible sign of God's ownership of His people. What it may be, Scripture does not say.

Although Scripture doesn't say this, one can reason that Adam and Eve's appearances were changed after their fall, considering that they dwelt in the presence of God, in holiness and perfection. I think it was more than them simply realizing they were naked; perhaps there was, in fact, a physical change when they lost their complete holiness and glorious radiance due to their rebellion. Also, considering that Cain received what seems to have been a visible mark that protected him from harm: see Gen. 4:15; furthermore, we read in Ex. 28:36-38 that the High Priest wore a seal on their turban which was indicated as being on their foreheads.

Something else to ponder: When the Church or Bride of Christ returns with Jesus at His Second Coming, we will be clothed in our new bodies and glorified state. What will this look like? Will we now possess a body after the likes of Jesus, after which He had risen from the grave, a body equipped to dwell on the earth, however, transcending mere physical limitations or that of earth-born creatures of God? Regarding this sealing, whatever it may or may not be, we know that God's people were sealed and made secure from His coming judgment upon the earth by this fifth angel and not by the Holy Spirit.

Revelation verse 4: Then I heard the number of those who were sealed: 144,000 (a completed or appointed numbering by God; this numbering by twelve represents God's governance or authority in heaven, whereas seven represent God's governance or authority on earth). *Continuing with* **verse 4**, *they were sealed* from all the tribes of Israel:

5 From the tribe of Judah, 12,000 were sealed; from the tribe of Reuben, 12,000,

from the tribe of Gad 12,000, **6** from the tribe of Asher 12,000,

from the tribe of Naphtali 12,000, from the tribe of Manasseh 12,000,

7 from the tribe of Simeon 12,000, from the tribe of Levi 12,000,

from the tribe of Issachar 12,000, **8** from the tribe of Zebulun 12,000,

from the tribe of Joseph (the replacement name for Ephraim) 12,000, from the tribe of Benjamin 12,000.

The tribe of Dan has been excluded from this land allotment and sealing. Dan was born from Racheal's maidservant; his conception was not connected with the promises of God; he was not conceived through faithfulness in God. Furthermore, Dan chose to live in the land of Bashan, which also was recognized as the territory of Dan; this land was not his inheritance, but rather the territory of the Nephilim – meaning giants, a wicked region belonging to Satan, and a demonic stronghold: see Deut. 33:22.

It was at this location where Jesus challenged Satan; Jesus said that He would build His church at this location and the gates of hell would not prevail against it, Matthew 16:19. What Jesus was actually doing was telling Satan and the other fallen angels or former sons of God that He was now declaring war against them, these forces of evil. Og, a giant king, aka Nephilim, was also killed within this cosmic territory: see. Gen. 6:1; Deut. 32:8,9 and Numbers 21:33 ESV. In Jesus' time, this region was called Caesarea Philippi.

Furthermore, it was the tribe of Dan who first turned to idol worship: see Judges 18:30 and 1 Kings 12:28,29, with the other tribes of Israel following suit in Dan's whoredom and rebellion against God. Side note: Sampson, this moral failure of a man was from the tribe of Dan. After his death, the history of the tribe of Dan seems to fade from the Bible, and they lose their significance.

This prophecy was given by Dan's dad – Jacob, concerning him: see Genesis 49:17: "Dan will be a snake by the roadside, a viper along the path that bites the horse's heels so that its rider tumbles backward." As indicated in this prophecy, Satan made great use of the tribe of Dan: see

Gen. 30:4; Gen. 49:17; Deut. 33:22; Judges 5:17; Jud. 18:29,30; 1 Kings 12:30 and Jud. Chap. 13. For these reasons mentioned, Dan is not listed among the sealed tribes of Israel. Considering the history of Dan and the prophecy concerning this tribe, it is believed that the ultimate Antichrist could come from the tribe of Dan. As we continue throughout this study, more will be said regarding the ultimate or this last Antichrist.

Remember, the Book of Revelation contains the promises or prophecies of what God has said He is going to do, what He has done, and also that which He has yet to do. God's word will not return to Him void. They will accomplish what He has said they will: see Isa.55:11).

The Great Multitude in White Robes:

9 After this (the sealing of 144,000), *John says* I looked, and there before me was a great multitude that no one could count, from every nation, tribe, people, and language, **standing** before the throne and before the Lamb. They were wearing white robes (garments of salvation) and were holding palm branches in their hands: *see John 12:12,13*. **10** And they cried out in a loud voice: "Salvation belongs to our God, who sits on the throne, and to the Lamb."

As for the word **standing** mentioned in verse 9, this reference indicates a different group of people than the Church, which had been raptured and who is seated with Christ: see Ephesians 2:8; Matthew 19:28.

Another indicator that points to these people not being the universal Church is that they are not described as wearing crowns as it was for the glorified Church, who will reign as kings and priests. And who will cast their crowns before the throne: see Rev. 4:10, and be given a victors crown: see 1 Corinthians 9:25. And neither had there been a blowing of the trumpet to call them to heaven, unlike the Church which had been raptured: see 1Thessalonians 4:16,17. Therefore, this group of people is to be understood as those coming out of the Great Tribulation; besides, Scripture says as much.

A Look at the Lamb:

In Revelation 14:1-5, we have the following: Then I looked, and there before me was the Lamb who stood on Mount Zion. Israel must see Jesus as their Passover Lamb before they can behold and have Him as their king. The Lamb is seen standing on Mount Zion; this is a picture of Jesus' Second Advent, and with him, 144,000 who had His name and His Father's name written on their foreheads – this number is a representation of all the Jews who will be saved as a result of having gone through the Great Tribulation, not to the exclusion of Gentile Believers.

The Church of this age has not replaced the Jews; the Jewish people will be saved. God has not broken His covenant with His people of ancient times – Abraham and his descendants: see Genesis 12:1-3; 17:7,8 and Hebrews 6:13-20. Romans 11:25-27 has this to say to the Church or Gentile Believers regarding the nation of Israel or the Jewish people: **25** "I do not want you to be ignorant of this mystery, brothers, and sisters, so that you may not be conceited: Israel has experienced a hardening in part until the full number of the Gentiles has come in, **26** and in this way, all Israel will be saved. As it is written: "The deliverer will come from Zion; he will turn godlessness away from Jacob *or Israel*. **27** And this is my covenant with them when I take away their sins."

The Book of Revelation reveals to us God's plan to save the Jews, resulting from His sealing them, and as shown by them going through and coming out of the Great Tribulation. The Jews, having received God's seal upon their foreheads, Jesus had therefore finally been seen by them as their Savior – the Lamb of God and also their risen King. And so He protects them when He pours out His final wrath against the nations when they will array themselves against Israel in a final attempt to destroy her. God had promised in His covenant with the Jews that He would not break His covenant with them. Therefore, in this Book of Revelation, God will prove to the ultimate Antichrist, the Devil, the fallen host of heaven, and all who war against Israel to destroy her that Israel is His chosen people who will be saved: see Psalm 2.

After those who cried out in a loud voice: "Salvation belongs to our God, who sits on the throne, and to the Lamb." **Verse 11 reads:** All the angels were *seen* standing around the throne and around the elders (a title given to the Church leaders, who represent the Church, Jewish people now included, which are in heaven) *along with* the four living creatures. They fell down on their faces before the throne and worshiped God, **12** saying: "Amen! Praise and glory and wisdom and thanks and honor and power and strength be to our God forever and ever. Amen!" **13** Then one of the elders asked me, "These in white robes—who are they, and where did they come from?" **14** I answered, "Sir, you know." And he said, "These are they who have come **out** of the great tribulation; they have washed their robes and made them white in the blood of the Lamb.

15 Therefore, "they are before the throne of God and serve him day and night in his temple; and he who sits on the throne will shelter them with his presence. **16** 'Never again will they hunger; never again will they thirst. The sun will not beat down on them,' nor any scorching heat (such things they had experienced during the great tribulation). **17** For the Lamb at the center of the throne will be their shepherd; 'he will lead them to springs of living water.' 'And God will wipe away every tear from their eyes.'

As for the springs of living water, this represents the Holy Spirit that the Church or a born-again Believer or Christ's Bride has now or had within them before its ascension. However, this is not so with those coming out of the Great Tribulation who will be led to this Living Water now that they are in heaven and before the throne of the Triune God, which this text has in view.

The sixth seal being opened; chapter 7 is drawn to a close. God's pattern of sevens begins and ends in Revelation 8.

CHAPTER 10

Outline and Revelation Chapter 8

The Seventh Seal and the Golden Censer:

1. **Verse 1-5:** The Seventh Seal and the Silence in Heaven
   - Introduction: When the Lamb opens the seventh seal, there is silence in heaven for about half an hour.
   - The Golden Censer: John sees the seven angels who stand before God, and they are given seven trumpets.
   - The Angel with the Golden Censer: Another angel comes and stands at the altar with a golden censer, and he is given much incense to offer with the prayers of all the saints on the golden altar before the throne. The smoke of the incense, with the prayers of the saints, rises before God from the hand of the angel.
2. **Verse 6-7:** The Seven Trumpets Prepared
   - Introduction: The angel takes the censer and, fills it with fire from the altar, and throws it on the earth.
   - The Seven Trumpets: There are peals of thunder, rumblings, flashes of lightning, and an earthquake.
   - The Announcement: The seven angels who had the seven trumpets prepare to sound them.

3. **Verse 8-13:** The First Four Trumpets: Hail, Fire, and Blood
   - Introduction: The first angel sounds his trumpet, and there is hail and fire, mixed with blood, thrown upon the earth.
   - The Second Trumpet: The second angel sounds his trumpet, and something like a great mountain burning with fire is thrown into the sea.
   - The Third Trumpet: The third angel sounds his trumpet, and a great star falls from heaven, blazing like a torch, and it falls on a third of the rivers and on the springs of water.
   - The Fourth Trumpet: The fourth angel sounds his trumpet, and a third of the sun, moon, and stars are struck so that a third of their light is darkened, and a third of the day is kept from shining, and likewise a third of the night.

This chapter describes the opening of the seventh seal, which brings about a period of silence in heaven, followed by the introduction of the seven angels with seven trumpets. It introduces the first four trumpet judgments, which bring about various calamities upon the earth, such as hail, fire, blood, and celestial disturbances.

Revelation Chapter 8

In the Book of Joshua, there are parallels with Rev. chap. 8. However, hear what Zephaniah has to say regarding the End of Days:

Zephaniah 1:14-16, 14 The great day of the Lord is near—near and coming quickly. The cry on the day of the Lord is bitter; the Mighty Warrior shouts his battle cry. **15** That day will be a day of wrath— a day of distress and anguish, a day of trouble and ruin, a day of darkness and gloom, a day of clouds and blackness— **16** a day of trumpet and battle cry against the fortified cities and against the corner towers.

As seen with the opening of the Six Seals, they unleash great bloodshed and destruction upon the earth; with the blowing of the trumpets here in

Revelation Chapter 8, the wrath of God will be intensified upon the world with the blowing of each trumpet; even so, the birth pains of this world will increase before the arrival of the Antichrist's rule. However, the World's birth pains will be magnified during this seven-year reign of the false Messiah; this period is also known as a time of Jacob's Troubles: see Matt. Chapter 24; Romans 8:22, and Jeremiah Chapter 30:7.

Still, the people who belong to this world will not repent from their evil, as in the days of Noah and Lot. Humanism, or mankind's self-reliance, will have replaced God. We are currently seeing this downward spiraling; nevertheless, this matter will have reached its limit during the Lawless One's seven-year rule. As a result of this great fallen away or exceeding rebellion from the wicked people of this world, God responds with His wrath...Enough is Enough, as it was during the time of Noah and God's flood judgment! And, as well, Sodom and Gomorrah's judgment by fire because of their sexual perversion and utter rebellion against God!

The Seventh Seal and the Golden Censer:

1 When he – *The Lamb ~ Jesus* opened the seventh seal, there was silence in heaven for about half an hour (once again, we have a pause or intermission of sorts with another subset of sevens beginning. In the previous chapter, there was praise in heaven. Now there is silence, the mood is somber...the terrible wrath of God is imminent; John's view is now directed back to the earth. As demonstrated in the book of Exodus and other places or situations throughout the Bible, God caused natural events to bring forth His judgment or to accomplish His purpose on earth against His rebellious creation – the people of His making. The blowing of these trumpets, I believe, will precede John's vision of the multitude seen around the throne of God – those who had been martyred by the Antichrist). **John says in verse 2,** And I saw the seven angels who stand before God, and seven trumpets were given to them.

3 Another angel, who had a golden censer, came and stood at the altar. He was given much incense to offer, with the prayers of all God's people, on the golden altar in front of the throne. **4** The smoke of the incense, together with the prayers of God's people, went up before God from the angel's hand. **5** Then the angel took the censer, filled it with fire from the altar, and hurled it on the earth; and there came peals of thunder, rumblings, flashes of lightning, and an earthquake.

With These 7 Trumpets, The Following Transpires:

Trumpet 1: 8:6 Earth scorched = Vegetation destroyed

Trumpet 2: 8:8 Explosion in the sea = Sea life destroyed

Trumpet 3: 8:10 Poisoned Waters = Land life affected

Trumpet 4: 8:12 Atmosphere Darkened = Season Altered

After the 4th trumpet, there is a pause, and the 3 woes are expressed, indicating the final 3 trumpet judgments will be worse than the previous 4!

Trumpet 5: 9:1 Abyss opens Locusts Ascends = Physical pain inflicted upon the people, but death is stayed

Trumpet 6: 9:13 Angels released = Invasion from the east

Revelation 10:7 Presents another pause or gap

Trumpet 7: Rev. 11:15 God's Wrath fully comes = Next to follow will be the last Seven Bowl Judgments

Revelation Chapter 8:6 reads, Then the seven angels who had the seven trumpets prepared to sound them. **7** The first angel sounded his trumpet, and there came hail and fire (see 2 Peter 3:7); *the hail and fire were* mixed with blood, and it was hurled down on the earth. A third of the earth was burned up, a third of the trees were burned up, and all the green grass was burned up.

What might this event and other cataclysmic events be? In July 2012, there was a notable solar event known as the "solar superstorm." However, it's important to note that the most significant aspect of this event did not occur on July 22 but rather in the late hours of July 23 and the early hours of July 24, 2012. The event was sparked by a series of solar flares and coronal mass ejections (CMEs) originating from the Sun. The solar flares were classified as X1.4 and X5.4, which are powerful classifications indicating high levels of energy release. These solar flares were associated with CMEs that released large amounts of charged particles into space.

Fortunately, the Earth was not in the direct path of these CMEs. However, the region of the Sun producing these events was turning toward Earth. If these CMEs had occurred a week earlier, they could have significantly impacted Earth's magnetosphere and potentially caused disruptions to communication systems, satellites, and power grids.

The July 2012 solar storm serves as a reminder of the potential risks associated with solar activity. While it wasn't as impactful as the famous Carrington Event of 1859, which was another powerful geomagnetic solar storm, it highlighted the vulnerability of modern technology to space weather events. It is quite possible that God will utilize such an event to bring forth His wrath upon the earth.

Verse 8: The second angel sounded his trumpet, and something like a huge mountain, all ablaze, was thrown into the sea. A third of the sea turned into blood, **9** a third of the living creatures in the sea died, and a third of the ships were destroyed.

Side note: The eruption of the Krakatoa Volcano in 1883 was one of the most powerful and devastating volcanic events in recorded history. Krakatoa is a volcanic island in the Sunda Strait, located between Java and Sumatra in Indonesia. Here are some key points about the eruption:

1. **Eruption Date:** The eruption began on the afternoon of August 26, 1883, and reached its climax on August 27, 1883.

2. **Nature of the Eruption:** Krakatoa's eruption was a series of cataclysmic explosions and volcanic activity. The event was marked by four massive explosions, which were heard as far as 3,000 miles away. This was the loudest recorded sound/explosion in modern history.

3. **Sound and Shockwaves:** The explosions generated extremely loud sounds, with reports of the noise reaching up to 180 decibels. The sound waves traveled around the Earth multiple times. The shockwaves produced by the explosions also caused atmospheric pressure changes that were recorded across the globe.

4. **Island Destruction:** The eruptions led to the collapse of much of the volcanic island. The northern two-thirds of the island disappeared into the sea, creating a caldera or crater. The explosion also caused tsunamis that reached coastal areas, causing widespread destruction.

5. **Tsunamis:** The tsunamis generated by the eruption were particularly devastating. Waves reached heights of up to 130 feet and affected coastlines as far away as South America, Africa, and the United States. In some areas, entire coastal communities were wiped out.

6. **Climate Effects:** The massive amounts of volcanic ash and aerosols ejected into the stratosphere had a significant impact on the global climate. The fine particles in the atmosphere caused spectacular sunsets around the world for several years. The volcanic aerosols also led to a temporary cooling effect on the Earth's surface.

7. **Casualties:** The eruption resulted in the deaths of tens of thousands of people, both from the immediate effects of the explosions and tsunamis and from longer-term impacts such as disease and famine caused by the destruction.

8. **Scientific Impact:** The Krakatoa eruption had a profound impact on the understanding of volcanic activity and its global consequences.

The Krakatoa eruption of 1883 is often cited as one of the most significant volcanic events in modern history due to its widespread and far-reaching impacts.

Side note: The eruption of Mount Tambora in 1815 is one of the most powerful volcanic eruptions in recorded history. Located on the island of Sumbawa in Indonesia, Tambora's eruption had significant global consequences. Here are key points about the Tambora eruption:

1. **Eruption Date:** The eruption began on April 5, 1815, and reached its climax on April 10, 1815.

2. **Explosive Power:** Tambora's eruption is classified as a VEI-7 event, the highest on the Volcanic Explosivity Index. It released an estimated 38 cubic miles of volcanic material.

3. **Catastrophic Effects:** The eruption resulted in the destruction of the volcano's summit, creating a caldera. The event caused massive pyroclastic flows, ashfall, and tsunamis. The pyroclastic flows devastated nearby settlements and caused widespread destruction.

4. **Tsunamis:** The eruption triggered tsunamis that affected coastal areas in the region, causing additional casualties and destruction.

5. **Global Climate Impact:** Tambora's eruption injected an enormous amount of volcanic ash and sulfur dioxide into the stratosphere. This led to the formation of sulfate aerosols, which reflected sunlight away from the Earth and caused a temporary cooling effect. The year following the eruption, 1816, is often referred to as the "Year Without a Summer" due to global climate abnormalities. Unseasonably cold temperatures, frosts, and crop failures occurred in various parts of the Northern Hemisphere.

6. **Global Consequences:** The cooling effect of the Tambora eruption had widespread impacts on agriculture, leading to food shortages and famines in various regions. The disrupted climate patterns contributed to social and economic hardships.

7. **Casualties:** The eruption is estimated to have resulted in tens of thousands of immediate casualties due to volcanic activity and tsunamis. The long-term impacts on climate and agriculture likely led to additional deaths.

8. **Scientific Understanding:** The Tambora eruption significantly advanced the understanding of the global effects of large volcanic eruptions. It highlighted the link between volcanic activity, atmospheric processes, and climate.

The eruption of Mount Tambora is considered one of the most powerful natural events in human history, and its effects had a profound impact on societies worldwide. It serves as a reminder of the potential for volcanic eruptions to influence global climate and have far-reaching consequences. These events are minuscule depictions of God's wrath that will be unleashed upon the earth! Once again, it is quite possible that God will utilize such an event or events to bring forth His wrath upon the earth...I believe this will be the case.

Revelation 8:10 The third angel sounded his trumpet, and a great star, blazing like a torch, fell from the sky on a third of the rivers and on the springs of water— **11** the name of the star is Wormwood. (Interestingly, some have associated the Chernobyl nuclear plant's name with Wormwood, and they believe this destruction here in verse 10 to be related to nuclear war or some form of nuclear devastation). *As a result of this falling great star,* a third of the waters turned bitter, and many people died from the waters that had become bitter: see Amos 5:6-8.

12 The fourth angel sounded his trumpet, and a third of the sun was struck, a third of the moon, and a third of the stars so that a third of them turned dark. A third of the day was without light, and also a third of the night. (As a result of such a cataclysmic event permitted or caused by God, there will be significant changes in the atmosphere). **Verse 13** *John says,* As I watched, I heard an eagle that was flying in midair call out in a loud voice: "Woe! Woe! Woe to the inhabitants of the earth because of the trumpet blasts about to be sounded by the other three angels!" (These three woes are an indication that things are about to worsen due to God's wrath)!

CHAPTER 11

OUTLINE AND REVELATION CHAPTER 9

The Fifth and Sixth Trumpets: The Locusts and the Army of Horsemen:

1. **Verse 1-12:** The Fifth Trumpet: The Locusts from the Bottomless Pit

   - Introduction: The fifth angel sounds his trumpet, and John sees a star fallen from heaven to earth. The star is given the key to the shaft of the bottomless pit.

   - The Release of the Locusts: The star opens the shaft of the bottomless pit, and smoke rises like the smoke of a great furnace. Out of the smoke come locusts on the earth, and they are given power like scorpions of the earth. They are commanded not to harm the grass or any green plant or tree, but only those people who do not have the seal of God on their foreheads.

   - Description of the Locusts: The appearance of the locusts is like horses prepared for battle, with crowns of gold on their heads, faces like human faces, hair like women's hair, teeth like lions' teeth, breastplates like iron breastplates, and the sound of their wings like the noise of many chariots with horses rushing into battle.

- Their Authority: They have tails like scorpions, and they have the power to torment people for five months but not to kill them.

2. **Verse 13-21:** The Sixth Trumpet: The Army of Horsemen
   - Introduction: The sixth angel sounds his trumpet, and John hears a voice from the four horns of the golden altar before God.

   - The Release of the Four Angels: The voice commands the sixth angel to release the four angels who are bound at the great river Euphrates. So, the four angels are released, and they are prepared for the hour, the day, the month, and the year to kill a third of mankind.

   - The Armies of Horsemen: The number of mounted troops is 200 million. John sees the horses in the vision, and he sees their breastplates of fiery red, dark blue, and yellow, and the heads of the horses are like lions' heads, and fire and smoke and sulfur come out of their mouths, killing a third of mankind.

   - The Unrepentant: Despite these plagues, the rest of mankind who were not killed by these plagues do not repent of the works of their hands or give up worshiping demons and idols of gold, silver, bronze, stone, and wood, which cannot see or hear or walk, nor do they repent of their murders, sorceries, sexual immorality, or thefts.

This chapter describes the sounding of the fifth and sixth trumpets, unleashing plagues upon the earth involving locusts and an army of horsemen. Despite the severity of these judgments, many people remain unrepentant in their idolatry and wickedness.

Revelation Chapter 9

Cosmic Conflict - Principalities and Powers:

As seen in this study and throughout the Bible. There is a pattern of sevens, wherein attention is given to the first three or four points, with extra emphasis closing out the writer's remaining thoughts. This pattern indicates a mystery God wants to reveal to His listeners and or readers regarding this division of seven. Here is one example for your review, as provided in Proverbs 30: 18-19.

The book of Revelation regarding Last Things is somewhat chronological or linear prophetic, unfolding history. Somewhat...because of the narrated intermissions provided to help the reader understand the unfolding future and events before us in this Book. And so, there is a beginning of a future event or narrative, as seen in this study regarding the Last Days. However, emphasis may be provided at different points of the unfolding story that seem to distinguish or establish a different revelation, order, or narrative period that John receives. That said, these events are to be viewed as a continuation or overlapping of the proceedings, highlighting or revealing a different perspective or characteristic of a person, place, or thing. It's, therefore, essential to understand this detail, or else the unfolding narrative can leave one confused about what is occurring, where, and or when.

In this chapter, John provides his readers with the re-emergence of the rebellious Fallen angels who were imprisoned in the pit. These and other events going forward relate to or are answers to three significant occurrences or rebellions early in mankind's history. Therefore, this 9th Chapter of the Book of Revelation is to be looked at with Genesis 6:1 in mind. Additionally, Revelation Chapter 12:9 should be read with consideration of the events of Gen. 3:1. And lastly, Rev. 13:18 should have attention considering Babylon's rebellion as provided in Gen. 11:3. These three rebellions are what Jesus is now about to respond to and counter. However, the matter of mankind's sins, Jesus had already addressed by giving Himself – as the Lamb Sacrificed for our atonement before the world was created.

Now John says here in verse 1: And the fifth angel blew his trumpet (signaling God's continuing judgment), and I saw a star (a fallen member of the angelic host an Elohim or former son of God: see Jude 1:6 and

Genesis 6:1- 4. *This* fallen *star* (or better translated, this rebellious angel or star had fallen) from heaven to Earth, and he (perhaps the Devil himself) was given the key to the shaft of the bottomless pit: see Isaiah 14: 12-14 and Luke 10:18,19.

2 He opened the shaft of the bottomless pit (see Luke 8: 30,31; 2 Peter 2:4 and Jude 1:6. This pit or hades is a prison housing some of the demons or Watchers or disembodied spirits from Gen. 6:1-4), and from the shaft rose smoke like the smoke of a great furnace and the sun and the air were darkened with the smoke from the shaft (which is an image of binding power, either good or evil). **3** Then, from the smoke came locusts (a symbol of destructive evil or demonic powers) on the Earth, and they were given power like the power of scorpions of the Earth (see Ex.10:12. This Locust judgment and others of Revelation parallels with God's judgment on Egypt. Additionally, nations that warred against Israel, who were enemies of God, were nevertheless used as God's instruments of judgment upon Israel and were identified as locusts: see Joel 1:1-6).

4 They – *the demonically possessed Locust or demons who resembled locusts,* were told not to harm the grass of the Earth or any green plant or any tree, but only those *rebellious* people who do not have the seal of God on their foreheads. **5** They were allowed to torment or torture them for five months (the same period of time that God judged the earth during the flood due to the great wickedness that was upon the earth during Noah's lifetime. And for which God's wrath will be unleashed upon the world at the end of this age for such wickedness as was in Noah's time and that of Sodom and Gomorrah) but – *the locusts were* not to kill them; *however,* their torment *would be* like the torment of a scorpion (again these demons had taken on the appearance as best described by John) when it *or they* stings someone. **6** And in those days, people will seek death and will not find it. They will long to die, but death will flee from them.

Amid their suffering, salvation is beckoning them to answer. But those who were not sealed by God would not or perhaps could not repent because of their wickedly altered disposition, both spiritually and very likely physically, nor could they find relief from their suffering; this torment foreshadowed these wicked, rebellious ones' eternal judgment and fiery suffering that is soon to come.

In case you are unaware. Some people have invested billions of dollars in the hopes of prolonging their lives or receiving immortality through advanced knowledge in the sciences and technological fields. In my view and others, this matter of acquiring such knowledge points back to the forbidden tree, wherein mankind desired knowledge apart from and outside the boundaries intended for what God had provided or permitted Adam and Eve to have. Furthermore, from the Jewish Book of Enoch, tradition holds that the Watchers or sons of God, these fallen angels – intelligent, malevolent heavenly beings seen in Gen. 6:1-7 provided knowledge to man by which to further corrupt and destroy themselves.

With regards to "the people seeking death and will not find it." They will long to die, but death will flee from them." What I and others believe could possibly be occurring at this point in mankind's history and through means beyond our current understanding, mankind in the future will have come up with some means to escape death or at least prolong life extensively. What we must bear in mind is that Satan's system or kingdom on earth with the Antichrist at its helm will be a counterfeit of Jesus' Kingdom. Everything that Jesus has offered to humanity both now and in the future. So, Satan will also convince the people that he can provide such things; therefore, some resemblance of extended life beyond what the norm currently is must be taken into consideration.

When we read through the Bible, particularly the Book of Exodus, where Moses and Aaron are squaring off with Pharaoh and his wise men, sorcerers, and magicians. Do we read this encounter with thoughts regarding Pharaoh's men, that they were merely performing magic or some form of trickery? If so, I will suggest that much more is taking place than the sleight of hand. A read through Deuteronomy Chapter 18:10-12 and elsewhere throughout the Bible, God strictly forbids His chosen people not to engage in divination, sorcery, witchcraft, and so on. Through these mediums and others, one can, in fact, consult with, be influenced by, and become one with the dark forces of spiritual wickedness and even be empowered by them. God knew and knows the danger of such entanglement. Therefore, our dependency is to be upon Him alone and His Holy Word.

Therefore, do not think it strange or believe that some trick is being played when false Antichrists and false prophets, who will be empowered by the Devil, perform signs and wonders: see Rev. 13:13,14. Matthew Chapter 24:24 reads, "For false messiahs and false prophets will appear and perform great signs and wonders to deceive, if possible, even the elect," also see Mark 13:22.

Look, something else to bear in mind regarding death fleeing from man. Scripture seems to suggest that the Tree of Life actually provided properties for extended life. We see from Genesis 3:24 that God drove Adam and Eve out of the Garden of Eden. But then He placed the cherubim – multiple guardians or super angels and a flaming sword that turned every way to guard the way or entrance to the Tree of Life. It is, therefore, reasonable to assume that God did not want mankind to have access to this tree, less they lived perpetually in wickedness until they totally destroyed one another. Another thing that we must bear in mind is that God will give fallen and rebellious humanity what they long for so that His purpose may ultimately be fulfilled through their wickedness and rebellion. This is what we see occurring in the Book of Revelation and elsewhere throughout the Bible.

Verse 7 In appearance, the locusts were **like** horses (a symbol of power, strength, and conquest) prepared for battle: on their heads were what looked like crowns of gold (symbols of ruling over death); their faces were **like** human faces, **8** their hair **like** women's hair, and their teeth **like** lions' teeth; **9** they had breastplates **like** breastplates of iron, and the noise of their wings was **like** the noise of many chariots with horses rushing into battle. **10** They have tails and stings **like** scorpions, and their power to hurt people for five months is in their tails. **11** They have as king over them the angel of the bottomless pit. (People as it was for John, some things we are unable to comprehend, yet God is in control: see Proverbs 30:27). *This king over them*; His name in Hebrew is Abaddon, and in Greek, he is called Apollyon (quite possibly this demonic power, as some think is called Gog: see Ezek. Chap. 38 and 39) who is believed to have been behind Nimrod's Babylon rebellion. Nimrod can be viewed as the first Antichrist or world's superpower to stand against God: see Gen. chap. 11. There were and are different religions. There may be different names associated with their varied gods and pagan practices. However, the same Elohim or gods or disembodied spirit entities are the evil and deceptive influence behind this world's corrupt government and this world's worship of idols and pagan religions.

Read Amos 7:1-7 and Ezekiel 38:1-3.

Rev. verse 12: The first woe has passed; behold, two woes are still to come.

The beginning of the second woe. And its ending is in Revelation 11:14,15. The information provided herein is the narration of this period.

13 Then the sixth angel blew his trumpet, and I heard a voice from the four horns (which is a symbol of power and strength) of the golden altar before God, **14** saying to the sixth angel who had the trumpet, "Release the four angels who are bound at the great river Euphrates. (This spiritual or demonic, geographical territory from which these demons or fallen angels are released is believed to be the location of present-day Iraq...And where the rebellious empire of Babylon was established. These four Elohim, or spirit beings, are going to unleash hell on Earth. Reminder: From under this altar came the martyrs' cry, as provided in Revelation Chapter 6, who were asking for God's vengeance, which is now to be answered. In God's judgment of nations, not only will He use other nations to perform His bidding, but He will also utilize evil spiritual powers, His loyal angels, and other created things to serve as His instruments of wrath or judgment.

15 So the four angels, who had been prepared for the hour, the day, the month, and the year (this being God's appointed time), were released to kill a third of mankind (believed to be numbered around 2 billion people). **16** The number of mounted troops (demon army or demon influenced or demon-possessed mankind is debated) was twice ten thousand times ten thousand; I heard their number (200 million). **17** And this is how I saw the horses in my vision and those who rode them: they wore breastplates the color of fire (a symbol of God's burning judgment, purifying and testing) and of sapphire (a symbol of hardness) and of sulfur, and the heads of the horses were **like** lions' heads, and fire and smoke and sulfur came out of their mouths. **18** By these three plagues, a third of mankind was killed by the fire and smoke and sulfur coming out of their mouths. **19** For the power of the horses is in their mouths and in their tails, for their tails are **like** serpents with heads, and by means of them, they wound: see Ezekiel 38: 1-15.

20 The rest of mankind, who were not killed by these plagues, **did not repent of the works of their hands** (Secular Humanism is in view – their self-will, or rule and Satan's influence has a stronghold on the minds of these lost, rebellious, and grossly perverted souls) nor *did they* give up worshiping demons (these Elohim through whatever the sort of mankind's making and beliefs and false-religions were worshipped; because of this God's judgment will come upon those belonging to this world's Babylon System) and *also their worship of* idols of gold and silver and bronze and stone and wood (materialism may also be in view, which neither can see or hear or walk but are idolized by fallen mankind) **21 nor did they repent** of their murders or their sorceries – *this being drug dependency* or their sexual immorality or their thefts.

Perhaps, because of the *Great Deception*, lies, and strong delusions that God gave mankind over to, they did not have within themselves or saw the need to repent. If we remain in rebellion against God, He will give us what we want, ultimately leading to our gross defilement and even self-destruction: see 2 Thessalonians 2:11 and Romans 1:26. Such debasement is a display of the lowest of our sinful human condition when humanity refuses God or rebels against Him and His truth. We, therefore, in essence, become gods unto ourselves, doing what is right in our own eyes – which is the work and aim of Satan. And the end result: Having sown the wind, they shall reap the whirlwind: see Hosea 2:9.

CHAPTER 12

OUTLINE AND REVELATION CHAPTER 10

Verses 1-11 offer another pause or intermission.

The Angel and the Little Scroll:

1. **Verse 1-4:** The Mighty Angel and the Little Scroll
   - Introduction: John sees another mighty angel coming down from heaven, clothed with a cloud, with a rainbow over his head, his face like the sun, and his legs like pillars of fire. He has a little scroll open in his hand.
   - The Angel's Cry: The angel cries out with a loud voice, and when he cries out, seven thunders sound their voices.
   - John's Instructions: When the seven thunders had sounded, John was about to write down what they said, but he heard a voice from heaven telling him to seal up what the seven thunders spoke and not to write it down.
2. **Verse 5-7:** The Angel's Oath and Declaration
   - Introduction: The mighty angel raises his right hand to heaven and swears by Him who lives forever and ever, who created heaven and what is in it, the earth and what is in it, and the sea and what is in it, that there would be no more delay.
   - The Mystery of God: The angel declares that in the days when

the seventh angel is about to sound his trumpet, the mystery of God will be fulfilled, as He announced to His servants, the prophets.

3. **Verse 8-11:** The Command to Eat the Little Scroll
    *   Introduction: Then the voice from heaven tells John to go and take the little scroll from the hand of the angel standing on the sea and on the land.
    *   John's Obedience: John goes to the angel and asks him to give him the little scroll. The angel tells John to take it and eat it; it will make his stomach bitter, but in his mouth, it will be sweet as honey.
    *   The Experience: John takes the little scroll and eats it. It is sweet in his mouth, but it makes his stomach bitter.
    *   The Prophetic Charge: The angel tells John that he must again prophesy about many peoples and nations and languages and kings.

This chapter introduces a mighty angel holding a little scroll, which he instructs John to eat. The chapter also highlights the angel's oath regarding the mystery of God and John's subsequent prophetic charge.

Revelation Chapter 10

The Angel and the Little Scroll:

1 Then I saw another mighty angel (perhaps this was Gabriel, Jesus' representative, or the archangel Michael or some other mighty angel also referred to as an Elohim or son of God. However, I'm inclined to believe this angel was Jesus) coming down from heaven, wrapped in a cloud (symbolic of divine covering and guidance. But again, this may be a different angel, an Archangel or Elohim), with a rainbow over his head (symbolic of God's covenant with His redeemed. Nonetheless also, around the throne of God, there was a rainbow: see Rev. 4:3), **Continuing verse 1**, and this – *mighty angel's* face was like the sun (symbolic of the glory of God), and his legs like pillars of fire (symbolic of strength, firmness and God's judgment; His purifying and or testing. In the New Testament, Jesus is not referred to as an angel. However, in the Old Testament, His designation is often the *Angel of The Lord* – indicating Deity when He took on physical form, aka, theophany, as seen in Genesis 16: 7-11 and Exodus 3:2-4. This is why some, myself included, think this mighty angel might be Jesus, which can also be compared with Revelation 1:14-16 and the attribute of the angel in this text before us. However, I will not be dogmatic with my opinion).

2 He – *the mighty angel*, had a little scroll open in his hand (indicating a different scroll from that of Revelation Chapter 5, which the Lamb possessed and, therefore, this is perhaps a different messenger or Archangel with additional information to be revealed). And *this mighty angel* – he set his right foot on the sea. (Rev. 13:1 speaks of a Beast - the Antichrist that is seen coming out of the sea), *and this – the mighty angel's* left foot was on the land. (Rev. 13:11 speaks to a 2nd Beast – the false prophet that is seen coming out of the earth, who is the 1st Beast's Minister of Propaganda and High Priest).

3 And he (the mighty angel or Jesus, you may choose whom you will, is now demonstrating all authority and power over the Antichrist and false prophet as He stands over both land and sea. Regardless of who is in view, this is a picture of Jesus reclaiming the earth and His judgment upon spiritual wickedness: see Romans 16:20). *And then He,* **verse 3 continues**, called out with a loud voice, like a lion roaring. (symbolic of Royalty and the King's anger: see Psalm 29:3,4; Job 37: 2-5, these Scriptures seemingly point to God. And still, this could be God's Angelic representative, an Archangel, son of God, or Elohim).

As we will see further along in our study, the Antichrist, who will claim to be God, has his own false prophet. And so, I say, yet again, don't be fooled by the giftings of false prophets, preachers, or pastors. ***Unless*** *you know the Holy Word for yourself, how else can you test those who claim to preach or those who claim to come or speak in the name or authority of Jesus?* Along with the Dragon – Satan himself, they will establish their own unholy or counterfeit trinity; having deceived the whole world, they will claim authority over the earth, politically and religiously – this one world government will be none other than "Babylon the Great." Furthermore, and generally speaking, "Sea" represents the nations of the world, and "Land" represents Israel or God's people).

Continuing with **verse 3**, *when he -* the mighty angel called out, the seven thunders sounded (the secret sayings of God or God speaking: see John 12:27-30 and Psalms 29:3-9). **4** And when the seven thunders had sounded (symbolic of God speaking forth His complete judgment), I was about to write, but I heard a voice from heaven saying, "Seal up what the seven thunders have said and do not write it down." (So did God command Daniel to secrecy in Daniel 7:28, 8:26, 12:4&9 and the Apostle Paul in 2 Corinthian 12:4-7. But soon enough, the mysteries or secret things of God will be revealed: see Deuteronomy 29:29).

5 And the angel whom I saw standing on the sea and on the land raised his right hand to heaven **6** and swore by him who lives forever and ever (this being God the Father who is seated on His throne), who created heaven and what is in it, the earth and what is in it, and the sea and what is in it, that there would be no more delay. (This was the delay or "rest a little longer" of Rev. 6:10,11; this delay is now over; God is about to move against the wicked and rebellious ones of this earth. Just as every Word of God is true, nor can He lie, this angel takes an oath as God's messenger that what He speaks for God will come to pass).

Remember that while Jesus was on the earth, He said that He came to bear witness of His Father who was in heaven: see John 6:38, 8:28, and John 14:24. There is nothing that suggests that Jesus cannot continue to bear witness of His Father while they are both in heaven. That said, I don't have a problem with this representative of God being an Archangel and not Jesus). *Regarding the delay, the angel proclaims in verse* **7** But that in the days of the trumpet call to be sounded by the seventh angel, the mystery of God (see verse 4) would be fulfilled, just as he announced to his servants the prophets."

Let's hear what the Prophet Daniel has to say regarding the mystery of the "End of Days:" **Chapter 12** reads as follows: **1** "At that time Michael, the great prince who protects your people, will arise. There will be a time of distress such as has not happened from the beginning of nations until then. But at that time, your people—everyone whose name is found written in the book—will be delivered. **2** Multitudes who sleep in the dust of the earth will awake: some to everlasting life, others to shame and everlasting contempt. **3** Those who are wise will shine like the brightness of the heavens, and those who lead many to righteousness, like the stars forever and ever. **4** But you, Daniel, roll up and seal the words of the scroll until the time of the end. Many will go here and there to increase knowledge."

5 Then I, Daniel, looked, and there before me stood two others, one on this bank of the river and one on the opposite bank. **6** One of them said to the man clothed in linen, who was above the waters of the river, "How long will it be before these astonishing things are fulfilled?" **7** The man clothed in linen, who was above the waters of the river, lifted his right hand and his left hand toward heaven, and I heard him swear by him who lives forever, saying, "It will be for a time, times and half a time *or 3.5 years*. When the power of the holy people has been finally broken, all these things will be completed."

8 I heard, but I did not understand. So, I asked, "My lord, what will the outcome of all this be?" **9** He replied, "Go your way, Daniel, because the words are rolled up and sealed until the time of the end. **10** Many will be purified, made spotless and refined, but the wicked will continue to be wicked. None of the wicked will understand, but those who are wise will understand. **11** "From the time that the daily sacrifice is abolished and the abomination that causes desolation – here, the Antichrist's rule is set up, there will be 1,290 days – according to the ancient Jewish calendar, 3.5 years. **12** Blessed is the one who waits for and reaches the end of the 1,335 days. (This period of time will be looked at when Jesus sets things in order or in place in Revelation Chapter 20, just before He establishes His millennial reign on earth.)

In Dan. 12:13, *the angel tells Dan,* "As for you, go your way till the end. You will rest, and then at the end of the days you will rise to receive your allotted inheritance." (We will see these things fulfilled in chapter 13 of this book of Revelation).

A Look at Various Mysteries of the Bible:

Mystery of the Rapture, 1 Cor. 15:50-52.
Mystery of Israel's blindness, Rom. 11:25-27.
Mystery of God's Wisdom, 1 Cor. 2:7-10.
Mystery of Christ and the Church, Eph. 5:31.
Mystery of Christ in us, Col. 1:25-27.
Mystery of the Kingdom of Heaven, Matt. 13:10,11.
Mystery of godliness, 1 Tim. 3:16.

As Christians, we will not understand everything in the Bible perfectly. However, if we hold fast to our faith in Jesus, as the Son of God, Who is our Lord and Savior...IN THE END WE WIN!

8 Then *Jonn says,* the voice that I had heard from heaven spoke to me again, saying, "Go, take the scroll that is open in the hand of the angel who is standing on the sea and on the land." **9** So I went to the angel and told him to give me the little scroll (John is now moved from being a spectator to becoming a participator in sharing the Word of God. This is the Great Commission of every Believer: see Matt. 28:18). And he (the angel) said to me, "Take and eat it; it will make your stomach bitter, but in your mouth, it will be sweet as honey." (The Word of God is in fact like a two-edged sword bringing the Good News of Salvation and the bitter news of His coming wrath and judgment). **10** And I took the little scroll from the hand of the angel and ate it. It was sweet as honey in my mouth, but when I had eaten it, my stomach was made bitter.

Regarding God's Word bringing sorrow or bitterness, see Ezek. 2:10 through 3:1-3 &14,15. Also, recall the difficult prophetic revelation given to Noah and Abraham. Additionally, the Word of God is as grievous to Daniel as seen in Dan. 7:28; 8:27; 10:8, and furthermore with Jeremiah the weeping prophet: see Jer. 15:15,16. Moreover, others, throughout Scripture, found God's Word to be troubling to their souls). *John continues here in verse* **11,** And I was told, "You must again (now pointing back to the unsealing of the first scroll, in Rev. Chapter 5 and the previous Trumpet Judgments) prophecy about many peoples and nations and languages and kings." (Now John going forward is to prophecy providing greater detail through the recapitulation of his narration).

CHAPTER 13

OUTLINE AND REVELATION CHAPTER 11

The Two Witnesses and the Seventh Trumpet:

1. **Verse 1-2:** The Measuring of the Temple and the Two Witnesses
   - Introduction: John is given a measuring rod and told to measure the temple of God, the altar, and those who worship there.
   - The Exclusion: The outer court of the temple is to be left out, as it is given over to the nations, and they will trample the holy city for forty-two months.
   - The Two Witnesses: They are given power to prophesy for 1,260 days, clothed in sackcloth, symbolizing a period of prophetic testimony.
2. **Verse 3-6:** The Ministry and Protection of the Two Witnesses
   - Introduction: Two witnesses are granted authority to prophesy for 1,260 days, clothed in sackcloth.
   - Their Abilities: They have the power to shut the sky so that no rain falls during the days of their prophesying, and they have power over the waters to turn them into blood and to strike the earth with every kind of plague as often as they wish.
   - Their Protection: They are protected from harm until their testimony is complete.

3. **Verse 7-10:** The Death and Resurrection of the Two Witnesses
   - Introduction: When their testimony is finished, the beast that rises from the bottomless pit will make war on them, conquer them, and kill them.
   - Public Display: Their dead bodies lie in the street of the great city where their Lord was crucified, and those from the peoples and tribes and languages and nations will gaze at their dead bodies and refuse to let them be placed in a tomb.
   - Celebration: Those who dwell on the earth rejoice over them and make merry and exchange presents because these two prophets had been a torment to those who dwell on the earth.

4. **Verse 11-14:** The Resurrection and Ascension of the Two Witnesses
   - Introduction: After three and a half days, the breath of life from God enters them, and they stand up on their feet, and great fear falls on those who see them.
   - The Call to Ascend: A loud voice from heaven calls the two witnesses, saying, "Come up here!" They ascend to heaven in a cloud, and their enemies watch them.
   - The Earthquake: At that hour, there is a great earthquake, and a tenth of the city falls. Seven thousand people are killed in the earthquake, and the rest are terrified and give glory to the God of heaven.

5. **Verse 15-19:** The Seventh Trumpet: The Kingdom Proclaimed
   - Introduction: The seventh angel sounds his trumpet, and loud voices in heaven declare, "The kingdom of the world has become the kingdom of our Lord and of his Christ, and he shall reign forever and ever."
   - Worship and Thanks: The twenty-four elders who sit on their thrones before God fall on their faces and worship God, saying, "We give thanks to you, Lord God Almighty, who is and who was, for you have taken your great power and begun to reign."

- The Nations' Anger: The nations rage, but God's wrath has come, and the time for judging the dead has come, for rewarding the saints and prophets, and for destroying those who destroy the earth.
- The Temple of God: The temple of God in heaven is opened, and the ark of his covenant is seen within his temple, accompanied by flashes of lightning, rumblings, peals of thunder, an earthquake, and hailstorm.

This chapter describes the ministry, death, resurrection, and ascension of the two witnesses, as well as the sounding of the seventh trumpet, signaling the proclamation of God's kingdom and the final judgment.

Revelation Chapter 11

Verses 1-14 offer another pause for John to elaborate.

In this chapter, we have continued prophetic recapitulation with greater detail or amplification of the revelation given to John of the events for the Day of the Lord and that which is yet to come.

The Two Witnesses:

1 Then I was given a measuring rod like a staff, and I was told, "Rise and measure the temple of God: see Zach. 2:1-5 and Ezek. Chapters 40 through 48. (A literal temple will be erected in Jerusalem: see Dan. 9:27; Matt. 24:15; 2 Thess. 2:3-12 and 2 Samuel 7:12,13. I recall your attention to prophetic history; it is cyclical. In 168 BC, the Greek King Antiochus desecrated the temple by erecting a statue of the Greek god Zeus and sacrificed a pig on the altar of incense. Although the 2nd temple was destroyed in AD 70 by General Titus, Scripture has informed us that another temple will be erected for the Jews. However, the ultimate Antichrist will also desecrate this temple. When this rebuilding project for this temple begins, this is a sure sign that the Antichrist is about to emerge if he isn't already on the scene. This temple should serve as no big deal for the Church of God. The reasons for our lack of concern: I believe the Church will have been Raptured before the temple's completion. Furthermore, and most importantly, as pertaining to our earthen bodies, *Born Again Believers* are Christ's living temples indwelt by the Holy Spirit: see 1 Cor. 3:16; 6:19).

Continuing with verse 1, *John was told to "Rise and measure the temple of God and the altar* and those who worship there – *undoubtedly the sealed of God, the Jewish people*); **2** but do not measure the court outside the temple; leave that out, for it is given over to the nations, and they will trample the holy city for forty-two months: see Luke 21:24-26. **3** And I will grant authority to my two witnesses. (God always provides two witnesses to establish His Word: see Num. 35:30; Matt. 18:16; Gen. 19:1; Ex. 5:1; Num. 14:6; Deut. 19:15; Josh 2:1 and Luke 20:4; moreover, the Apostles were sent out by two's), and so, they – *the two witnesses* will prophesy for 1,260 days (or a Time – 1yr., Times – 2 years and half a time – ½ year or forty-two months or 3.5 years: see Dan. 7:25). *These two witnesses will be* clothed in sackcloth (which is symbolic of mourning, sorrow, or judgment. There is a pattern of 3.5 years throughout Scripture; the most notable is the period or duration of Jesus' ministry and the prophetic ministry of these two witnesses in our text).

4 These are the two olive trees (who will be *Spirit-filled Light Bearers* of God's Truth. Although debated, they are believed to be Moses and Elijah based on their job descriptions: see 2 Kings 1:10; James 5:7 and regarding Moses: see Ex. 5:3; and 17:17. The fact that these two appeared on the mountain of transfiguration: see Matt. 17:1-8 and Luke 9:28-36, there these two were speaking of Jesus' departure. One can, therefore, reason that these two will be prophesying about Jesus' reign as King and His 2nd Coming), and *they,* the two lampstands (God's Light of the world and His Truth tellers), stand before the Lord of the Earth.

5 And if anyone would harm them, fire (literally) pours from their mouth and consumes their foes. If anyone would harm them, this is how he is doomed to be killed. (Like it was during the life and ministry of Moses and Elijah, here once again, they will be calling down fire from heaven: see Malachi 4:4,5). *Additionally,* **6** They have the power to shut the sky that no rain may fall during the days of their prophesying (which is believed by some, me included, as occurring during the first 3.5 years of the 7-year tribulation period. God is longsuffering; He's still trying to reach lost souls before He unleashes His righteous fury or wrath through the blowing and outpouring of His Trumpet and Bowl judgments upon this rebellious world).

Just as Jesus proclaimed His authority and power for 3.5 years. God also gives the world what they want: their counterfeit or false Messiah – the Antichrist, judicially 3.5 years to rule and further deceive the people. Once again, the people – the unbelieving Jews, in particular, are about to get what they want: figuratively their Saul, Ceasar, and Barabas). *Continuing with verse 6*, and they – the two witnesses, have power over the waters to turn them into blood and to strike the Earth with every kind of plague as often as they desire. **7** And when they have finished their testimony (for 3.5 yrs. under God's witness protection program), the beast (who is Satan's representative and believed by some to be his very seed: see Gen. 3:15, this, the Antichrist and member of Satan's counterfeit trinity) *this one* that rises from the bottomless pit (also see Jude 6 and 2 Pet.2:4,5) *as for this beast he* will make war on them (which will at this time be permitted by God. God will have given rebellious mankind one final time to repent. Instead, they rejected the grace of God extended by these two witnesses) and (this Beast, again believed by some to be the Antichrist who will come from the tribe of Dan) *will* conquer them and kill them,

8 and their dead bodies – *the two witnesses*, will lie in the street of the great city that symbolically is called Sodom and Egypt (a picture of the world's sexual immorality, vileness, idolatry, and self-will), *this being the utter corruption of the people and location* where their Lord was crucified. **9** For three and a half days, some from the peoples and tribes and languages and nations will gaze at their dead bodies *of the two witnesses* and refuse to let them be placed in a tomb (this being an open display of ultimate disrespect and rejection of God and His servants and an act of intimidation), **10** and those who dwell on the Earth will rejoice over them and make merry and exchange presents because these two prophets had been a torment to those who dwell on the Earth.

Currently, we are witnessing a world that is increasingly rejecting God and perverting His Truth. I raise the questions. How are you seeing evil celebrated in this world? Are you among the number of those who celebrate wickedness?

11 But after the three and a half days, a breath of life from God entered them, and they stood up (resurrected from the dead) on their feet, and great fear fell on those who saw them. **12** Then they heard a loud voice from heaven saying to them, "Come up here" (or the wording Harpazo in Greek, meaning they were caught away or raptured). And they - *the two witnesses*, went up to heaven in a cloud, and their enemies watched them. (These two witnesses were on the winning team – God's team. Each of us desires to be successful or a winner or on the winning team. If we remain faithful...In the end, we win! If we are one with Jesus, no matter our situation on this side of glory, we are winners! We are on the winning team; death, being our ultimate adversary, has been defeated, and we are now seated with the Lion of Judah – Jesus, our Conquering King; already, we are Conquers and winners but not yet eternally glorified. Already and not yet, it is termed, but Victors, we are)!

13 And at that hour – *following the witnesses' Rapture*, there was a great earthquake, and a tenth of the city fell. (Perhaps God is reminding or pointing out to the Jews, through the teaching of Moses, that the tenth of the Levitical priesthood belonged to Him). Seven thousand people were killed in the earthquake (which may be a reminder of the seven thousand prophets God told Elijah that was reserved for Him. In destroying this precise number of unbelieving Jews, perhaps Gentiles as well, God is indicating that His dispensational period of grace has come to an end.

They, the rebellious people, were now to get what they wanted, the complete rule of this unholy trinity – Satan, his Antichrist, and false prophet, which will lead to their ultimate rejection by God. And their subsequent banishment or imprisonment to eternal suffering in the Gehenna – the Lake of Fire). ***Continuing with verse 13*** and, the rest were terrified and gave glory to the God of heaven. (Regarding this last statement, it may lead one to believe that these individuals turned to God; however, the text does not say this; instead, earlier we read, the people did not repent. I will point out Scripture where such acknowledgment or acclaim was made of God; however, repentance did not follow: see Pharaoh's recognition of God's power in Ex. 8:15,32, and 9:27,28. Nebuchadnezzar's praise of God: see Dan. 4:34-37, and the Demoniac's acknowledgment of Jesus: see Mark 5:1-20; however, in this instance, repentance from Demons is not an option unto Salvation. As it were, they willingly, of complete free will and without enticement and without having a sin-nature, as it is with fallen mankind, these Demons or fallen angels chose to rebel against their God and Creator. Nevertheless, regarding the statement of the people who "gave glory to God." Some take the position that their praise was in reverence to God.

14 The second woe has passed; behold, the third woe is soon to come (these horrendous events will be seen unfolding in chapter 14 onward).

The Seventh Trumpet:

15 Then the seventh angel blew his trumpet, and there were loud voices in heaven, saying, "The kingdom of the world has become the kingdom of our Lord and of his Christ, and he shall reign forever and ever." (Here is what **1 Cor. 15: 24-26** reads regarding Christ's triumph over evil: **24** "Then the end will come when he – *Jesus* hands over the kingdom to God the Father after he has destroyed all dominion, authority, and power. **25** For he – *again Jesus* must reign until he has put all his enemies under his feet. **26** The last enemy to be destroyed is death." In the following 16th verse, John begins narrating the events he saw regarding Jesus' victory; however, before we are provided the coming Bowl Judgements, occurring during the last 3.5 years of the Great Tribulation). ***Here in verse 16, John now says,*** And the twenty-four elders who sit on their thrones before God fell on their faces and worshiped God, **17** saying,

"We give thanks to you, Lord God Almighty, who is and who was, for you have taken your great power and begun to reign: see Rev. chap. 19.

18 The nations raged, but your wrath came, and the time for the dead to be judged, and for rewarding your servants, the prophets and saints, and those who fear your name, both small and great, and for destroying the destroyers of the Earth." **19** Then God's temple in heaven was opened, and the ark of his covenant was seen within his temple. There were flashes of lightning, rumblings, peals of thunder, an earthquake, and heavy hail. (Read Psalms Chapter 2 regarding God's judgment of the nations).

Verse 19 of this closing chapter provides us an image of God's Holy Heavenly Temple and the ark of His covenant, upon which God appeared in ancient times. Before Israel's forty years of wilderness wandering, God had meticulously instructed Moses how they were to fashion and erect His portable Tabernacle. This was God's temporary dwelling place and Tent of Meeting so that He may dwell amongst His covenant people; in this sense, heaven was on earth. Now, John is provided a look at the actual temple and ark of the covenant. This view into the Holy of Holies offers some semblance of this temple of God when it will once again be established on the earth during Jesus' millennial reign and rule. Even so, "God's will being done on earth as it is in heaven." Jesus will be seated on the throne of King David! Thus fulfilling Biblical prophecy! From John's view of the Ark of the Covenant, this serves as a reminder to the Jews that

God's covenant with Israel – His chosen people is unfailing even amongst the great persecution they will have to endure.

CHAPTER 14

OUTLINE AND REVELATION CHAPTER 12

The Woman, the Child, and the Dragon:

1. **Verse 1-6:** The Woman and the Dragon
   - Introduction: John sees a great sign in heaven: a woman clothed with the sun, with the moon under her feet, and on her head a crown of twelve stars.
   - The Woman's Labor: She is pregnant and cries out in birth pains and the agony of giving birth.
   - The Dragon's Appearance: Another sign appears in heaven: a great red dragon with seven heads and, ten horns, and seven diadems on his heads.
   - The Dragon's Actions: The dragon's tail sweeps down a third of the stars of heaven and casts them to the earth. He stands before the woman, ready to devour her child as soon as it is born.
2. **Verse 7-12:** War in Heaven
   - Introduction: War breaks out in heaven; Michael and his angels fight against the dragon.
   - Victory of Michael: The dragon and his angels are defeated and thrown down to the earth.

- Rejoicing in Heaven: A loud voice in heaven proclaims salvation, power, and the kingdom of our God and the authority of his Christ.

- The Accuser Cast Down: The accuser of the brothers is thrown down, who accuses them day and night before God.

- The Overcomers: They have conquered him by the blood of the Lamb and by the word of their testimony, for they loved not their lives even unto death.

- Rejoice, O Heavens: Heaven and those who dwell in it rejoice, but woe to the earth and the sea, for the devil has come down to you in great wrath, knowing that his time is short.

3. **Verse 13-17:** The Dragon Persecutes the Woman and Her Offspring
   - Introduction: When the dragon saw that he had been thrown down to the earth, he pursued the woman who had given birth to the male child.

   - Protection of the Woman: The woman is given the two wings of the great eagle so that she might fly to the wilderness, where she is nourished for a time and times, and half a time, away from the presence of the serpent.

   - The Dragon's Fury: The dragon pours out water like a river to sweep the woman away with a flood, but the earth came to the help of the woman, and the earth opened its mouth and swallowed the river that the dragon had poured from his mouth.

   - The Dragon's Wrath: The dragon became furious with the woman and went off to make war on the rest of her offspring, on those who keep the commandments of God and hold to the testimony of Jesus.

This chapter presents a symbolic vision of cosmic conflict, featuring a woman representing the people of God, a child representing Christ, and a dragon representing Satan. It also describes the victory of Michael and his angels over the dragon and the subsequent persecution of the woman and her offspring.

Revelation Chapter 12

This chapter offers a pause for John to elaborate.

The Woman and the Dragon: These signs or imagery provided to John and us is an overview of humanity's history and cosmic battle with the Devil beginning in the book of Genesis and concluding here in the book of Revelation.

1 And a great sign appeared in heaven. (As Bible students, I remind you, we can only come to understand these signs in light of their meaning as found in Scripture or through Biblical Exegesis. Even so, interpretations may differ). *This sign –* a woman (who is believed to be representing the people of Israel through which Jesus and the Church will be birthed or brought forth) *was* clothed with the sun (symbolic of God's glory and presence upon Jacob, his wife and his descendants), *and she had* under her feet the moon (a picture of Rachael, Jacob's bride, collectively Israel and perhaps the universal Church is also in view) and on her head a crown of twelve stars (representing the twelve tribes of Israel – Jacob's sons). **2** She was pregnant and was crying out in birth pains and the agony of giving birth: see Isa. 26:17,18; 66:7; Micah 4:10, additionally Jeremiah Chapters 2 and 3; Ezek. chap. 23 and Hosea Chapters 1 through 3. Within the provided Scripture, Israel's historical suffering caused by the Dragon is in view. Regarding the imagery of the stars, sun, and moon, see Gen. 37:9-11.

From this reading, we see that Jacob, his wife, and his twelve sons – who make up the nation of Israel- represent this woman. This woman or Israel, God's chosen people and Yahweh's Bride, can be understood from Jer. 31:31 – 33. This woman – Israel, gives birth through the virgin Mary, a son, Jesus, the Savior of the world, through whom is birthed or brought forth the Church or the Bride of Christ; Jesus is therefore described as the Bridegroom of His Church. Regarding the woman or Israel giving birth to the Messiah, see Gen. 3:15,16, where we have the first announcement of the Protoevangelium – the Good News of the world's Savior – Jesus the Son of God, prophesied; also see Isaiah 9:6,7.

Additionally, with regards to Israel's birth pains, as mentioned in the Old Testament, prophetically points to this time of Jacob's troubles, seen here in the book of Revelation; also, see Micah 4:9-11 and 5:3,4. Many references are found in the Old Testament regarding this state of Israel – her agony and birth pains). **3** And another sign appeared in heaven: behold, a great red dragon, with seven heads (representing Satan's kings or kingdoms or empires who are influenced by him. Even so, a picture of Israel's historical oppressors of the past, present and future, but also the Church's enemy) and *this dragon had* ten horns, and on his heads seven diadems (the ten horns are symbolic of the coming alliances or amalgamation of these ten powerful beastly and devouring national superpowers, their essence being from the empires as seen in Daniel Chapter 2 and chap. 7. This New World Order or One World Government will be united under Satan's rule, thus inaugurating a change in the world's balance of power and a resurgence or emergence of "Babylon the Great" or "The Revived Roman Empire," these being Satan's systems and his rule upon the earth through the Antichrist.

The Seven oppressive Empires or Beast who reign over Israel with their Antichrist Kings:

Egypt = Pharaoh – Gen. 1:7
Assyria = Shalmaneser and Sennacherib – 2 Kings 17:5
Babylon = Nebuchadnezzar – Jer. 21:10
Persia = Cyrus – 2 Chr. 36:20
Greece = Alexander the Great – Dan. 10:20

Rome = The Caesars – Luke 2:1. Rome was never destroyed. It merely morphed into modern Europe, which maintains its global influence.

The Ancient Roman Empire = Papal rule with Church Dominance

Lastly, The Revived Roman Empire or Babylon the Great = The Antichrist or Beast system of Rev. 13:1, a unification of these world powers with its capital city being open to debate.

Rebellious Babylon first rose to prominence under Nimrod, as seen in Gen. 10:10. It reemerged as an oppressive empire under Nebuchadnezzar but lost its radiance or dominance after Persia seized it. Still, Babylon, the city, was not destroyed, unlike the other empires that Daniel prophesied about in Chapters 2 and 7 of the Book of Daniel. However, Babylon will meet its end; in the Book of Revelation, we see that this world power makes its final appearance and stands against God on the earth as Babylon the Great. Revelation Chapter **17:8a.** has an angel describing this one-world government to John because he could not comprehend what this final reemergence of Babylon was. The angel, therefore, says to John, "The beast – *dragon or unified world government*, which you saw, now is not, and yet will come up out of the Abyss and go to destruction..." According to the Bible, Babylon – this self or man-ruling government, which was operating under the influence of the Devil or this Dragon was the start or first of this world's rebellion. Babylon shows up again in the middle of the Bible, under Nebuchadnezzar's reign, and this final time in the Book of Revelation as Babylon the Great.

Rev. 17:8b-11 The inhabitants of the earth whose names have not been written in the book of life from the creation of the world will be astonished (or will be in admiration and marvel) when they see the beast because it once was, now is not, and yet will come. **9** "This calls for a mind with wisdom. The seven heads are seven hills on which the *harlot* woman – *the false prophet and Antichrist's system* sits. **10** They are also seven kings. Five have fallen (Egypt, Assyria, Babylon, Persia, and the

Grecians); one is (this was Rome's dominance during John's time and), the other has not yet come (this will be the revived Roman empire under the Antichrist), but when he does come, he must remain for only a little while. **11** The beast who once was, and now is not, is an eighth king (the Antichrist, Satan's man, even Satan's seed, and his kingdom or one-world government). He belongs to the seven (other or past world empires) and is going to his destruction.

Revelation Chapter 12 verse 4 His – the Devil's or Dragon's tail (had) swept down a third of the stars of heaven (fallen angels who rebelled with the Devil) and cast them to the Earth. (Some understand this casting down of the stars to be God's judgment upon these rebellious angels. While others view this as the fallen angels who followed the Devil in his rebellion against God, their Creator. These rebellious Elohim or fallen angels had lost their positions in heaven. However, they may have still had access to God, mainly the Devil, who acts as the accuser of God's people). Verse 4 continues: And the dragon – *the Devil* stood before the woman who was about to give birth so that when she bore her child, he might devour it. (Remember Satan's agent, the proto-Antichrist Herod, wanted to kill Jesus. Therefore, he massacred all male children aged 2 and under; so was this the case with Pharoah, the King of Egypt, who decreed the midwives to kill all male Hebrew babies: see Exodus 1:22.

Satan Wanted the Messiah – the World's Redeemer and King, his Feared Nemesis Destroyed:

Genesis 3:15: herein, eternal enmity is portrayed between the woman's or Israel's *Seed* and Satan and his seed.

Genesis Chapter 6: here, the fallen sons or angels of God produced Nephilim or hybrid offspring through their forbidden and unholy marriage with women by which to corrupt humanity biologically or by altering mankind's DNA to prevent the woman's *Seed* – the Messianic King from being born.

Exodus 1:22: therein we have Pharoah's infanticide to prevent the woman's *Seed* from coming forth.

Dan. 3:11: herein Nebuchadnezzar's edict to destroy the Jews and the potential *Seed* of the woman.

Esther 3:6: Haman's attempt at committing genocide of the Jews.

Matt. 2:16: we have Herod's Bethlehem Massacre of Jewish male babies, 2 years of age and under

Luke 19:43: therein we have the record of Titus's destruction of Jerusalem and persecution of the Jews; the persecution of Christians would soon follow.

Although Satan failed to prevent the woman's *Seed* ~ Jesus, from being born and fulfilling His purpose, Satan still has it in for the Jews; even so, he has it in for the bride of Christ – Jesus' Church encompassing all who have accepted Jesus as their King and Savior. This also goes for innocent and vulnerable children – all who are created in the image of God; Satan longs to annihilate or at the least corrupt these potential Believers of Christ.

Verse 5 She (Mary, who is one with Israel and representative of the woman in our text) gave birth to a male child (who is Jesus: see Rev. 19:11-16 and Isaiah 9: 5-7), *the* one – *this child* who is to rule all the nations with a rod of iron, but her child was caught up (Harpazo or Raptured, snatch or caught up) to God and to his throne, **6** and the woman fled into the wilderness; (After Jesus' ascension, the Jews fled Judea due to Roman persecution in AD 70, this was the second destruction of Israel's temple. Additionally, there was a final fleeing and dispersion of the Jews during the 2nd Century by Ceasar Hadrian due to the Kokhba Revolt, where the Jewish people were scattered throughout the known world.

However, the Jewish people began returning to their promised land in the 1600s. Nevertheless, Satan has remained biting at their heels, as seen during The Middle Ages, The Spanish Inquisition of 1492, the Pogroms of the 1800s by Russia, the 20th Century Holocaust under

Hitler, and the ongoing Islamic threat and anti-Semitism now occurring and increasing globally. Satan hates Israel! He has always warred against her as God said it would be in Genesis 3:15. The essence of Satan's hatred is anti-Semitism and their ultimate destruction. Also, bear in mind Satan's hatred for the True Church of God. His hatred is witnessed all around us, and it will only increase as we see the opposition of the godless people of this world who are and who will stand against God and His people, both His chosen people – the Jewish nation and all who truly belongs to Jesus – namely the universal Church belonging to the Christ, the Messianic King – Jesus.

Resuming with verse 6: and the woman fled into the wilderness where she has a place prepared by God, in which she is to be nourished for 1,260 days. (The Jewish persecution after Jesus' ascension – here being the ancient past, was a foreshadowing of their later persecution during the 3.5 years of the Great Tribulation, as seen after the prophetic pattern of Elijah's flight to safety for 3.5 years: see 1 Kings Chapters 17 & 18. But there is an answer for Israel's agony: see Jer. 30: 6-9 and Zec. 13:8,9, which are also presented here in the Book of Revelation. Israel will turn back to God, and her enemies will be destroyed by Jesus!

Satan Thrown Down to Earth:

7 Now war arose in heaven, Michael (Israel's chief and protecting Mighty Archangel) and his angels *were seen* fighting against the dragon – *the Devil:* see Dan. 10:13&21; Dan. 12:1 and Jude 9. (Understand that unseen battles are occurring in the spiritual realm at any given time); and the dragon and his angels fought back **8,** but he was defeated (there had been and continues to be an ongoing celestial battle for cosmic territorial claim, with spiritual powers influence over nations – most notably the land that God promised to the Jews, land that Muslims wrongly claim as theirs.

From the text, we are shown that all Satanic powers will be cast to the earth before their pending damnation. Dan. 10:20,21 presented a present cosmic conflict during his time. Dan. 12:1-4 speaks of a future conflict we are now reading about. However, Jesus has yet to fully engage with His opposition – the Devil. When Jesus finally decides to stand against Satan, Satan will be done or doomed merely by Jesus' word being spoken. There will be no contest!

Repeating verses **7 and 8.** Now, war arose in heaven, Michael and his angels fighting against the dragon. And the dragon and his angels fought back, **8** but he was defeated, and there was no longer any place for them in heaven.

9 And the great dragon was thrown down, that ancient serpent, who is called the Devil and Satan, the deceiver of the whole world—he was thrown down to the Earth, and his angels were thrown down with him. (Regarding deception, see Mark 13:5-6 and 2 Thes. 2:3-8). **10** And I heard a loud voice in heaven, saying, "Now the salvation and the power and the kingdom of our God and the authority of his Christ have come, for the accuser of our brothers has been thrown down, who accuses them day and night before our God. (When Jesus becomes our Adjudicator, there is no longer any condemnation or accusation that can be held or hurled against those who have been cleansed by His blood. Nevertheless, that didn't stop Satan, and neither has it prevented him from trying. Even now, he tries to make those who belong to Jesus feel guilt and condemnation for the wrongs that we have repented from...but don't fall for Satan's deceit and lies).

11 And they – the martyred saints (those who maintained their faith under the tyrant Antichrist) have conquered him by the blood of the Lamb and by the word of their testimony, for they loved not their lives even unto death. **12** Therefore, rejoice, O heavens and you who dwell in them! But woe to you, O earth and sea (both unbelieving Jews and Gentiles), for the Devil has come down to you in great wrath because he knows that his time is short!" (This is what the world is currently experiencing – Satan's fury, as immorality runs rampant, along with great deception, lying, death, and destruction being upon us throughout the world. However, as I've already mentioned, things are only going to worsen leading up to Jesus' Second Coming or His Parousia).

13 And when the dragon saw that he had been thrown down to the Earth (now having lost all access to God and his former dwelling place), he pursued the woman (the Jewish people) who had given birth to the male child. **14** But the woman (the remnant Jews or those during The Great Tribulation) was given the two wings of the great eagle: see Exodus 19:4 (these two wings are symbolic of God's care and provision during this time) so that she – *some of the persecuted Jewish people* might fly from the serpent into the wilderness, to the place where she is to be nourished for a time, and times, and half a time – 3.5 years).

15 The serpent poured water like a river out of his mouth after the woman to sweep her away with a flood (meaning to war against her). **16** But the Earth came to the help of the woman, and the Earth opened its mouth and swallowed the river (or Satan's armies) that the dragon had poured from his mouth. (Remember, Pharaoh's army was swallowed up by the sea; it is an earthquake that will swallow up this army – those nations who attempt to wage war against Israel during the final Battle at Armageddon).

17 Then the dragon became furious with the woman (the Jewish people) and went off to make war on the rest of her offspring (here meaning End-time Saints, not the Church or Jesus' Bride, which was last mentioned in Rev. chap. 3, who the Devil could not prevail against: see Matt. 16:18 and 1 Thes. 5:9. However, on this side of glory, we – the people of God, His universal Church will have to endure trials or troubles and even deadly persecution). **18** Then the dragon became furious with the woman (the Jewish people) and went off to make war on the rest of her offspring on those (all the Saints) who keep the commandments of God and hold to the testimony of Jesus. And he – the dragon stood on the sand of the sea (preparing to marshal his might against these Faithful ones – the Tribulation Saints: see Rev. 7:1-7 & 9 and Rev. 20: 4).

CHAPTER 15

OUTLINE AND REVELATION CHAPTER 13

The First Beast from the Sea and The Second Beast From Earth:

1. **Verse 1-10:** The Beast from the Sea
   - Introduction: John sees a beast rising out of the sea, having ten horns and seven heads, with ten diadems on its horns and blasphemous names on its heads.

   - The Beast's Appearance: The beast resembles a leopard, with feet like a bear's and a mouth like a lion's. The dragon gives it his power and throne and great authority.

   - The Beast's Wounded Head: One of its heads appears to have been mortally wounded, but the wound was healed. The whole earth marvels after the beast, worshiping the dragon who gave authority to the beast.

   - The Beast's Authority: The beast is given authority to make war on the saints and to conquer them. Authority is given to it over every tribe and people and language and nation.

   - The Worship of the Beast: All who dwell on earth worship it, everyone whose name has not been written before the foundation of the world in the book of life of the Lamb who was slain.

- The Call to Hear: John calls for the endurance and faith of the saints in light of the persecution by the beast.

2. **Verse 11-18:** The Beast from the Earth
   - Introduction: John sees another beast rising out of the earth. It has two horns like a lamb but speaks like a dragon.
   - The False Prophet's Authority: This beast exercises all the authority of the first beast in its presence and makes the earth and its inhabitants worship the first beast, whose mortal wound was healed.
   - Deception through Signs: The second beast performs great signs, even making fire come down from heaven in front of people.
   - The Mark of the Beast: It deceives those who dwell on earth, telling them to make an image of the first beast and to receive a mark on their right hand or forehead so that no one can buy or sell unless he has the mark, which is the name of the beast or the number of its name.
   - The Number of the Beast: This calls for wisdom: let the one who has understanding calculate the number of the beast, for it is the number of a man, and his number is 666.

This chapter presents the rise of two beasts: one from the sea and another from the earth. The first beast represents political power, while the second beast represents religious deception. Both beasts exert authority over the world and lead many to worship them, ultimately leading to the persecution of the saints and the enforcement of the mark of the beast.

Revelation Chapter 13

This chapter offers a pause for John's elaboration.

The Antichrist or the Beast out of the sea, and his rule, has already been seen during the opening of the first seal, this being the white horse and its rider. The fallen angel, Apollyon the Destroyer, who was released from the bottomless pit, is believed by some to somehow influence or be one with the Antichrist. Whatever one's presupposition may be, Scripture states that the Antichrist receives his authority and power from Satan. His kingdom is a counterfeit of Christ's kingdom. Satan, along with his Antichrist and the false prophet, will seek to imitate God and His kingdom on earth, thereby establishing their counterfeit and unholy trinity.

1 The dragon (which is actually a picture of Satan, the false representation of the 1st Person of the Trinity – God the Father. However, the mention of the dragon in other translations is a beast, which affords a clearer understanding of this text. It is, therefore, the beast who receives power and authority from the Devil or the Dragon, both are beasts). *Thus, this beast* stood on the shore of the sea. (Here, the sea is a representation of the unruliness and chaos of all people or nations of the earth over which Satan, through his political system, will have gained influence). *John says*, And I saw a beast (which is the ultimate Antichrist, or the little horn according to the book of Daniel, a picture of the false representation of the 2nd Person of the trinity – Jesus, the Son of God. Additionally, this beast represents a kingdom or ruling system) coming out of the sea. It had ten horns (a representation of earthly rulers and an amalgamation of their 10 kingdoms, economically and otherwise. They will have one leader – the Antichrist, who will have absolute authority and power given to it by Satan to rule over these nations of the world) and *this beast had* seven heads (or seven rulers. Three of these kingdom leaders will have passed from history.

And this beast with ten crowns (representing earthly or worldly completion and its leaders or kingdoms) on its horns and on each head a blasphemous name *which is a display of opposition and defiance against God.* **2** The beast I saw resembled a leopard (a picture of Greece) but had feet like those of a bear (a picture of Medo-Persia) and a mouth like that of a lion – *Babylon is now in view.* (Here, we have three empires, three

Kings, and their amalgamation of other ancient Biblical empires. These systems can be likened to the first rebellious Babylonian system under Nimrod because they established their own empires apart from God: see Daniel Chapter 7 and Gen. chap. 11).

The dragon – *Satan, or the Devil,* gave the beast – the Antichrist, his power and his throne and great authority. **3** One of the heads of the beast seemed to have had a fatal wound, but the fatal wound had been healed (this, in part, is picturing the revival of the Roman Empire, however, specifically the Antichrist who receives a deadly wound, which makes him appear as rising from the dead, akin to Jesus' resurrection; with this feat of the Antichrist, he will be revered because he like Jesus possess supernatural power. Bear in mind that a kingdom or empire can be used synonymously with its ruler and vice versa). The whole world was, *therefore,* filled with wonder and followed the beast (the Antichrist and embraced him and his system that will be greater than all the world powers preceding His). **4** People worshiped the dragon (or Satan, knowingly or not) because he had given authority to the beast, and they also worshiped the beast and asked, "Who is like the beast? Who can wage war against it?" (Again, the Antichrist and his kingdom, the people of the world will believe is the answer to all their problems).

5 The beast was given a mouth (his words will be persuasive; he will have charisma like Hitler, and people will believe in him as people have believed in other persuasive people, even such people who are dictators, liars, and who are corrupt at their core); *the Antichrist will have a mouth or speech* to utter proud words and blasphemies and to exercise its authority for forty-two months (or 3.5 years of the Antichrist's tyranny and his false claim to be God. History records many mere men who claimed to be a god and required worship of their subjects or else they would be killed). **6** It – *this world dictator, the Antichrist, opened* its mouth to blaspheme God (which according to Levitical law was to be punished by stoning: see Lev. 24:16 and Rev. 16:21) and *the Antichrist* *opened its mouth* to slander his – God's name and his dwelling place and those who live in heaven.

7 It was given power to wage war against God's holy people (the people of Israel during their time of great tribulation and others who come to Christ in faith, who are called Saints. However, this is not the Church; nevertheless, they are called God's holy people) and to conquer them *will be the Antichrist's demonic and destructive aim.* (In **Rev. 3:10,13,** Jesus spoke to the Church in Philadelphia, saying, **10** "Since you have kept my command to endure patiently, I will also keep you from the hour of trial that is going to come on the whole world to test the inhabitants of the earth." Verse **13**: "Whoever has ears, let them hear what the Spirit says to the churches. (God's faithful followers – His Church or Bride at this time in history will be safe in heaven).

Revelation Chapter 13, Verse 7, And it – *the Antichrist* was given authority over every tribe, people, language, and nation. **8** All inhabitants of the earth will worship the beast—all whose names have not been written in the Lamb's book of life, the Lamb who was slain from the creation of the world. **9** Whoever has ears, let them hear. (Notice, we don't have the words "To the churches"; instead, "all inhabitants." Why?... It has been raptured. God's Bride, the church will not be defiled or come against by the Antichrist. As a reminder, after Revelation Chapter 3, we no longer hear the Church being mentioned; the seven-fold statement, "The Spirit's sayings to the churches," ended there).

10 "If anyone is to go into captivity, into captivity they will go (perhaps a reference to those who take the mark of the beast will be eternally condemned). If anyone is to be killed with the sword, with the sword, they will be killed." This calls for patient endurance and faithfulness on the part of God's people. (God will bring vengeance upon those who harm His people. However, those going through the Great Tribulation will have to endure in faith and, through faith, their belief in Jesus without retaliation. Vengeance belongs to the Lord, He will repay: see Romans 12:19).

The Beast out of the Earth:

11 Then I saw a second beast (a picture of the false representation of the 3rd Person of the Trinity, God – the Holy Spirit. This second beast, who is a false prophet and who serves as a High Priest of sorts, the Antichrist's Minister of Propaganda, is the head of their religious system, which holds religious influence and is one with the government. Hence, together, they become the revived Roman Empire or Babylon the Great. This one world government and unified religious system point back to Genesis 11:1-6. These two beasts are Babylon or Antichrist systems); *unlike the first beast described as coming from the sea, this second beast will be* coming out of the earth. It had two horns (representing the joining or uniting of the two powers or systems) like a lamb (the Antichrist and false prophet will appear innocent, thereby bringing a false sense of unity, peace, and hope to this deceived world), but it – *the false prophet* spoke like a dragon. (Satan, along with these two beasts or systems of power and authority, will oppose Yahweh, the True God, and His people. Together, the Devil's systems of unified power will establish a counterfeit trinity before their worldly church – those fooled and those embracing the lies through their deceitful preaching and politics of propaganda).

12 It – *the false prophet* exercised all the authority of the first beast on its behalf and made the earth and its inhabitants worship the first beast (the Antichrist or son of perdition), whose fatal wound had been healed. (Again, some form of counterfeit resurrection, perhaps involving artificial intelligence and other technological and biological advancements; man's acquired knowledge, here pointing back to the tree of forbidden knowledge within the Garden of Eden. It is also worth mentioning that some ancient manuscripts suggest that when the fallen angels or sons of God took women as their wives, they also exchanged or provided mankind with increased and forbidden knowledge or technology in order to engage in these illicit unions. There will very well be a parallel, as are already taking place in illegal unions of varying sorts, not short of fallen angels mingling with mankind occurring during these end-time events, thereby also prompting God to destroy the world as he did in the days of Noah and with Sodom and Gomorrah because of these forbidden unions – fallen angels uniting with or marrying women and gross wickedness – homosexuality or sexual perversions occurring in the world by those who have been deceived or lead astray. See the Book of 1 Enoch Chapters 1-36; here, the fallen angels are called "Watchers." Also, see Genesis Chapter 6).

13 And it – *the false prophet* performed great signs, even causing fire (like the prophets Moses and Elijah) to come down from heaven to the earth in full view of the people. (See Numbers 16:28-35; 1 Kings 18:24; 2 Kings 1:10 and Luke 9:55,56). **14** Because of the signs, it was given power to perform on behalf of the first beast; it deceived (like Eve was deceived in Genesis 3:13) it – *this beast or false prophet* deceived the inhabitants of the earth. (The people were deceived because they did not know or embrace the truth of the Bible.

Regarding Deception:

Matthew 24:3-5, verses 10,11, and 24 & 25 reads. Verse **3:** "As Jesus was sitting on the Mount of Olives, the disciples came to him privately. "Tell us," they said, "when will this happen, and what will be the sign of your coming and of the end of the age?" **4** Jesus answered: "Watch out that no one deceives you. **5** For many will come in my name, claiming, 'I am the Messiah,' and will deceive many. (Messiah means anointing or the Anointed One – ultimately the title befitting of Jesus and exclusively belonging to Him. People, I remind you, don't be deceived by one's seemingly anointing or their giftings and talents). Mattew continues here in verse **10:** "At that time, many will turn away from the faith and will betray and hate each other, **11** and many false prophets will appear and deceive many people. And verse **24:** For false messiahs and false prophets will appear and perform great signs and wonders to deceive, if possible, even the elect. **25** See, I have told you ahead of time. (Notice the text didn't say these deceivers will perform false signs and wonders).

Now let's consider **1 Corinthians 6:9, 10,** which reads **9:** "Or do you not know that wrongdoers will not inherit the kingdom of God? Do not be deceived: Neither the sexually immoral nor idolaters nor adulterers nor men who have sex with men **10** nor thieves nor the greedy nor drunkards nor slanderers nor swindlers will inherit the kingdom of God.

Continuing with **Revelation Chapter 13 and Verse 14**, It – *the false prophet* ordered them to set up an image in honor of the beast who was wounded by the sword and yet lived. (Just as mankind is created in the image of God, hence He indwells His born-again children – His living temples who are one with Him; Satan also desires to inhabit and influence man by additionally marking or defiling them in some unusual manner. To also control his imagers, Satan used Nebuchadnezzar to erect an image to be worshipped; now through this false prophet, Satan once again erects a statue and an image in the likeness of himself for the people to worship or else be killed: see Daniel 3:1-6).

Satan desires to put his image or mark on or in man; this is his ultimate aim to indwell or pervert the bodies of humanity and to have ultimate control over God's creation. All who covenant with or take Satan's mark or pervert themselves, as seen in Genesis Chapter 6, where we have the fallen angels marrying women and giving birth to their Nephilim offspring, and as it was with Sodom and Gomorrah and their sexual immorality, which is also believed to have been incited by these Nephilim. As it was with these two ancient examples, mankind during the End of Days will be destroyed because they no longer bear the image of God because of their irreversible defilement of whatever the making – hence some marking or perversion of the beast.

It is also believed by some, I'm in this number, that perhaps mankind would have likely chosen to undergo some extreme biological or gene manipulation and or technological transitioning or implants in the likes of Nanotechnology merging with Transhumanism, thereby, in some manner, corrupting mankind's essence and thereby giving themselves over to the Antichrist's complete control not to exclude sexual perversion occurring in the likes of what happened in Genesis Chapter 6 and therefore, God's subsequent judgment and destruction of this hybrid race of genetically altered people and those rebellious angels. **2 Peter 2:4-6,** reads. **4** For if God spared not the angels that sinned, but cast them down to hell, and delivered them into chains of darkness, to be reserved unto judgment. **5** And spared not the old world, but saved Noah the eighth person, a preacher of righteousness, bringing in the flood upon the world of the ungodly; **6** And turning the cities of Sodom and Gomorrah into ashes condemned them with an overthrow, making them an ensample unto those that after should live ungodly. (The end of this age will once again, as it was in the days of Noah and the cities of Sodom and Gomorrah, be inundated with sexual corruption, sexual perversion, and all sorts of wickedness).

Additionally, **Jude** has this to say, verse **6:** And the angels which kept not their first estate, but left *or changed* their own habitation, he hath reserved in everlasting chains under darkness unto the judgment of the great day. **7** Even as Sodom and Gomorrah, and the cities about them in like manner, giving themselves over to fornication and going after strange flesh (in the Hebrew language, this means foreign flesh, and this being why some believe there was Nephelim entanglement) *and therefore these fallen angels*, are set forth for an example, suffering the vengeance of eternal fire (KGV). This kind of corruption and yielding to fleshly defilement, as seen in the texts provided, once again foreshadows what will occur here in Rev. Chapter 13; these forbidden mixing with angels – hence pointing to the people taking the mark of the beast or some form of bodily corruption to make themselves to bear Satan's image: see Daniel 2:43 and Gen. 3:15 (KGV). In Genesis Chapter 19, therein, we have the sexual perversion of Sodom and Gomorrah. Matt. 24:37-39 reference Noah's generation's corruption or sexual defilement, while Luke 17:28-30 reference the corruption or sexual defilement of Sodom and Gomorrah; these perversions or base deviations will no doubt reach their pinnacle before the return of Christ and his final judgment upon such wickedness).

Revelation Chapter 13: verse 15 The second beast - the false prophet (who will now mimic Jesus) was given power to give breath to the image of the first beast (who is an image of the Antichrist, Satan's son) so that the image could speak (a lifeless and counterfeit existence of the ultimate idol or image of Satan's and fallen man's creation likely through technological and biological and medical advancement is seemingly brought to life) and *the false prophet* cause all who refused to worship the image to be killed (as it was with King Nebuchadnezzar and the image he erected: see Daniel Chapter 3.

Colossians 1:15 reads: "The Son – Jesus is the (exact) image of the invisible God, the firstborn over all creation." As born-again Believers, we now bear our restored image of God, through Whom our spirits are made anew by our Creator Jesus. Therefore, we dare not make nor bow to anything or anyone except the Son of God: see Exod. 20:4-6! And so it is, this false prophet's image is made in the likeness of the Antichrist and Satan; they now stand in total defiance against God); **16** this image also forced all people, great and small, rich and poor, free and slave, to receive a mark on their right hands or on their foreheads, **17** so that they could not buy or sell unless they had the mark, which is the name of the beast or the number of its name. (Anyone not taking the mark of the beast was considered an enemy of the state. These Saints of God were persecuted and forbidden to earn a living through what had been free commerce).

Regarding the understanding or the lack thereof of the mark of the beast, **verse 18 reads:** This calls for wisdom. Let the person who has insight calculate the number of the beast, for it is the number of a man. That number is 666 (a registration of sorts that further represents man's vain attempt at establishing utopia on earth, along with Satan and his chosen ruler – the Antichrist and the world's systems of governmental operation that is in full support and one with the religious system of this fallen world, which thereby, was to bring peace, unity, and prosperity upon the earth. The ultimate Kingdom of Babylon, here, has risen with its dictator – the man of sin, the Lawless one, or the Antichrist as its tyrant King. But this kingdom will soon be brought to ruin.

Here is something else we must be careful or mindful about – that is, not becoming Nationalists. We see this with people who say they worship God. But they also worship or have made their country an idol; in our case – America, the so-called greatest nation in the world. Listen, God never claims this as so in the Bible; neither has He established any other people besides Israel as His "chosen people;" furthermore, with emphasis being placed on their territory or the land that He gave and promised to them so that they may be identified perpetually as a nation – His uniquely covenant people, although remaining a rebellious nation until this day).

Lastly, regarding what has been mentioned thus far on the matter of deception and the arrival of the Antichrist, **2 Thessalonians Chapter 2,** beginning at verse **3,** has this to say, **3** Don't let anyone deceive you in any way, for that day will not come (meaning God's wrath upon the earth or The Day of the Lord) until the rebellion (the great apostasy of the world and gross rebellion against God) occurs and the man of lawlessness is revealed, the man doomed to destruction. **4** He will oppose and will exalt himself over everything that is called God or is worshiped so that he sets himself up in God's temple, proclaiming himself to be God. **5** Don't you remember that when I was with you, I used to tell you these things? **6** And now you know what is holding him – *the final Antichrist* back so that he may be revealed at the proper time. **7** For the secret power of lawlessness is already at work, but the one – *likely the Holy Spirit* who now holds it back will continue to do so till he – *God the Holy Spirit* is taken out of the way.

8 And then the lawless one will be revealed, whom the Lord Jesus will overthrow with the breath of his mouth and destroy by the splendor of his coming. **9** The coming of the lawless one (or Antichrist) will be in accordance with how Satan works. He will use all sorts of displays of power through signs and wonders that serve the lie, **10** and all the ways that wickedness deceives those who are perishing. They perish because they refuse to love the truth and so be saved. **11** For this reason, God sends them a powerful delusion so that they will believe the lie **12** and so that all will be condemned who have not believed the truth but have delighted in wickedness.

When a person or people utterly rejects God, He will allow them to have what they want – the desires of their wicked hearts, even so, this being a judgment against themselves. This is what we are seeing in this chapter of the Book of Revelation. And what we are witnessing in this present perverse world. The people are doing and getting what they want, and the consequences will follow their wicked rebellion against God.

Ways to Identify the Antichrist or an Antichrist:

A look at Judas, who is also identified as the son of perdition, will help determine the ultimate Antichrist and lesser antichrist.

First, They are already among us	**John 13:2**
They are not recognized as deceivers	**John 13:22**
They possess power or influence	**Luke 9:1**
They may be chosen by God	**Luke 6:13**
They may be philanthropic	**John 12: 5**
They appear to love Jesus	**Luke 22:47**
They appear to be Believers	**1 John 2:18,19**

CHAPTER 16

OUTLINE AND REVELATION CHAPTER 14

The Lamb and the 144,000, the Three Angels, and the Harvest of the Earth:

1. **Verse 1-5:** The Lamb and the 144,000 on Mount Zion
    *   Introduction: John sees the Lamb standing on Mount Zion with 144,000 people, who have his name and his Father's name written on their foreheads.
    *   Their Description: They sing a new song before the throne and before the four living creatures and the elders. No one could learn that song except the 144,000 who had been redeemed from the earth.
    *   Their Purity: They are described as those who have not defiled themselves with women, for they are virgins. They follow the Lamb wherever he goes. They have been redeemed from mankind as firstfruits for God and the Lamb.
    *   Their Honor: In their mouth, no lie was found, for they are blameless before the throne of God.
2. **Verse 6-13:** The Messages of the Three Angels
    *   Introduction: John sees another angel flying directly overhead, with an eternal gospel to proclaim to those who dwell on earth, to every nation and tribe and language and people.

- The First Angel's Message: He proclaims with a loud voice, "Fear God and give him glory because the hour of his judgment has come, and worship him who made heaven and earth, the sea and the springs of water."

- The Second Angel's Message: Another angel follows, saying, "Fallen, fallen is Babylon the great, she who made all nations drink the wine of the passion of her sexual immorality."

- The Third Angel's Message: A third angel follows them, saying with a loud voice, "If anyone worships the beast and its image and receives a mark on his forehead or on his hand, he also will drink the wine of God's wrath, poured full strength into the cup of his anger, and he will be tormented with fire and sulfur in the presence of the holy angels and in the presence of the Lamb."

- The Call to Endurance: John hears a voice from heaven saying, "Blessed are the dead who die in the Lord from now on. 'Blessed indeed,' says the Spirit, 'that they may rest from their labors, for their deeds follow them!'"

3. **Verse 14-20:** The Harvest of the Earth
    - Introduction: John sees a white cloud and seated on the cloud, one like a son of man, with a golden crown on his head and a sharp sickle in his hand.

    - The Harvest of the Earth: Another angel comes out of the temple, calling with a loud voice to him who sits on the cloud, "Put in your sickle and reap, for the hour to reap has come, for the harvest of the earth is fully ripe."

    - The Angel's Reaping: So, he who sat on the cloud swung his sickle across the earth, and the earth was reaped.

    - The Grape Harvest: Then another angel comes out of the temple in heaven, and he, too, has a sharp sickle. And another angel comes out from the altar, the angel who has authority over the fire, and he calls with a loud voice to the one who has the sharp sickle, "Put in your sickle and gather the clusters from the vine of the earth, for its grapes are ripe."

- The Grapes of Wrath: So, the angel swung his sickle across the earth and gathered the grape harvest of the earth and threw it into the great winepress of the wrath of God. And the winepress was trodden outside the city, and blood flowed from the winepress, as high as a horse's bridle, for 1,600 stadia.

This chapter presents various visions, including the Lamb and the 144,000, the messages of the three angels, and the harvest of the earth, signaling the culmination of God's judgment and the finality of His redemption.

Revelation Chapter 14

This chapter directly contrasts those taking the mark of the Beast in chapter 13. This is a continuation of John's pause or narration.

Reminder: we are being provided information in John's narrative about what is occurring on earth with the ending of the Trumpet Judgment. And just before the Bowl Judgments during or overlapping this period.

The Lamb and the 144,000:

John says, 1 Then I looked, and there before me was the Lamb (this was Jesus and not the false lamb of chapter 13), *this Lamb – representing Jesus, was* standing on Mount Zion, and with him 144,000 (this is not the Church but rather God's remnant Jews and Saints – Gentile believers from Rev. 7:4) who had his name and his Father's name (unlike the Beast's number) written on their foreheads. (This name, whatever it may be, is associated with familiarity and oneness with God, unlike the number utilized by Satan for the purpose of tracking and identifying his people who will be seen as mere commodities. Nevertheless, these delusional, deceived, and lost souls of this world will be one with the Antichrist).

Without going into the many specifics, this Antichrist system and the false prophet overseeing his church merely see the people as a number by which to increase their wealth and status. They have no love for God or the people...they instead have a love for money and celebrity. Whereas with the true church of God, we are protected and beloved family members with Jesus. In our Father's house, we are not just a number; instead, we are accounted as invaluable and God's offspring! On this matter of numbering, Hitler also numbered or marked the Jews as slaves to be identified and ultimately killed. It's also worth pointing out that prisons assign numbers to their inmates; our government tracks us by our SS# and other numbers associated with us. **But God knows us by His name**, which has been given to us. And we are sealed by the Holy Spirit. How reassuring this should be for the children of God!

2 And I heard a sound from heaven like the roar of rushing waters and like a loud peal of thunder. The sound I heard was like that of harpists playing their harps. **3** And they sang a new song before the throne and before the four living creatures and the elders. No one could learn the song except the 144,000 who had been redeemed from the earth. **4** These are those who did not defile themselves with women, for they remained virgins (meaning they did not become one with Satan or this world's adulterous and corrupt systems ruled by the Antichrist and false prophet. Instead, they remained faithful to the Lamb – Jesus amongst great difficulty, even unto death. Throughout the Bible, Satan had always sought to defile the woman, or the Church – all who belong to the Lamb. Satan's desire is to lead mankind to destruction. Jesus' desire is to bring us with Him unto eternal life). They – *the 144,000* follow the Lamb wherever he goes. (These faithful ones had accepted Jesus as their Great Shepherd amid persecution coming from the Antichrist). *As a result of their faithfulness,* they were purchased by Jesus from among the loss of this world and offered as firstfruits. (They had been gathered as one with the Bride) to God – *the Father* and the Lamb – Jesus. **5** No lie was found in their mouths (in our culture of rampant lies and deception, they came to the truth of God and lived by His truth. How are you measuring up? See John 17:17) *Choosing to follow Jesus,* they – *those numbering among the 144,000* are *seen as being* blameless or the righteous of God.

The Proclamation of these Seven Angels Before us:

Rev. 14:6 The Gospel is Preached.

Rev. 14:8 Satan's Babylon, this world's last government and religious systems destruction.

Rev. 14:9 Warns those who take the mark of the beast that God's wrath will come upon them.

Rev. 14:13 God's Blessing upon His faithful Martyrs.

Rev. 14:15 God will harvest His faithful ones.

Rev. 14:17 God's harvest of the wicked and rebellious ones.

Rev. 14:18 God's final judgment of eternal suffering for the wicked; into the Gehenna or Lake of Fire they will be cast.

6 Then I saw another angel flying in midair, and he had the eternal gospel to proclaim to those who live on the earth—to every nation, tribe, language, and people. **7** He said in a loud voice, "Fear God and give him glory because the hour of his judgment has come. Worship him who made the heavens, the earth, the sea and the springs of water" (nevertheless, the people of the world will not repent after hearing the eternal gospel: see Rev. 16:11).

8 A second angel followed and said, " 'Fallen! Fallen is Babylon the Great,' which made all the nations drink the maddening wine of her adulteries." **9** A third angel followed them and said in a loud voice: "If anyone worships the beast and its image and receives its mark on their forehead or on their hand, **10** they, too, will drink the wine of God's fury, which has been poured full strength into the cup of his wrath. They will be tormented with burning sulfur in the presence of the holy angels and of the Lamb. **11** And the smoke of their torment will rise forever and ever. There will be no rest day or night for those who worship the beast and its image, or for anyone who receives the mark of its name." **12** This calls for patient endurance on the part of the people of God who keep his commands and remain faithful to Jesus.

If you haven't noticed, society is being primed for the acceptance of the mark of the beast, whatever it may be. We see this from the world's embrace of tattoos, drugs to enhance human capabilities, surgical body augmentation or cosmetic surgery, and even so, technological implants and other advanced medical and scientific methods embraced by mankind merely to prolong their lives and enhance their abilities and outward appearance. Mankind has, in fact, rejected how wonderfully they have been made by God. They are, in essence, saying that what God has done isn't good enough!

13 Then I heard a voice from heaven say, "Write this: Blessed are the dead (those that refuse the mark of the beast) who die in the Lord from now on." "Yes," says the Spirit, "they will rest from their labor, for their deeds will follow them." (See 1 Thessalonians 4:13-18).

Harvesting the Earth and Trampling the Winepress:

14 I looked, and there before me was a white cloud, and seated on the cloud was one like a son of man with a crown of gold on his head and a sharp sickle in his hand. (This is believed by some to be Jesus, the Sovereign Ruler and Judge. Or this just may be an Elohim aka angel who represents Jesus). **15** Then another angel came out of the temple and called in a loud voice to him who was sitting on the cloud, "Take your sickle and reap because the time to reap has come, for the harvest of the earth is ripe." **16** So he who was seated on the cloud swung his sickle over the earth, and the earth was harvested (of those who are God's righteous people).

Views on the subject of Harvesting:

There are those within the varied eschatological framework who are proponents of this harvesting as being God's separation or the reaping of His righteous ones as opposed to those who belong to Satan, who will soon experience God's ending judgment upon these rebellious ones at their reaping. Those holding this view believe that this harvesting or reaping is to distinguish between those at the final judgment who will dwell with Jesus for all eternity, as opposed to those individuals who will spend eternity with Satan and the other rebellious angels or Elohim (gods) in the lake of fire at the close of history as we know it. With this view on harvesting, I do not have any objection.

Additional views:

These views hold that there may be "another rapture" and resurrection event, as seemingly depicted in Revelation 14:16 along with Rev. 7:9-17, which is distinct from the rapture traditionally associated with the universal Church occurring before the seven-year tribulation period. These views are often associated with the mid-tribulation or pre-wrath rapture positions. However, in the place of the wording "another rapture," the preferred wording is a continuation of the rapture and resurrection, with Jesus being the first to be resurrected and raptured or the first stage of three raptures – hence, Jesus being called the firstfruits from the dead: see James 1:18 and 1 Cor. 15:20-23 followed by the resurrection and rapture of the universal Church and this final event or stage concluding here in verse sixteen with a look back at Rev. 7:9-17. Verse **3** of this 14th chapter of Revelation states that they – the 144,000 were "redeemed from the earth." Continuing with verse **4**, we read they were "redeemed from mankind as firstfruits..." Our conundrum is identifying when this redemption and the people being identified as firstfruits actually occur. When did their resurrection and rapture take place? It is debatable. However, we have the following in **Revelation**

Chapter 20:4-6: "I saw thrones on which were seated those who had been given authority to judge. And I saw the souls of those who had been beheaded because of their testimony about Jesus and because of the word of God. They had not worshiped the beast or its image and had not received its mark on their foreheads or their hands. They came to life and reigned with Christ a thousand years. **5** The rest of the dead did not come to life until the thousand years were ended. This is the first resurrection. **6** Blessed and holy are those who share in the first resurrection. The second death has no power over them, but they will be priests of God and of Christ and will reign with him for a thousand years.

In light of the belief that the universal Church will be raptured before the period of the seven-year Great Tribulation, subsequently, this current age of God's grace and mercy coming to a close because of the Great Apostasy and wickedness of this age, although those numbering among the 144,000 will come to faith in Christ at some point during the seven years of the tribulation period and this era culminating with the Great Tribulation ending with the Bowl Judgments. It stands to reason, I believe, as the Church or Bride of Christ will experience persecution and many even death leading to the time of the rapture and the resurrection of the dead in Christ; therefore, so it will be, for many going through these seven years of tribulation, they will likewise experience persecution and even death and then or like the universal Church will be raised to new-life or the living Saints united with Jesus when He arrives on earth contrasting the Church or Bride of Christ that was brought or rapture to me Him in the air: see 1 Thes. 4:16,17.

I reason that those numbering among the 144,000 will not experience, at least not directly, the worst of God's wrath that will be unleashed upon the rebellious and wicked people during God's Trumpet Judgments nor His Bowl Judgments of this ending period identified as the Great Tribulation. In my understanding and view of the Pretribulation Rapture of the Church – Christ Bride, I see a potential pattern with God dealing with His people who will come to faith in Him during this unprecedented time. Yes, those making up the number of 144,000 will experience persecution, and many will be killed for their faith.

However, again, I put forth that they will not directly experience the worst of God's wrath to be unleashed upon their murderers and the wicked of this world. We were told in Rev. 12:14 that many will be protected from God's wrath, as it was for Noah and Lot's family by God Himself as they were instructed to flee to the wilderness: see Rev. 12:6-14. However, it yet remains unclear to some when the faithful dead in Christ will be restored to life. But again, Revelation Chapter 20:4 has this to say: "I saw thrones on which were seated those who had been given authority to judge. And I saw the souls of those who had been beheaded because of their testimony about Jesus and because of the word of God. They had not worshiped the beast or its image and had not received its mark on their foreheads or their hands. **They came to life and reigned with Christ a thousand years.**" One can, therefore, postulate from this reading that the martyred Saints are resurrected at Jesus' Second Coming.

In other views, the Jews and believing Saints are raptured at some point during the tribulation period but before the outpouring of God's wrath, as described in the latter part of the time of the Great Tribulation. This timing places the rapture event somewhere in the middle of the tribulation period, or the 3.5-year mark, hence the term "mid-tribulation rapture." Similarly, the pre-wrath rapture position holds that Believers will be raptured before the pouring out of God's wrath in the form of the seven Bowl Judgments described in Revelation Chapters 15 and 16. This view places the timing of the rapture just prior to the final portion of the tribulation or the Great Tribulation, with this era concluding with the Bowl Judgments.

As seen, proponents of these views often interpret Revelation 14:16 as describing a separate gathering or rapture event that occurs at a specific point during the tribulation, distinct or in opposition from the rapture traditionally associated with the universal Church occurring before the tribulation period. This interpretation allows for the possibility of multiple rapture events or, as I prefer, a continuation of the first rapture beginning with Jesus, then His Bride, and possibly concluding here in Revelation 14:16. Just the same, all who will be resurrected or rapture regardless of when are among the firstfruits with Christ.

It's important to note that the mid-tribulation and pre-wrath rapture positions occurring during the seven-year tribulation are minority views within Christian eschatology, and interpretations of Revelation 14:16 vary among different theological traditions and scholars. These alternative views, such as pre-tribulation rapture or post-tribulation rapture, as seen offer different understandings of the timing and nature of the rapture event in relation to the events described or understood by others here in this 14th chapter of the book of Revelation. Regardless of when and how these events occur. If we remain faithful to Jesus...In the end, we win!

Continuing with verse 17, Another angel came out of the temple in heaven, and he too had a sharp sickle. **18** Still another angel, who had charge of the fire, came from the altar and called in a loud voice to him who had the sharp sickle, "Take your sharp sickle and gather the clusters of grapes from the earth's vine because its grapes are ripe." (This is a picture of those belonging to Satan who are about to be harvested). **19** The angel swung his sickle on the earth, gathered its grapes, and threw them into the great winepress of God's wrath. **20** They were trampled in the winepress outside the city, and blood flowed out of the press, rising as high as the horses' bridles for a distance of 1,600 stadia. (Here before us is God's judgment and response to the martyrs or the faithful dead's cry as presented in Rev. 6:10; we will see this proclamation further fulfilled in the coming chapters. Read Isaiah 63:2-6. 1,600 stadia points to a significant amount of bloodshed and loss of life).

An Outline Pattern of End Times:

In Revelation Chapters 11 and 12, God responds to man's historical dilemma. Working backward, beginning with Genesis Chapter 11, we can see in this outline God dealing with the three rebellions.

The Rebellions: Genesis Chapter 3, Genesis Chapter 6, and Genesis Chapter 11:

Gen. 11 The 1st Babylon Built	Revelation The Last Babylon Falls
Gen. 10 The 1st Antichrist – Nimrod	Rev. Last Antichrist is dealt with
Gen. 9 The 1st Remnant saved – Noah	Rev. Last Remnant saved – 144,000 and others
Gen. 8 The Dove can't find land	Rev. the Holy Spirit is removed, the earth is under judgment
Gen. 7 The 1st Wrath of God	Rev. The Final Wrath of God
Gen. 6 The Fallen Angels	Rev. Fallen Angels released and destroyed
Gen. 5 The 1st Rapture – Enoch	Rev. Last Rapture
Gen. 4 Mark upon Cain	Rev. Mark of the Beast
Gen. 3 Satan Deception	Rev. Satan is Bound and cast into the Lake of Fire

CHAPTER 17

OUTLINE AND REVELATION CHAPTER 15

1. **Verse 1-4:** The Prelude to the Seven Plagues
   - Introduction: John sees another sign in heaven, great and amazing: seven angels with seven plagues, which are the last, for with them, the wrath of God is finished.
   - The Victorious Saints: John sees those who had conquered the beast and its image and the number of its name, standing beside the sea of glass with harps of God in their hands.
   - The Song of Moses and the Lamb: They sing the song of Moses, the servant of God, and the song of the Lamb, saying, "Great and amazing are your deeds, O Lord God the Almighty! Just and true are your ways, O King of the nations! Who will not fear, O Lord, and glorify your name? For you alone are holy. All nations will come and worship you, for your righteous acts have been revealed."
2. **Verse 5-8:** The Temple of the Tabernacle of the Testimony
   - Introduction: After this, John looks, and the sanctuary of the tent of witness in heaven is opened.
   - The Seven Angels: Out of the sanctuary come the seven angels with the seven plagues, clothed in pure, bright linen, with golden sashes around their chests.

- The Temple Filled with Smoke: The sanctuary is filled with smoke from the glory of God and from his power, and no one can enter the sanctuary until the seven plagues of the seven angels are finished.

This chapter serves as a prelude to the pouring out of the seven bowls of God's wrath, highlighting the victorious saints who stand beside the sea of glass and sing the song of Moses and the Lamb. Additionally, it portrays the heavenly sanctuary and the arrival of the seven angels with the seven plagues, indicating the imminent judgment of God upon the earth.

Revelation Chapter 15

We have now concluded the narration of John following the Seventh Trumpet, beginning in Revelation Chapter 11 and ending in Chapter 14. Here is a reminder of what John stated in Rev. 11:15.

The Final Seventh Trumpet:

15 Then the seventh angel blew his trumpet, and there were loud voices in heaven, saying, "The kingdom of the world has become the kingdom of our Lord and of his Christ, and he shall reign forever and ever." And verse **19**, "Then God's temple in heaven was opened, and the ark of his covenant was seen within his temple. There were flashes of lightning, rumblings, peals of thunder, an earthquake, and heavy hail." (Beginning with these verses and concluding with Rev. Chapter 14, we were provided events occurring in heaven and on earth. We were also provided prophecy regarding what is to take place from this point on).

Revelation 15: Seven Angels With Seven Plagues – The last 3.5 years of God's wrath:

1 I saw in heaven another great and marvelous sign: seven angels with the seven last plagues—last because with them God's wrath is completed.

(The first great sign John saw was the woman clothed with the son, representing Israel as provided in Rev. 12:1; the second sign was a great red dragon, representing the beast of Rev. 12:3. These signs were seen in heaven; however, they were manifested on earth. Even so, God's kingdom will come unto the earth as it is in heaven: see Rev. 5:10). **2** And I saw what looked like a sea of glass glowing with fire and, standing beside the sea, those – *the tribulation Saints* who had been victorious over the beast and its image and over the number of its name. They held harps given them by God **3** and sang the song of God's servant Moses and of the Lamb: "Great and marvelous are your deeds, Lord God Almighty. Just and true are your ways, King of the nations (see Ex. 15:1-18 and Deuteronomy Chapter 32). **4** Who will not fear you, Lord, and bring glory to your name? For you alone are holy. All nations will come and worship before you, for your righteous acts have been revealed."

God's millennial kingdom will be established on earth; as Scripture says, "Thy kingdom come, Thy will be done on earth as it is in heaven" see Matthew 6:9-13. God says He will be worshipped here on earth, and His words will not return to Him void or empty: see Isa. 55:11. God's intended rule of a Man – here meaning Jesus the Messianic King, and the very Son of God with His reign with and over mankind on earth, is going to be re-established. A do-over of the fall occurring in Genesis, chap. 3 is going to take place. Nimrod's kingdom, this being the first of fallen mankind or Satan's kingdoms as seen in Genesis chap. 10 with additional mentioning of such kingdoms throughout the Bible and known throughout man's history, will come to ruin; Babylon the Great, this world's or Satan's final Antichrist system or kingdom, will be no more! God's counter-defense to the Devil's systems with the emergence of His earthly or physical kingdom began with Abraham in Genesis chap. 12, and his descendants – the Israelites or Jewish people. And God's kingdom will be re-established and perfected through Jesus, who will reign as King of kings over the Jews and all nations, here on this earth for one thousand years: see Ezekiel 37:22; Daniel 2:44; Isaiah 9:6,7; Luke 1:31-33; and Matthew 8:11.

5 After this, I looked, and I saw in heaven the temple (from Rev. 11:19) —that is, the tabernacle of the covenant law—and it was opened. **6** Out of the temple came the seven angels with the seven plagues. They were dressed in clean, shining linen and wore golden sashes around their chests. **7** Then one of the four living creatures (a mighty Cherub, a higher order of angelic beings) gave to the seven angels seven golden bowls filled with the wrath of God, who lives forever and ever. **8** And the temple was filled with smoke from the glory of God and from his power, and no one could enter the temple until the seven plagues of the seven angels were completed. (Access to God and His grace and mercy is now denied. God's final Bowl Judgments are imminent. His longsuffering had reached its limit; now, His final judgment is to roll to its completion).

CHAPTER 18

OUTLINE AND REVELATION CHAPTER 16

The Seven Angels Bowls of God's Wrath:

1. **Verse 1-2:** The First Bowl: Harmful Sores
   - Introduction: The first angel pours out his bowl on the earth, and harmful and painful sores break out on the people who bore the mark of the beast and worshiped its image.
2. **Verse 3:** The Second Bowl: The Sea Turns to Blood
   - Introduction: The second angel pours out his bowl into the sea, and it becomes like the blood of a corpse, and every living thing in the sea dies.
3. **Verse 4-7:** The Third Bowl: The Waters Turn to Blood
   - Introduction: The third angel pours out his bowl into the rivers and the springs of water, and they become blood.
   - The Angel's Declaration: The angel declares, "You are just, O Holy One, who is and who was, for you brought these judgments. For they have shed the blood of saints and prophets, and you have given them blood to drink. It is what they deserve!"
   - The Altar's Response: John hears the altar saying, "Yes, Lord God the Almighty, true and just are your judgments!"

4. **Verse 8-9:** The Fourth Bowl: Scorching Heat
   - Introduction: The fourth angel pours out his bowl on the sun, and it was allowed to scorch people with fire.

   - The People's Reaction: They were scorched by the fierce heat, and they cursed the name of God, who had power over these plagues. They did not repent and give him glory.

5. **Verse 10-11:** The Fifth Bowl: Darkness and Pain
   - Introduction: The fifth angel pours out his bowl on the throne of the beast, and its kingdom was plunged into darkness. People gnawed their tongues in anguish and cursed the God of heaven for their pain and sores. They did not repent of their deeds.

6. **Verse 12:** The Sixth Bowl: The Euphrates Dried Up
   - Introduction: The sixth angel pours out his bowl on the great river Euphrates, and its water was dried up to prepare the way for the kings from the east.

7. **Verse 13-16:** The Three Unclean Spirits and Armageddon
   - Introduction: John sees three unclean spirits, like frogs, come out of the mouth of the dragon, the beast, and the false prophet. They are demonic spirits performing signs, and they go to the kings of the whole world to assemble them for battle on the great day of God the Almighty.

   - Warning: Jesus interjects, saying, "Behold, I am coming like a thief! Blessed is the one who stays awake, keeping his garments on, that he may not go about naked and be seen exposed!"

   - Gathering at Armageddon: The spirits assemble the kings at the place that in Hebrew is called Armageddon.

8. **Verse 17-21:** The Seventh Bowl: The Great Earthquake and Hailstorm
   - Introduction: The seventh angel pours out his bowl into the air, and a loud voice comes out of the temple from the throne, saying, "It is done!"

- The Earthquake: There is a great earthquake, such as there had never been since man was on the earth, so great was that earthquake.
- The Cities Collapse: The great city is split into three parts, and the cities of the nations fall. God remembers Babylon the Great to make her drink the cup of the wine of the fury of his wrath.
- The Hailstorm: Huge hailstones, about one hundred pounds each, fall from heaven on people, and they curse God for the plague of the hail because the plague was so severe.

This chapter depicts the pouring out of the seven bowls of God's wrath upon the earth, each resulting in severe judgments and calamities. Despite the intensity of these plagues, many people continue to blaspheme God and refuse to repent of their sins.

Revelation Chapter 16

The Seven Bowls of God's Wrath:

This, being the finale of God's wrath, will be poured out on the earth with increased severity. All life will be affected, unlike the 1/3 of the environment affected by the Trumpet Judgments. With the pouring out of the last bowl, we will then have the Second Coming of Jesus to decimate the nations who will come against Israel in her perceived defeat at or of the battle Armageddon. At the crying out of Israel to God, from fear of these armies, Jesus returns: see Romans Chapter 10:13; 11:26 and Zech. 14:3,4. Moreover, Christ will return with His bride – the universal Church and with all the faithful dead of God brought forth out of the Great Tribulation. After this, Jesus – the Messianic King, will set up His kingdom on earth for 1,000 years for His millennial reign, followed by the condemnation of the wicked dead and the rebellious spirit beings into eternal darkness and the Lake of Fire. Then God will create His New Heaven and New Earth!

1 Then I heard a loud voice from the temple saying to the seven angels, "Go, pour out the seven bowls of God's wrath on the earth." **2** The first angel went and poured out his bowl on the land, and ugly, festering sores *or boils* broke out on the people who had the mark of the beast and worshiped its image. (These plagues primarily follow the pattern of God's judgment on Pharoah and Egypt as seen in Exodus Chapters 5:1-3 and 9:11,12).

3 The second angel poured out his bowl on the sea, and it turned into blood like that of a dead person, and every living thing in the sea died. **4** The third angel poured out his bowl on the rivers and springs of water, and they became blood (see Ex. 7:20,21). **5** Then I heard the angel in charge of the waters say: "You are just in these judgments, O Holy One, you who are and who were; **6** for they have shed the blood of your holy people and your prophets, and you have given them blood to drink as they deserve." (Throughout Scripture, God has shown Himself to be a loving and merciful Father; lest we forget or choose not to acknowledge, He has also displayed that He is a Righteous Judge, therefore, unrepentant evil does not go unpunished).

7 And I heard the altar respond: "Yes, Lord God Almighty, true and just are your judgments."**8** The fourth angel poured out his bowl on the sun, and the sun was allowed to scorch people with fire. **9** They were seared by the intense heat, and they cursed the name of God, who had control over these plagues, but they refused to repent and glorify him. (This is precisely what we saw with Pharoah and other rebellious nations who withstood Yahweh; they saw and even acknowledged His mighty acts, and yet, they refused to turn from their wicked rebellion, nor did they worship Him). **10** The fifth angel poured out his bowl on the throne of the beast, and its kingdom was plunged into darkness (see Ex. 10:21-23). People gnawed their tongues in agony **11** and cursed the God of heaven because of their pains and their sores, but they refused to repent of what they had done.

12 The sixth angel poured out his bowl on the great river Euphrates, and its water was dried up – *like the Red Sea was dried and the Jordan River was halted. However, in this case,* to prepare the way for the kings from the East: see Isa. 11:15,16. (These are a coalition of nations who will set themselves up to battle against Israel). **13** Then I saw three impure spirits that looked like frogs; they came out of the mouth of the dragon (they are the essence of evil – the Devil himself), *and* out of the mouth of the beast (the Antichrist they came) and out of the mouth of the false prophet (this unholy and false trinity was at work with all of its vengeful rage and evil to destroy Israel, but it will not be so).

14 *These three images of frogs:* They are demonic spirits that perform signs, and they go out to the kings of the whole world to gather them for the battle on the great day of God Almighty. (Satan's hatred for Israel and his desire for her land is manic. So has he stirred the people of the world throughout Israel's history to be against Israel. We saw this with the Pharoah of Egypt, the Philistines, Assyria, Babylon and Nebuchadnezzar, and Persia, with Hamon trying to exterminate the Jews and the Greeks through Hellenization, and the tyrant king and mad-man, Antiochus, Rome and its dictator kings, and others.

However, 2000 years after Rome dominated the Jews, on May 14th, 1948: see Jer. 30:1-9, the Jewish people, on this date, became a sovereign state and declared its independence after centuries of dispersion and persecution as a nation or people group. After their Six Day War in 1967 with Arab countries, Israel acquired more of the land that God had promised to her: see Joel Chapter 3:1,2 and verses 12-17. God saw to it that Israel would be reestablished as a nation within the land He promised and gave to them: see Jeremiah Chapter 31:35,36. In this 16th chapter of the Book of Revelation, we will see that God is going to defend Israel and His land, which He gave them, leading to Jesus reclaiming all the land promised to Israel and there establishing His kingdom and millennial reign.

15 "Look, I come like a thief! Blessed is the one who stays awake and remains clothed *or spiritually prepared*, so as not to go naked and be shamefully exposed." (This is a message from Jesus forewarning us that He is coming like a thief – this can point to Him rapturing the church, but also His sudden arrival to rescue Israel His chosen people from the Devil and their enemies who will be arrayed against them. In Rev. 3:10, Jesus says to all who belong to Him, "Since you have kept my command to endure patiently, I will also keep you from the hour of trial that is going to come on the whole world to test the inhabitants of the earth. Even so, in Rev. 22:7, we see Jesus prepping the world – His Bride, for His imminent return; He says, "Look, I am coming soon! Blessed is the one who keeps the words of the prophecy written in this scroll," and who remains clothed in His blood and righteousness. Whom God saves, He clothes – we see this with Adam and Eve, demon-possessed people, the prodigal son, and His Saints who are clothed in salvation and righteousness, even in fine white linen; God's people are seen as being clothed by Him: see Isaiah Chapter 61:10 and Rev. 19:8).

16 Then they gathered the kings together to the place that in Hebrew is called Armageddon (aka the Mount of Megiddo, for the Day of the Lord, in the valley of Jezreel, the location of Israel's major military airbase – Ramat David and the location of their nukes. This battle is when and where the Antichrist-led world comes against Israel: see Zech. Chapter 12:1-3 verses 9-11 and chap. 14:1,2. This is not the war of Gog and Magog. (Here, it is believed that Russia will be allied with Turkey and Iran in particular) that occurs before the seven-year tribulation period: see Ezekiel Chapters 38-39. However, this campaign will be the world's last assault against Israel, but not the universal Church, which will be returning with Jesus at His 2nd Coming to deal with Israel's enemies: see Zech. chap. 14:3-9: Isaiah 10:20,21; Dan. 12:1; Matt. 24:22 and Zech. 13:8,9).

17 The seventh angel poured out his bowl into the air, and out of the temple came a loud voice from the throne, saying, "It is done!" (John, at a loss for words and struck by what he saw possibly a nuclear holocaust, we don't know, responds…) **18** Then there came flashes of lightning, rumblings, peals of thunder and a severe earthquake. No earthquake like it has ever occurred since mankind has been on earth, so tremendous was the quake. (See Romans 8:22, 23; here, labor pains are likened to earthquakes; Israel at this time was experiencing such pain resulting from her enemies. Also, look back at Rev. 12:16). **Verse 19:** The great city split into three parts – *resulting from this earthquake,* and the cities of the nations collapsed. God remembered Babylon the Great (this Antichrist's world system) and *therefore* gave her the cup filled with the wine of the fury of his wrath. **20** Every island fled away, and the mountains could not be found. **21** From the sky, huge hailstones, each weighing about a hundred pounds, fell on the people. (See Ex. 9:22-26 and Lev. 24:16 regarding punishment by stoning; in this case, it was hailstones). And they cursed God on account of the plague of hail because the plague was so terrible. (Jesus says in Matthew Chapter 24:22, "If those days – *referring to these end times and the nations thirst for war* had not been cut short, no one would survive, but for the sake of the elect these days will be cut short." Jesus is going to return; His Second Coming is as sure as His First Parousia).

CHAPTER 19

OUTLINE AND REVELATION CHAPTER 17

The Great Prostitute and the Beast:

1. **Verse 1-2:** The Great Prostitute and the Beast
   - Introduction: One of the seven angels who had the seven bowls comes and speaks to John, saying, "Come, I will show you the judgment of the great prostitute who is seated on many waters, with whom the kings of the earth have committed sexual immorality, and with the wine of whose sexual immorality the dwellers on earth have become drunk."
   - The Invitation: The angel carries John away in the Spirit into a wilderness, where he sees a woman sitting on a scarlet beast that is full of blasphemous names, having seven heads and ten horns.
2. **Verse 3-6:** The Woman and the Beast's Description
   - Introduction: The woman is arrayed in purple and scarlet and adorned with gold, jewels, and pearls, holding in her hand a golden cup full of abominations and the impurities of her sexual immorality.
   - Her Name: On her forehead was written a name of mystery: "Babylon the great, mother of prostitutes and of earth's abominations."

- Her Drunkenness: John sees the woman drunk with the blood of the saints, the blood of the martyrs of Jesus. And when he saw her, he marveled greatly.

3. **Verse 7-18:** The Interpretation of the Vision
   - Introduction: The angel explains the mystery of the woman and the beast to John.

   - The Beast's Description: The beast that John saw was, and is not, and is about to rise from the bottomless pit and go to destruction. Those who dwell on earth whose names have not been written in the Book of Life from the foundation of the world will marvel at seeing the beast because it was and is not and is to come.

   - The Seven Heads and Ten Horns: The seven heads are seven mountains on which the woman is seated. They are also seven kings, five of whom have fallen, one is, and the other has not yet come. And when he comes, he must remain only a little while. As for the beast that was and is not, it is an eighth, but it belongs to the seven, and it goes to destruction.

   - The Ten Horns: The ten horns are ten kings who have not yet received royal power, but they are to receive authority as kings for one hour or a short period, together with the beast. They are of one mind and hand over their power and authority to the beast. They will make war on the Lamb, but the Lamb will conquer them, for He is Lord of lords and King of kings, and those with him are called and chosen and faithful.

   - The Waters: The waters that the woman is seated on are peoples and multitudes and nations and languages.

   - The Judgment of the Great Prostitute: The ten horns and the beast will hate the prostitute. They will make her desolate and naked and devour her flesh and burn her up with fire, for God has put it into their hearts to carry out his purpose by being of one mind and handing over their royal power to the beast until the words of God are fulfilled.

- The Woman's Identity: The woman is the great city that has dominion over the kings of the earth.

This chapter unveils the vision of the great prostitute seated on the beast with seven heads and ten horns. The angel interprets the mystery, explaining the significance of the woman, the beast, and the waters. It also portrays the ultimate judgment of the great prostitute by the beast and the ten horns, as orchestrated by God's divine plan.

Revelation Chapter 17

Once again, in chapter 17 and later in chapter 18, we are provided narrations from John. In these chapters, we will first see the Prostitute, the harlot church – Mystery Babylon, and also the city united with the Antichrist's united nations – Babylon the Great, and these two systems intermingling. In this final stage of human history, we will see the merging of the two systems or influential powers: the Antichrist's political or world rule and the false prophet's religious system or the false church that is pictured in chapter 18. This merging gives rise to Babylon the Great. As we attempt to see these systems function, their distinction blur, making it a challenge at times to distinguish which Babylon system is in view. Nevertheless, the Antichrist system – Babylon, is in full view.

Keep in mind that the Bible is the tale of two cities: Jerusalem – the kingdom of God, and Babylon – which is any nation or, in the case before us, the whole world establishing its own rule apart from God. Regarding the original Babylon, under Nimrod's rule and its religious system, which was established when they erected the Tower of Babel to reach the heavens so that they may entangle themselves with other gods or Elohim. This is what we see occurring once again in the Book of Revelation during the end of time as we know it; mankind rejecting God's rule over them so that secular humanism – that is, man doing what they want to do and hence becoming gods unto themselves and even one with the dark and wicked spiritual under-world. Such towers or pyramids, as described in Genesis, are seen throughout the world, here indicating Satan's influence or Babylon's system upon fallen humanity.

The original Babylon under Nimrod was dispersed by God, and Nebuchadnezzar's Babylonian Rule was lost to Medo-Persia, but it wasn't destroyed. Babylon never went away; it simply ceased to be a central world power. Nevertheless, its influence continued until Christ's First Coming, and it is seen even now at work. And is slowly being brought back together as a one-world government under Satan's influence. In **Zechariah 5:6-11**, we are informed that Babylon will return. Zechariah has a vision, and he asks the angel about his vision, " The angel replied, **6** "It is a basket." And he added, "This is the iniquity of the people throughout the land." **7** Then the cover of the lid was raised, and there in the basket sat a woman! **8** He said, "This is wickedness," and he pushed her back into the basket and pushed its lead cover down on it. **9** Then I looked up—and there before me were two women, with the wind in their wings! They had wings like those of a stork, and they lifted up the basket between heaven and earth. **10** "Where are they taking the basket?" I asked the angel who was speaking to me.

11 He replied, "To the country of Babylonia to build a house for it. When the house is ready, the basket will be set there in its place." (Here in our study of the Book of Revelation, it's time for the basket – this woman and false church to be set back in its place or its reunion with the ultimate Antichrist system, Babylon, where man seeks to establish its own government under the rule of the final Antichrist, Satan's hybrid man).

Babylon, the Prostitute on the Beast:

1 One of the seven angels who had the seven bowls came and said to me, "Come, I will show you the punishment of the great prostitute, who sits by many waters. (Waters globally represent the people of the world).

2 With her, the kings of the earth committed adultery, and the inhabitants of the earth were intoxicated with the wine of her adulteries." (The influence of this false or harlot church – which is believed to be the revival of the ancient Roman Catholic Church, seizes the minds of its vast followers).

3 Then the angel carried me away in the Spirit into a wilderness (considered as the abode or haunt of demons; location, possibly Southern Iraq and Kuwait, the region of ancient Babylon: see Isa. 21:1-17). *John continues,* and I saw a woman (the false prophet's religious system – the false church of this world. The next time John is carried away in the Spirit, as seen in Rev. 21:10 & 15,16, he sees the true Church – the Bride of the Lamb or New Jerusalem). *But now, John sees the woman* who is seated on the scarlet beast (that represents the Antichrist's united world governmental system) that was covered with blasphemous names and had seven heads and ten horns (this being a picture of the unification of these world powers under the Antichrist). **4** The woman was dressed in purple and scarlet and was glittering with gold, precious stones, and pearls. She held a golden cup in her hand, filled with abominable things and the filth of her adulteries. (John is describing this harlot religious system that benefited from the one-world government and this system that mutually benefitted from the harlot – hence, their joining together and rejection of the *One True God* is viewed as spiritual prostitution as they pursued their own ways and wicked, lustful fleshly indulgences. The following Scriptures identify some ways of spiritual prostitution: Deut. 31:16-18; 23:17,18; Ex. 34:15-17; Isa. 1:21-24; Jer. 2:20; Eze. 16:15,16 and James 4:4).

5 The name written on her forehead was a mystery: BABYLON THE GREAT, THE MOTHER OF PROSTITUTES, AND OF THE ABOMINATIONS OF THE EARTH.

6 I saw that the woman was drunk with the blood of God's holy people, the blood of those – *martyrs or the faithful dead whom this false church or Babylon system murdered* who bore testimony of Jesus. (The ancient Roman Catholic Church, throughout its history, with its Popes, was morally corrupt and responsible for killing countless true Christians or those who believed in the deity of Christ and who rejected this false church's religious idolatrous and spiritual adulterous system. Also, the religious faith of Islam is guilty of the same offenses that some believe will be integral to this false and Antichrist church. There are other nations or state churches that have killed Christians; however, the ancient Roman Church and Islam are the greatest massacres of Christians).

Continuing with **verse 6,** *John says,* When I saw her, I was greatly astonished. **7** Then the angel said to me: "Why are you astonished? I will explain to you the mystery of the woman and of the beast she rides, which has the seven heads and ten horns (again, this is a representation of a united coalition of world powers and their unprecedented evil). **8** The beast, which you saw, once was, now is not, and yet will come up out of the Abyss (this beastly system or the Antichrist will be demonically influenced or the Antichrist, even demon possessed as he establishes his Babylonian kingdom); *however, it will* go to its destruction (he – the beast and his kingdom). **Verse 8** continues, The inhabitants of the earth whose names have not been written in the Book of Life from the creation of the world will be astonished when they see the beast (and its system of autocratic or authoritarian global rule) because it once was, now is not, and yet will come – *this one-world government under the Antichrist's rule.*

In light of the statement, "whose names have not been written in the Book of Life," I take the position that for every child born of a woman, his or her name is written in the Book of Life; however, there are extraordinary exceptions as found in Scripture and as shown before us, where some are excluded from "the Book of Life from the creation of the world." My response to this, God is Sovereign. If this statement speaks to Predestination and/or Election, as some argue that it does. My response regarding this matter, "This idea is beyond my comprehension." Nevertheless, there arises a time or age of accountability for every person to freely choose Christ for themselves as their Lord and Savior when He presents Himself to them or as He the Holy Spirit moves upon their hearts. One's acceptance of Christ or exercise of free will as free moral agents will determine if their name remains in the Book of Life or if their names are blotted out. See Ex. 32:32,33; Ps. 69:28; Dan.12:1and Rev.3:5.

Regarding this beast's description, **verse 9** *says,* "This calls for a mind with wisdom. The seven heads are seven hills on which the woman sits. (This image is believed to be a representation of ancient Rome, which was described as a nation with seven cities built on seven hills, which also had seven kings). **10** They are also seven kings. Five have fallen (the Greek nation and the four preceding world powers identified in the Old Testament); one is (at the time ancient Rome), the other has not yet come, but when he does come, he must remain for only a little while. (Many believe this will be Babylon the Great, the amalgamation of the preceding world powers, led by the Antichrist: see Dan. 7:7,8 and verses 24,25. However, another view suggests that this image points to Emperor rule during the time of John's writings.). **11** The beast who once was, and now is not, is an eighth king. He belongs to the seven and is going to his destruction. **12** "The ten horns you saw are ten kings who have not yet received a kingdom, but who for one hour – *or for a short period* will receive authority as kings along with the beast. (This will be the future and final confederation of nations or one-world government). **13** They have one purpose and will give their power and authority to the beast – *the Antichrist.* **14** They – *the Antichrist's system of rule* will wage war against the Lamb, but the Lamb will triumph over them because he is Lord of lords and King of kings—and with him will be his called, chosen and faithful followers." (We will see this event unfold in chapter 19).

15 Then the angel said to me, "The waters you saw, where the prostitute sits, are peoples, multitudes, nations, and languages. (This prostitute or false church that has united with these political powers together will have global reign before she is betrayed by this ambitious and narcissistic government). **16** The beast and the ten horns you saw will hate the prostitute. (This united government, led by the Antichrist, will use the religious system for its benefit, and when she is no longer useful, He is going to turn against the woman – this counterfeit church and its false prophet. The world led by the Antichrist, this abuser, and ultimate megalomaniac and narcissist, will want all things to be about him; therefore, he will destroy the woman or harlot church who also wielded great power and influence. However, it will be God who will destroy the Antichrist and all he represents. It is the All-Supreme God who permits the Antichrist to take out the false prophet. However, Jesus is going to deal with the Antichrist and the Devil personally)! *Concluding verse 16*. They – *the Antichrist and his government* will bring her – *the false prophet* to ruin and leave her naked; they will eat her flesh and burn her with fire. (This is a picture of the false prophet and harlot church being brought to utter devastation resulting from God's judgment for her whoredom and wicked rebellion).

17 For God has put it into their – *this world's government or Antichrist's* hearts to accomplish his purpose by agreeing to hand over to the beast their royal authority until God's words are fulfilled. **18** The woman (or this false religious system) you saw is the great city (likened to the ancient Roman Empire, which was ruling during John's writing of the Book of Revelation; however, at the end of this age, it will be the revived harlot Roman Catholic Church, with power such that ancient Roman Catholic Church had will be reestablished) that rules over the kings of the earth."

Such was the influence of the ancient Roman Catholic Church. However, some maintain that this false church will be established in Mecca and, therefore, this being Islamic world dominance at the end of the age. Whichever position one holds, this church is an amalgamation or a World Council of churches or religions. I call your attention back to Revelation 2:20-25. Remember the church of Thyatira, which tolerated Jezebel? "And unless they repent, will be cast into the great tribulation. Jezebel was the wicked woman who taught false doctrines, rejected true prophecy from God, and who was married to the Antichrist, Ahab, the evil king of Israel. The world is currently under Babylon's system; however, it is yet to reach maturity as described before us. And yet, it is sure to come; the alignment for such governmental unification is slowly underway.

CHAPTER 20

OUTLINE AND REVELATION CHAPTER 18

The Fall of Babylon the Great:

1. **Verse 1-3:** The Announcement of Babylon's Fall
   - Introduction: After these things, John sees another angel coming down from heaven, having great authority, and the earth was made bright with his glory.
   - The Angel's Cry: The angel calls out with a mighty voice, "Fallen, fallen is Babylon the Great! She has become a dwelling place for demons, a haunt for every unclean spirit, a haunt for every unclean bird, a haunt for every unclean and detestable beast."
   - The Reason: For all nations have drunk the wine of the passion of her sexual immorality, and the kings of the earth have committed immorality with her, and the merchants of the earth have grown rich from the power of her luxurious living.
2. **Verse 4-8:** The Call to God's People to Flee Babylon
   - Introduction: John hears another voice from heaven, saying, "Come out of her, my people, lest you take part in her sins, lest you share in her plagues; for her sins are heaped high as heaven, and God has remembered her iniquities."

- The Retribution: Pay her back as she herself has paid back others, and repay her double for her deeds; mix a double portion for her in the cup she mixed.

- The Boasts of Babylon: As she glorified herself and lived in luxury, so give her a like measure of torment and mourning, since in her heart she says, 'I sit as a queen, I am no widow and mourning I shall never see.'

- The Judgment: For this reason, her plagues will come in a single day, death and mourning and famine, and she will be burned up with fire, for mighty is the Lord God who has judged her.

3. **Verse 9-19:** The Lamentation of Kings, Merchants, and Sailors

   - Introduction: The kings of the earth who committed sexual immorality and lived in luxury with her will weep and wail over her when they see the smoke of her burning.

   - The Merchants' Lament: The merchants of the earth weep and mourn, for no one buys their cargo anymore, cargo of gold, silver, jewels, pearls, fine linen, purple cloth, silk, scarlet cloth, all kinds of scented wood, all kinds of articles of ivory, all kinds of articles of costly wood, bronze, iron, and marble, cinnamon, spice, incense, myrrh, frankincense, wine, oil, fine flour, wheat, cattle and sheep, horses and chariots, and slaves, that is, human souls.

   - The Riches Gone: The fruit for which your soul longed has gone from you, and all your delicacies and your splendors are lost to you, never to be found again.

   - The Merchants' Grief: The merchants of these wares, who gained wealth from her, will stand far off, in fear of her torment, weeping and mourning aloud, "Alas, alas, for the great city that was clothed in fine linen, in purple and scarlet, adorned with gold, with jewels, and with pearls! For in a single hour, all this wealth has been laid waste."

4. **Verse 20-24:** Heaven's Response to Babylon's Fall
   - Introduction: Rejoice over her, O heaven, and you saints and apostles and prophets, for God has given judgment for you against her!
   - The Finality: Then a mighty angel took up a stone like a great millstone and threw it into the sea, saying, "So will Babylon the great city be thrown down with violence, and will be found no more."
   - The Silence: And the sound of harpists and musicians, of flute players and trumpeters, will be heard in you no more, and a craftsman of any craft will be found in you no more, and the sound of the mill will be heard in you no more, and the light of a lamp will shine in you no more, and the voice of bridegroom and bride will be heard in you no more, for your merchants were the great ones of the earth, and all nations were deceived by your sorcery.
   - The Guilt: And in her was found the blood of prophets and of saints, and of all who have been slain on earth.

This chapter depicts the fall of Babylon the Great, a symbol of the world's system of rebellion against God. The chapter highlights the announcement of Babylon's fall, the call for God's people to flee her, the lamentation of kings, merchants, and sailors over her destruction, and the rejoicing of heaven over her judgment.

Revelation Chapter 18

What John has been shown and what he further reveals to us in this chapter is a repeat of the prophecies of Isaiah, in Chapters 13 & 14, and Jeremiah, Chapters 50 & 51, to include prophecies of Ezekiel, Daniel, Zechariah, and others, not the least of which, the prophecies of Jesus.

Old Testament Prophecies Concerning Babylon and its Fall:

Isa. 21:9; Jeremiah 51:49 .... Revelation 18:2

Leave Babylon's System:

Isa. 48:20; Jer. 50:8 .... Rev. 18:4

The Pride of Babylon:

Isa. 13:19; Jer. 51:41 .... Rev. 18:7

Babylon as The Woman:

Isa. 47: 7,8; Jer. 51: 33; Zech. 5: 7,8 .... Rev. 18: 7,9

Babylon is Doomed:

Isa. 14:22,23; Jer. 51:64 .... Rev. 18:10

Babylon is Called Sodom:

Gen. 19:4-10; Isa. 13:19; Jer. 50:40 .... Rev. 11:8

New Testament Scripture Regarding the End-Time Sodom and Gomorrah:

Luke Chapter 17 records the following, verse **28:** "It was the same in the days of Lot (Jesus is now speaking of the Last Days and the sexual perversion that will have seized the world as it was within the time and location of Lot's place of dwelling). *The text continues:* People were eating and drinking, buying and selling, planting and building. **29** But the day Lot left Sodom, fire and sulfur rained down from heaven and destroyed them all. (This was because of the people's gross sexual perversion and wickedness of other sorts; therefore, God judged the city). **30** "It will be just like this on the day the Son of Man is revealed. (This is a reference to Jesus' 2nd Coming. With the so-called legalization of "Homosexual

Marriages" and the growing acceptance of bodily perversion and so-called gender dysphoria, which the Bible calls delusional, hence the people of this world, having therefore been given over to their wicked hearts and lies, looking at the condition of this world presently, it seems to me that the time for Jesus' return to judge the earth is nearing. See Rom. 1:28; John 12:40, and 2 Thes. 2:9-12).

Jude verse 6 reads as follows: "And the angels who did not keep their positions of authority but abandoned their proper dwelling (meaning having rebelled against God their Creator, therefore, left their natural habitation or nature or designed purpose of God)—these – *fallen angels* he has kept in darkness, bound with everlasting chains for judgment on the great Day. 7 In a similar way, Sodom and Gomorrah and the surrounding towns gave themselves up to sexual immorality and perversion (these people, like the fallen angels, abandoned their designed order or purpose and engaged in unnatural sexual relations – namely homosexuality or sodomy and other sexual perversions were the sins of rebellious mankind). They serve as an example of those who suffer the punishment of eternal fire. (People, this matter of eternal fire is not annihilation, where mankind, after death, cease to exist...to the contrary. As we will see continuing this lesson, eternal fire or the Lake of Fire will be a place of consciousness, where all who rebel against God will suffer in torment without end or relief.

2 Peter 2:6-9 also has something to say about such times of wickedness; verse **6** reads: "If he – *Jehovah God* condemned the cities of Sodom and Gomorrah by burning them to ashes, and made them an example of what is going to happen to the ungodly; **7** and if he rescued Lot, a righteous man, who was distressed by the depraved conduct of the lawless **8** for that righteous man, living among them day after day, was tormented in his righteous soul by the lawless deeds he saw and heard— **9** if this is so, then the Lord knows how to rescue the godly from trials and to hold the unrighteous for punishment on the day of judgment." (See Genesis Chapter 19 and Luke 17:31-35, where the End-time rapture,

I believe, is in view, with Lot's family rescue as a foreshadowing of the rapture of the Church before God's judgment of this wicked and rebellious world).

Here's something that the United States and, in particular, those who are Nationalists should bear in mind: God does not seek to reform the inhabitants of Sodom and Gomorrah, these governmental and religious systems that were given to wickedness and hell-bent on their evil ways or practices that opposed Lot's worldview and Jehovah God, their Creator and now Judge. I also call your attention to this fact: God had no political system to be established by a vote to remedy or control these people's sinful perversions and great wickedness. For this simple reason, man cannot manage mankind's spiritual ills through legislation or in any other manner. Instead, from these cities, God had entirely given over to Satan and/or the wickedness of mankind's heart; God rescued His chosen – righteous Lot from this evil system before condemning and destroying these rebellious people.

He then destroys or judges these cities and their perverse system of operation! God had determined that enough was enough! Because of their own doing, these people were now beyond repentance and redemption. This same fate, soon enough, is about to befall this world. Perhaps you recall Lot's family rescue from God's judgment of Sodom and Gomorrah. However, from this story, we are told that Lot's wife looked back at the city, which God had forbidden them to do; this indicated that her heart was still one with Sodom as she showed contempt for God; therefore, He destroyed her. People, where is your heart? To whom do you give your allegiance to? Whose system are you embracing? God's judgment is nearing!

Lament Over Fallen Babylon's System:

1 After this, I – *John* saw another angel coming down from heaven. He had great authority, and the earth was illuminated by his splendor. **2**

With a mighty voice, he shouted: "Fallen! Fallen is Babylon the Great! She has become a dwelling for demons and a haunt for every impure spirit, a haunt for every unclean bird, and a haunt for every unclean and detestable animal. **3** For all the nations have drunk the maddening wine of her adulteries. The kings of the earth committed adultery with her, and the merchants of the earth grew rich from her excessive luxuries." (This is a taunt of Babylon and a picture of those of this world who were living their best lives in sinful indulgences and rejection of God; nevertheless, they and this city Babylon's imminent destruction is upon them. See Isa. 21:9; Jer. 50:39; 51:8).

Warning to Escape Babylon's Judgment:

4 Then I heard another voice from heaven say: " 'Come out of her, my people,' so that you will not share in her sins so that you will not receive any of her plagues; **5** for her sins are piled up to heaven, and God has remembered her crimes *or iniquities*. **6** Give back to her as she has given; pay her back double for what she has done. Pour her a double portion from her own cup. **7** Give her as much torment and grief as the glory and luxury she gave herself. In her heart, she boasts, 'I sit enthroned as queen. I am not a widow; I will never mourn.'

People, we are told that pride comes before the fall, such was Satan's sin leading to his expulsion from heaven: see Isaiah 14:12-15 and Ezekiel 28:12-17. And so will the Antichrist fall into utter destruction along with Satan and this boastful capital city. In contrast to the boastful arrogance of this Babylon system and her statement, "I will never be a widow." We know from Scripture God lovingly and graciously uses these faithful widows of Jesus' genealogy: Bathsheba, Abigail, Tamar, Ruth, and Mary, women who were dead to this world's system or Satan but who instead faithfully united with God, who is viewed in one sense their Husband. Therefore, all such women and all who join with Christ – their Bridegroom will forever be with Him and never left alone or found wanting. Yet, the Antichrist's radiant and decadent city boasts that it will never end; nevertheless, it will be found wanting, and it will come to nothing: see Daniel 5:27! **8** Therefore, in one day, her plagues will overtake her: death, mourning, and famine. She will be consumed by fire, for mighty is the Lord God who judges her.

Threefold Woe Over Babylon's Fall:

9 "When the kings of the earth who committed adultery with her and shared her luxury see the smoke of her – *this city's* burning, they will weep and mourn over her. **10** Terrified at her torment, they will stand far off and cry: " 'Woe! Woe (these woes indicate God's certain destruction and the seriousness of the matter) *therefore* Woe! Woe to you, great city, you mighty city of Babylon! In one hour, your doom has come!' (It is thought that this city will likely have a major shipping port; some believe this city may very well be Jerusalem).

11 "The merchants of the earth (the idolatrous wealthy or self-indulgent wicked) will weep and mourn over her (this great capital city of Babylon) because no one buys their cargoes anymore (there will be a collapse of the world's economy and trade system) **12** cargoes of gold, silver, precious stones, and pearls; fine linen, purple, silk and scarlet cloth; every sort of citron wood, and articles of every kind made of ivory, costly wood, bronze, iron, and marble; **13** cargoes of cinnamon and spice, of incense, myrrh, and frankincense, of wine and olive oil, of fine flour and wheat; cattle and sheep; horses and carriages; and human beings sold as slaves – *impoverished people who were exploited or taken advantage of.* (A study of each of these items mentioned will reveal that they hold religious significance. This Babylonian city – being as it were, a false representation of heaven; to no surprise, she has its counterfeit use of such items to represent her fading worth and glory that is destined for destruction)!

14 "They will say, 'The fruit you longed for is gone from you. All your luxury and splendor have vanished, never to be recovered.' **15** The merchants who sold these things and gained their wealth from her will stand far off, terrified at her torment. They will weep and mourn **16** and cry out: " 'Woe! Woe to you, great city, dressed in fine linen, purple and scarlet, and glittering with gold, precious stones, and pearls! **17** In one hour, such great wealth has been brought to ruin!' "Every sea captain, and all who travel by ship, the sailors, and all who earn their living from the sea, will stand far off. **18** When they see the smoke of her burning, they will exclaim, 'Was there ever a city like this great city'? (Like Lot's wife, the people of this world's hearts were one with this wicked or adulterous city).

19 They will throw dust on their heads and, with weeping and mourning, cry out: " 'Woe! Woe to you, great city, where all who had ships on the sea became rich through her wealth! In one hour, she has been brought to ruin!' **20** "Rejoice over her, you heavens! Rejoice, you people of God! Rejoice, apostles and prophets! For God has judged her with the judgment she imposed on you."

The Finality of Babylon's Doom:

21 Then a mighty angel picked up a boulder the size of a large millstone (here, and as seen elsewhere throughout the Bible, the millstone represented God's judgment and it pointed towards the end-times), and *so here the mighty angel* threw it – *the large millstone* into the sea, and said: "With such violence, the great city of Babylon will be thrown down, never to be found again: see Jer. 51:63,64. **22** The music of harpists and musicians, pipers and trumpeters, will never be heard in you again. (The world's partying, banqueting, and the likes will forever cease). No worker of any trade will ever be found in you again. The sound of a millstone will never be heard in you again (man's labor force will come to an end).

23 The light of a lamp will never shine in you again. The voice of bridegroom and bride will never be heard in you again (such things were to be used to glorify God. These things will no longer be defamed. And neither will the witness or light of the faithful nor the Spirit of God be seen at work in Babylon any longer). Your merchants were the world's important people. By your magic spell (or its embrace of demonic deception and seduction), all the nations were led astray. **24** In her was found the blood of prophets and of God's holy people, of all who have been slaughtered on the earth."

CHAPTER 21

OUTLINE AND REVELATION CHAPTER 19

The Rejoicing in Heaven and the Marriage Supper of the Lamb:

1. Verse 1-5: The Multitude in Heaven Praises God
   - Introduction: After these things, John hears what sounds like the roar of a great multitude in heaven, praising God.
   - The Multitude's Praise: They cry out, "Hallelujah! Salvation and glory and power belong to our God, for his judgments are true and just; for he has judged the great prostitute who corrupted the earth with her immorality and has avenged on her the blood of his servants."
2. Verse 6-10: The Marriage Supper of the Lamb
   - Introduction: Then John hears what seems to be the voice of a great multitude, like the roar of many waters and like the sound of mighty peals of thunder, crying out, "Hallelujah! For the Lord our God, the Almighty reigns. Let us rejoice and exult and give him the glory, for the marriage of the Lamb has come, and his Bride has made herself ready."
   - The Bride's Attire: John is told, "Blessed are those who are invited to the marriage supper of the Lamb." And he said to John, "These are the true words of God."

- John's Reaction: John falls down at the feet of the angel to worship him, but the angel says to him, "You must not do that! I am a fellow servant with you and your brothers who hold to the testimony of Jesus. Worship God. For the testimony of Jesus is the spirit of prophecy."

3. Verse 11-16: The Rider on the White Horse
   - Introduction: Then John sees heaven opened, and behold a white horse! The one sitting on it is called Faithful and True, and in righteousness, he judges and makes war.

   - The Rider's Description: His eyes are like a flame of fire, and on his head are many diadems, and he has a name written that no one knows but himself. He is clothed in a robe dipped in blood, and the name by which he is called is The Word of God.

   - His Army: The armies of heaven, arrayed in fine linen, white and pure, follow him on white horses.

   - His Authority: From his mouth comes a sharp sword with which to strike down the nations, and he will rule them with a rod of iron. He will tread the winepress of the fury of the wrath of God the Almighty.

   - His Title: On his robe and on his thigh, he has a name written, King of kings and Lord of lords.

4. Verse 17-21: The Defeat of the Beast and False Prophet
   - Introduction: Then John sees an angel standing in the sun, and with a loud voice, he calls to all the birds that fly directly overhead, "Come, gather for the great supper of God, to eat the flesh of kings, the flesh of captains, the flesh of mighty men, the flesh of horses and their riders, and the flesh of all men, both free and slave, both small and great."

   - The Beast and False Prophet: Then John sees the beast and the kings of the earth with their armies gathered to make war against him, who was sitting on the horse and against his army.

- Their Defeat: And the beast was captured, and with it, the false prophet who in its presence had done the signs by which he deceived those who had received the mark of the beast and those who worshiped its image. These two were thrown alive into the lake of fire that burns with sulfur.

- The Rest: And the rest were slain by the sword that came from the mouth of him who was sitting on the horse, and all the birds were gorged with their flesh.

This chapter depicts the rejoicing in heaven over the judgment of the great prostitute and the impending marriage supper of the Lamb. It also portrays the triumphant return of Christ as the rider on the white horse, accompanied by the armies of heaven, and the defeat of the beast and the false prophet.

Revelation Chapter 19

The Main Event – The Return of Jesus, The Bridegroom:

If you recall, it was at the final Bowl Judgment that the battle of Armageddon or the gathering at Megiddo, where the nations of the world had come against Israel: see Rev. 16:16. This event marks Jesus's return to earth – His Second Coming, to deal with Israel's and His enemies; this was John's view of what would occur on earth during the Last Days. Now, we are about to see what was happening in heaven as Jesus was preparing to return to earth to bring an end to these nations who came against Israel and finally for Jesus to judge the Antichrist and Babylon's world order.

Threefold Hallelujah Over Babylon's Fall:

John says, **1** After this (those things regarding Babylon, the Antichrist's world systems as seen in chapters 17 and 18), I heard *declares John* what sounded like the roar of a great multitude in heaven shouting:

"Hallelujah! Salvation and, glory, and power belong to our God (this doxology is a trinitarian statement of praise in honor of the Father, Son, and Holy Spirit), **2** for true and just are his – *our God's* judgments. He has condemned *or sentenced* the great prostitute who corrupted the earth by her adulteries. He has avenged on her the blood of his servants." **3** And again they shouted: "Hallelujah (because of the righteous judgment of God that is coming upon Babylon's rebellious system of evil)! The smoke from her – *burning destruction* goes up forever and ever." **4** The twenty-four elders and the four living creatures (or Cherubim) fell down and worshiped God, who was seated on the throne. And they cried: "Amen, Hallelujah!" (The worship of God requires giving ourselves over to Him and yielding our bodies to His service. How would you assess your worship of God)?

5 Then a voice came from the throne, saying: "Praise our God, all you his servants, you who fear him, both great and small!" **6** Then I heard what sounded like a great multitude, like the roar of rushing waters and like loud peals of thunder, shouting: "Hallelujah! For our Lord God Almighty reigns. (Unlike in Revelation Chapter 4, where the angels are leading worship, now the Church, or Bride of Christ, is seen in heaven and is leading worship). *The praise and worship leader proclaims,* **7** Let us rejoice and be glad and give him glory (even so, this should be for the church as anticipation arises at our coming before God to hear from Him during corporate worship. And to behold His marvelous acts, we must beforehand extend praise due to Him)! **Continuing with verse 7,** For the wedding of the Lamb has come, and his Bride has made herself ready.

The Church – those of us who are currently Christians are now seen in heaven. We – the Church or Bride of Christ, as previously mentioned, are raptured before the Great Tribulation, and then we are wedded to our Bridegroom – Jesus, while in the presence of His Father and ours, who has approved of this eternal union. It is from this point on in the book of Revelation that we only hear about or from the Bride and no longer the Cherubim, living creatures, and elders.

Pictures of the rapture through Biblical Marriages: Just as the patriarchs whose brides, Sarah, Rebecca, Rachel, and Leah, were sent for and called from their homes to marry these individuals, God the Father will also send for or call forth or rapture from the earth Christ's Bride or His betrothed – which is the Church who is to be formally wedded to His Son Jesus for all eternity. Currently, the universal Church is betrothed or engaged to Jesus. However, soon enough, we will become perfected through our formal marriage with Jesus as His Bride when we are called to be with Him and the Father in heaven: see Matthew 24:40 through 25:10.

Pictures of Israel's Restoration to Jehovah God: Rachel's husband Jacob, after purchasing her, had to wait seven years before actually making her his bride. It will be the ending of the seven years of the Great Tribulation before Israel is restored to Jesus and Jehovah, their God. At this time of Jesus' return to the earth with His Bride, He will right the wrongs of Adam and Eve and reverse the curse by restoring the Garden of Eden. Once again, heaven will be united with the earth, and Israel will also be united with her Messianic King and reunited with Yahweh, her God: see Romans 11:11,12.

Just as Ester, in the book bearing her name, had to wait through her wedding preparation before becoming the official bride to the gentile King - Xerxes, which led to Israel being saved; Ester's life, therefore, foreshadowing the universal Church and Jesus' marriage to her. In a reversal of the lineage of kingship, so must Jesus – the Jewish King, formally marry and return with His Bride – the Church – gentile Believers before the Jews can be saved and restored to Jesus their King. As Ester was chosen by the gentile king and set apart for him, so has the Church been chosen in Christ the Jewish King and set apart as a chaste virgin for Jesus: see 2 Cor. 11:2 and Eph. 5:26,27. Even as Ester was made beautiful before being taken into the presence of the king, God's chosen people had to be purchased and cleansed and made holy before being brought into the presence of God the Father by the Holy Spirit: see Rev.

5:9. Read the story of Ester to see how God was working behind the scene. No mention was made of God in this book; nevertheless, He was clearly at work, and His divine providence is evident; Israel was saved from Haman's attempted genocide!

Verse 8: Fine linen, bright and clean, was given her – *for the Bride to wear.*" (This linen represents the righteous acts of God's holy and faithful people. Even so, symbolizing the people's purity. This garment also indicated honor bestowed upon a person: see Est. 6:7-9; linen being a blessing: see Gen. 27:27, and linen viewed as a garment of salvation: see Isa. 61:10. Linen was also a garment of praise: see Isa. 61:3, and this attire additionally indicated that one belonged to God's family: see Luke 15:22. Even so, the priest of God wore linen garments: see Ex. 28:2-4. In Christ, the Church of God is called a royal priesthood and kings. As seen in the Bible, the priests of the Old Testament were not given land as an inheritance; likewise, neither is this earth Christ's Bride's home or inheritance; we are merely sojourners here on earth; Jesus has, in fact, become our inheritance; through Him, we have been promised a new home where He, our Bridegroom will care for us forever)!

9 Then the angel said to me, "Write this: Blessed are those who are invited to the wedding supper of the Lamb:" See Matt. 22:2; 25:10; Luke 12:35; 14:8 and verse 15. (For all who belong to Jesus – here the Church, or His Bride, we will now receive all the promises offered by God in His eternal kingdom. Those belonging to the universal Church had accepted God's proposal for marriage and/or salvation. Additionally, those who will be at the wedding banquet through invitation will be the ones who remained faithful to Him, even unto death; these Tribulation Jews and Saints will also have a seat at the table.

Restoration of things is at hand: Just as the Book of Genesis begins with a wedding, the Book of Revelation ends with a wedding in the New Jerusalem. Just as Jesus began His ministry at the wedding in Cana: see John 2:4, He is going to end His ministry with a wedding; Jesus invites all to His wedding; He's going to end His ministry by seating people at the wedding...it's all about the Great Wedding Supper where God's people will be restored to Him! Will you be in attendance...Will you have a seat at the table)? **Concluding verse 9:** And, he – *the angel* added, "These are the true words of God."

10 At this, I fell at his feet to worship him (John was likely overwhelmed by all that he saw). But he – the angel said to me, "Don't do that! I am a fellow servant with you and with your brothers and sisters who hold to the testimony of Jesus. Worship God! For it is the Spirit of prophecy who bears testimony to Jesus." (Or the testimony of Jesus is the spirit of true prophecy. Every time we give witness to Jesus, we are prophesying...This is no light matter; souls are at stake!

Our exercise of faith and witness in this manner is considered to be the first level of prophecy. The second level of prophecy is the spiritual gift of prophecy: this is when one speaks, perhaps even with spiritual discernment, comfort, exhortation, and edification to others or the church. The third level of prophecy is the gift or office of Prophecy; see Eph. 4:11...This is where God has gifted someone to see into the future; this will always be without Biblical contradiction. This gifting is given to prepare or warn the church or someone about something impending. Lastly, the fourth level of prophecy, and the most important, is the very Word of God: Rev. 22:7 reads, "Look, I am coming soon! Blessed is the one who keeps the words of the prophecy written in this scroll." (This scroll – the Book of Revelation contains a summary of the Bible).

The Heavenly Warrior Defeats the Beast

11 I saw heaven standing open (Perhaps these experiences of John can be likened to what occurred in 2 Kings 6:16,17, where God allowed Alijah and Elisha to see into the spiritual or unseen realm, including the experiences of Ezekiel and the Apostle Paul). *Heaven now open, John says,* and there before me was a white horse (representing the fullness of God's grace and might), whose rider (Jesus the conquering King) is called

Faithful – *hence all of Scripture will be* fulfilled and True. (Jesus is the foundation of all that is; He is the Word, the Alpha, and Omega, who is Faithful and True). **Ending verse 11:** With justice, he - *Jesus* judges and wages war.

God is gracious. However, there will be a time, not too distant, for His righteous justice to be executed. Grace standing alone, apart from repentant obedience to God, many people, therefore, use and abuse God's grace to justify their sinful ways. Notwithstanding, to recognize God's justice or judgment of sin, only then will people see the necessity to repent from their immoral practices. **Regarding war:** Generally, war is not viewed as a good thing. However, God justifies righteous wars so that evil does not prevail amongst humanity nor within the spiritual realm against mankind or evil and rebellion aimed at Him. Evil must be dealt with, or else it will only continue leading to the total destruction of mankind: see Matt.24:22. However, when Jesus deals with Satan, this will not be a contest. Jesus will do Satan in by His mere word. When Jesus returns, He is going to deal with Babylon – Satan's system.

We will now review a few of the prophecies regarding Israel and God dealing with the rebellious nations. Beginning with **Isaiah 13:1-9** God has this to say: **1** A prophecy against Babylon that Isaiah, son of Amoz, saw: **2** Raise a banner on a bare hilltop, shout to them; beckon to them to enter the gates of the nobles. **3** I have commanded those I prepared for battle; I have summoned my warriors to carry out my wrath—those who rejoice in my triumph. Listen, a noise on the mountains, like that of a great multitude! **4** Listen, an uproar among the kingdoms, like nations massing together! The Lord Almighty is mustering an army for war.

5 They come from faraway lands, from the ends of the heavens—the Lord and the weapons of his wrath—to destroy the whole country. **6** Wail, for the day of the Lord, is near; it will come like destruction from the Almighty. **7** Because of this, all hands will go limp, every heart will melt with fear. **8** Terror will seize them; pain and anguish will grip them; they will writhe like a woman in labor. They will look aghast at each other, their faces aflame. **9** See, the day of the Lord is coming a cruel day, with wrath and fierce anger—to make the land desolate and destroy the sinners within it.

From **Zechariah's prophecy, in Chapter 12**, we have the following: **2** "I am going to make Jerusalem a cup that sends all the surrounding peoples reeling. Judah will be besieged, as well as Jerusalem. **3** On that day, when all the nations of the earth are gathered against her, I will make Jerusalem an immovable rock for all the nations. All who try to move it will injure themselves." **Zech. continues in Chapter 14:1-4, 1**: "A day of the Lord is coming, Jerusalem, when your possessions will be plundered and divided up within your very walls. **2** I will gather all the nations to Jerusalem to fight against it; the city will be captured, the houses ransacked, and the women raped. Half of the city will go into exile, but the rest of the people will not be taken from the city. **Verse 3 begins to present to us the End of Days: 3** Then the Lord will go out and fight against those nations as he fights on a day of battle. **4** On that day, his feet will stand on the Mount of Olives, east of Jerusalem (the very place where Jesus was rejected as Messiah and will ascend as the risen Lord and will return as King of kings: see Acts 1:11), and the Mount of Olives will be split in two from east to west, forming a great valley, with half of the mountain moving north and half moving south. **5** You will flee by my mountain valley, for it will extend to Azel (believed to be modern-day Jordan: see Jer. 49:22 and Micah 2:12,13). You will flee as you fled from the earthquake in the days of Uzziah, king of Judah. Then the Lord my God will come, and all the holy ones with him.

Zechariah also prophesied regarding the return of Jesus, chapter 12:10-14: "And I will pour out on the house of David and the inhabitants of Jerusalem a spirit a of grace and supplication. They will look on me, the one they have pierced, and they will mourn for him as one mourns for an only child and grieve bitterly for him as one grieves for a firstborn son. **11** On that day, the weeping in Jerusalem will be as great as the weeping of Hadad Rimmon in the plain of Megiddo. **12** The land will mourn, each clan by itself, with their wives by themselves: the clan of the house of David and their wives, the clan of the house of Nathan and their wives, **13** the clan of the house of Levi and their wives, the clan of Shimei and their wives, **14** and all the rest of the clans and their wives.

Joel had this to say in chapter 3, beginning at verse **12**: "Let the nations be roused; let them advance into the Valley of Jehoshaphat – which means Yahweh judges (aka the Kidron Valley, located at the bottom of the Mt. of Olives), for there I – *Jesus*, will sit to judge all the nations on every side. **13** Swing the sickle, for the harvest is ripe. Come, trample the grapes – *or wicked people*, for the winepress is full, and the vats overflow— so great is their wickedness!" **14** Multitudes, multitudes in the valley of decision! For the day of the Lord is near in the valley of decision.

15 The sun and moon will be darkened, and the stars no longer shine. **16** The Lord will roar from Zion and thunder from Jerusalem; the earth and the heavens will tremble. But the Lord will be a refuge for his people, a stronghold for the people of Israel. Blessings for God's People. **17** "Then you will know that I, the Lord your God, dwell in Zion, my holy hill. Jerusalem will be holy; never again will foreigners invade her.

Returning to Revelation verse 12: His – Jesus' eyes are like blazing fire (fixed to display His righteous indignation and judgment), and on his head are many crowns (unlike the Antichrist who has one crown). He – *Jesus* has a name written on him that no one knows, but he himself (in this sense, Jesus' character as the Supreme Judge and King will be revealed unlike ever before). **13** He is dressed in a robe dipped in blood (representing His blood of atonement for His Bride – the Church), and his name is the Word of God. (See Psalm 2). **14** The armies of heaven were following him, riding on white horses and dressed in fine linen, white and clean: see Rev. 17:14; John 18:36; 1 Thess. 3:13 and Isaiah 61:10. (The following Scriptures will show Jesus returning to earth from heaven with His Bride: see Matt. 24:30; Mark 13:26; 14:62 and Luke 21:27).

15 Coming out of his – *Jesus'* mouth is a sharp sword with which to strike down the nations. "He will rule them with an iron scepter." He treads the winepress of the fury of the wrath of God Almighty. **16** On his robe and on his thigh (a banner or sash will be draped over Jesus' leg), he has this name written: KING OF KINGS AND LORD OF LORDS.

17 And I saw an angel standing in the sun, who cried in a loud voice to all the birds flying in midair, "Come, gather together for the great supper of God, **18** so that you may eat the flesh of *the dead* kings, generals, and the mighty, of horses and their riders, and the flesh of all *rebellious* people, free and slave, great and small."

19 Then I saw the beast and the kings of the earth and their armies gathered together to wage war against the rider on the horse – *which will be Jesus* and *his heavenly* army. **20** But the beast (the Antichrist) was captured, and with it, the false prophet who had performed the signs on its behalf. With these signs, he had deluded those who had received the mark of the beast and worshiped its image. The two of them were thrown alive into the fiery lake of burning sulfur. **21** The rest were killed with the sword coming out of the mouth of the rider on the horse, and all the birds gorged themselves on their flesh. (Jesus will merely speak, and His enemies will be destroyed)!

CHAPTER 22

OUTLINE AND REVELATION CHAPTER 20

The Thousand Years and the Judgment of Satan:

1. **Verse 1-3:** The Binding of Satan
   - Introduction: John sees an angel coming down from heaven, holding in his hand the key to the bottomless pit and a great chain.
   - The Binding: The angel seizes the dragon, that ancient serpent, who is the devil and Satan, and binds him for a thousand years and throws him into the pit, and shut it and seals it over him so that he might not deceive the nations any longer until the thousand years were ended.

2. **Verse 4-6:** The Reign of the Saints with Christ
   - Introduction: Then John sees thrones, and seated on them were those to whom the authority to judge was committed. Also, he sees the souls of those who had been beheaded for the testimony of Jesus and for the word of God and those who had not worshiped the beast or its image and had not received its mark on their foreheads or their hands. They came to life and reigned with Christ for a thousand years.
   - The First Resurrection of the wicked dead: The rest of the dead did not come to life until the thousand years were ended. This is the first resurrection for the wicked dead.

- Blessed and Holy: Blessed and holy is the one who shares in the first resurrection! Over such, the second death has no power, but they will be priests of God and of Christ, and they will reign with him for a thousand years.

3. **Verse 7-10:** The Release and Defeat of Satan
   - Introduction: When the thousand years are ended, Satan will be released from his prison and will come out to deceive the nations that are at the four corners of the earth, believed by some to be led by the evil demonic prince, Gog, with the nation Magog and other nations who gather themselves for a final battle against Israel.
   - The Army's Number: Their number is like the sand of the sea.
   - The Defeat: They marched up over the broad plain of the earth and surrounded the camp of the saints and the beloved city, but fire came down from heaven and consumed them, and the devil who had deceived them was thrown into the lake of fire and sulfur where the beast and the false prophet were, and they will be tormented day and night forever and ever.

4. **Verse 11-15:** The Great White Throne Judgment
   - Introduction: Then John sees a great white throne and him who was seated on it. From his presence, earth and sky fled away, and no place was found for them.
   - The Books Opened: And John sees the wicked dead, great and small, standing before the throne, and books were opened. Then, another book was opened, which is the Book of Life. And the dead in Christ were judged by what was written in the books, according to what they had done.
   - Death and Hades: Then the forces of Death and Hades – the holding place of the dead were thrown into the lake of fire. This is the second death, the lake of fire. And if anyone's name was

not found written in the Book of Life, he was thrown into the lake of fire.

This chapter describes the thousand-year reign of Christ and his saints, the release and final defeat of Satan, and the Great White Throne Judgment, where all the wicked dead are judged according to their deeds. It portrays the ultimate victory of God over evil and the establishment of His eternal kingdom.

Revelation Chapter 20

We have seen that after the end of the seven years of the Great Tribulation, Jesus will return to the earth for a second time. However, following the final 3.5 years, or 1,260 days, additional days have been added; this period can be viewed as a transfer of power as Jesus sets things in order for His new administration or millennial Rule and Reign as King. Daniel 12:11,12 reads: **11** From the time that the daily sacrifice is abolished and the abomination that causes desolation is set up (when the Antichrist desecrates the temple), there will be 1,290 days. **12** Blessed is the one who waits for and reaches the end of the 1,335 days."

We see that 30 days plus an additional 45 days have been added, a total of 75 days. During this period of time, Jesus had work that He must fulfill at His 2nd Advent. Some of these things have been seen in His end-time mission: beginning with His arrival at the Mount of Olives, there is the casting into fire the Antichrist and false prophet, Jesus judging the nations, and rescuing Israel from Bozrah.

Additionally, and although not shown in this chapter of the Book of Revelation, much about the millennial period is only provided by the Old Testament prophets, i.e., the Jewish priests would have to undergo consecration during this added 30-day period, and the Jews had to get prepared to meet with Jesus – their Passover Lamb and Atonement: see 2 Chron. 30:2-4; Ex. 12:2 and Lev. 23:5. During this time, the Jews will come to understand that their Passover celebration of old actually pointed to the True Passover Lamb ~ Jesus, God tabernacling or dwelling with mankind on earth: see John 7:1-8 and Zech. 14:16-19.

Also, the 3rd rebuilt Jewish temple and altar that the last Antichrist will defile has to be consecrated. John 10:22 speaks of the Feast of Dedication, which was established in the New Testament, also known as Hanukkah or the Festival of Lights; this feast was instituted after the pseudo-antichrist, Antiochus Epiphanes, who set himself up as a god in the Jew's 2nd temple. He oppressed the Jews, erected a statue or idol, and sacrificed a pig on the altar, thereby desecrating this holy space. This led to the Maccabean revolt; as a result of their victory, they rededicated the second temple, inaugurating the celebration of Hanukkah, which was 75 days after Yom Kippur, or Day of Atonement. And so, the rebuilt temple that stands when Jesus returns at His 2nd Coming has to also be consecrated because the Antichrist defiles it. However, when Jesus inaugurates His kingdom, His temple will be an imposing structure surrounded by a great city: see Ezek. Chapter 40 through Chapter 48. In this 20th Chapter of the book of Revelation, we will see additional tasks that Jesus has to carry out during these 75 days.

The Thousand Years:

John says, verse 1 And I saw an angel coming down out of heaven, having the key to the Abyss and holding in his hand a great chain. **2** He seized the dragon, that ancient serpent, who is the devil, or Satan, and bound him for a thousand years.

On the subject of binding Satan:

As for man being able to bind Satan – the Prince of the power of the air, this is not the case, and it's unscriptural. Only Jesus can imprison Satan. Spiritually speaking, regarding "binding and loosening," this authority given to Christians has to do with our obedience to the Word of God and our actions and/or church governance lived out according to God's Word. In our obedience and submission to God, we, therefore, receive authority and are empowered over evil). **3** *He – the angel* threw him – *Satan* into the Abyss and locked and sealed it over him to keep him from deceiving the nations anymore until the thousand years were ended.

In chapter 19, the Antichrist and false prophet were cast into the lake of eternal fire; on the other hand, we see that Satan is imprisoned for a thousand years. Now, Jesus is about to restore order and/or His administration on the earth: see Isa. 9:6,7 and 11:4,5. However, before establishing His kingdom on earth, Jesus first had to deal with the false trinity; only then would He reestablish His new and temporary Eden or heaven on earth. **Concluding verse 3:** After that – *the thousand years,* he – *Satan* must be set free for a short time.

At Jesus' return, heaven indeed meets with earth; hence, Jesus will establish His kingdom on earth, thereby fulfilling Biblical prophecy as the one to sit on and Rule from King David's throne. And so, this is not the new earth and heaven, which is to follow King Jesus' millennial rule on earth. However, during this time, the earth will be habitable, and its atmosphere and geography will have been significantly changed, thereby providing long life and harmony with all of creation: see Ezek. 47:7-12; Isa. 2:2-5 and 65:20.

During this time, earthly children will be born to those who are the remaining inhabitants of the earth, who are unlike Christ's Bride during this 1000-year reign of Jesus, who will be clothed in their glorified bodies. It is debatable whether the Bride of Christ or the children of God are able to reproduce during Jesus' millennial reign. According to Micah 4:3 and Dan. 2:44, there will be world peace. Satan nor demonic evil will be present to tempt or influence mankind during these 1,000 years of Christ's rule.

On the matter of world peace:

Micah Chapter 4:3 reads: "They will beat their swords into plowshares and their spears into pruning hooks. Nation will not take up sword against nation, nor will they train for war anymore," also see Isaiah 2:4. This very Scripture is written on a large plaque on the outside wall of the United Nations building in New York. Nonetheless, human secularism – mankind's best efforts cannot establish world peace or bring about utopia on earth. With all of mankind's advancements, look at the mess and unrest this world currently faces...People, this world needs Jesus!

Micah's and Isaiah's prophecies foresaw Jesus and Him alone, bringing peace or heaven on earth. During Jesus' millennial reign, life expectancy will increase exponentially, and health, well-being, and prosperity on earth will become the new norm: see Zech. 8:4; Isa. 65:20-23 and Amos 9:13,14. There will also be peace within the animal kingdom: see Isa. 11:6-9, and lastly, the environment will be restored: see Ezek. 47:8,9 and Isa. 51:3, but again, the new earth and heaven are yet to be established, but this harmony on earth will be its temporary restored condition during Jesus' millennial kingdom.

Why the 1000-year reign of Christ? God, showing us His pattern of operation, says in 2 Peter 3:8, "But do not forget this one thing, dear friends: With the Lord, a day is like a thousand years, and a thousand years are like a day." This is God's time scale. Even so, Just as Adam lived just shy of a thousand years, his age was 930, and at that time, death reigned upon the earth. Jesus – the new Adam will reign on earth for 1000 years, temporarily reversing the curse upon the earth before restoring all of creation to new life and eternal life in and through Himself – who is Life. That which Adam failed to do; the earth will be entrusted to Jesus for 1000 years, and He will rule victoriously and steward the earth impeccably, therefore fulfilling all Biblical prophecy concerning Himself and this dispensation, thereby thwarting Satan's plan of attempting to keep the Messianic King from ruling the earth and sitting on King David's throne! That said, God has made it clear that Jesus will reign on earth for a millennium; therefore, the matter is settled. "God's will...will be done on earth as it is in heaven!"

During Christ's millennial reign on earth, children born of still, fallen, or mortal parents during this dispensation will not have been perfected in heart or body either. Mankind, as it has always been, will be able to exercise free will as free moral agents. **The test:** Will such ones be unfaithful to God and do evil, which was the case with Adam and Eve? Or will they choose to be faithful to Jesus, thereby being granted access to the new heaven and earth that will come at the conclusion of Jesus' 1000-year reign? What we must understand, during Christ the King's rule on earth, is that earth-born or mortal mankind's hearts and thoughts are still bent toward evil. However, during this time, spiritual wickedness influence or Satan will be bound.

God's reason for releasing Satan is to show and remind the Church, even those who will be living and born during the millennial, that man, apart from Jesus or the indwelling Spirit, is prone to evil. Many during the millennial era will, in fact, follow Jesus, while others will choose to follow the Devil upon his release, who remains the Great Deceiver of the people. The pattern from the Garden of Eden is yet again present before humanity. Everything that man would ever need during the millennial – this new Eden will be provided by Jesus. But mankind or mortal man will still have a choice and the free will to choose Life – Jesus. Or to choose to follow their unregenerated hearts or Satan, aka Death.

Resuming with verse 4 of chapter 20, John says I saw thrones on which were seated those (members of the Church, who share in Christ's authority) who had been given authority to judge: see Matt. 19:28 and 1 Cor. 6:2,3. And I saw – *says John*, the souls of those (the resurrected martyrs of the Great Tribulation. Also, during this time, things must be sorted out with the Jews, including their inheritance or land allotment for the 144,000 from the tribes of Israel: see Gen. 15:18; Ezek. 34:13 and 36:24-28. Furthermore, the nations or people of the world have to be judged: see Matt. 25:31-34 & 40,41. Repeating Dan. 12:12: "Blessed is the one who waits for and reaches the end of the 1,335 days. (This is a reference to those Jews and Saints who will come through the Great Tribulation and who will be standing with Jesus just before He establishes His kingdom).

Repeating and completing verse 4, John says I saw thrones on which were seated those who had been given authority to judge. And I saw the souls of those who had been beheaded because of their testimony about Jesus and because of the word of God. They had not worshiped the beast or its image and had not received its mark on their foreheads or their hands. They came to life and reigned with Christ a thousand years. (Those who will be resurrected during this time will be welcomed into the holy city of God).

5 The rest of the dead (a different grouping – the wicked dead; this will be the final and a separate resurrection for them – the condemned dead who will be cast into the Lake of Fire); *however, they* did not come to life until the thousand years were ended. (These individuals remained in Hades or the grave during the 1,000-year reign of Jesus. However, at the first resurrection, these wicked dead individuals will be brought separately before the Great White Throne of God to receive judgment unto eternal suffering, as will be seen in Rev. 20:11. Following this event, God will bring forth the new heaven and earth). **Verse 5 concludes:** This is the first resurrection (all, no matter when or who...who have been raised from the dead to reign with Jesus). *And so,* **6** Blessed and holy are those who share in the first resurrection – *that is, apart from the resurrection of the damned dead.*

With regards to the first resurrection as pertaining to the Church and all who died in Christ, what we are now reading here should be viewed as a characterization and not a single event, but rather a continuation of an event – the resurrection of the Church occurring before the Great Tribulation, followed by the resurrection of the dead or martyrs of the Great Tribulation before Jesus establishes His kingdom on earth. And lastly, the wicked dead, who will be resurrected – consequently also called the first resurrection but a separate resurrection for those who are condemned to Eternal Torment.

Examples to help understand the ideal of the First Resurrection: When I turned 18, I thought I was a man, and by society's standards, I was. However, over the years, I matured as a man and into Biblical manhood; there has been a continuation from my 18th birthday with my identity with manhood. Nevertheless, the process of my biblical manhood or spiritual maturity is ongoing until I reach glorified perfection or am clothed in my imperishable body. Another example: When my son was born, I became a father. For every child I would have had after that, I wouldn't become a father each time; instead, there would be a continuation of that aspect of who I'd become – a dad because of the birth of my first child.

Jesus' statement clears this matter up for us. Not only does He say, "I am the Resurrection," but He is also described as being the first fruit of the resurrection process, with there being others who would follow after Him; therefore, Jesus is the first who has been resurrected from the dead and glorified or perfected in body: see Romans 8:29; Acts 26:23; 1 Cor. 15:20-23; Col. 1:18 and Rev. 1:5. Matthew 27:52,53 informs us that when Jesus was resurrected from the dead "that the bodies of many holy people who had died were raised to life" and that "they went into the holy city and appeared to many." However, Scripture does not indicate that these people received their glorified bodies. Now, simply reiterating. There will be subsequent resurrections: see 1 Thess. 4:14-17. Therefore, in **verse 6**, we are told or reminded, "Blessed and holy are those who share in the first resurrection. The second death has no power over them, but they will be priests of God and of Christ and will reign with him for a thousand years."

The Judgment of Satan:

7 When the thousand years are over, Satan will be released from his prison (this may very well include others from the demonic realm being active during this time as well) **8** and (these forces of evil) will go out to deceive the nations in the four corners of the earth—Gog (perhaps a demon power) and Magog (an actual territory or nations as previously mentioned)—and *Satan will* gather them for battle (for a final time these forces of evil who will rebel against the kingdom of God. This futile standoff of evil against Jesus and His people will show forth those who will remain faithful to Jesus as opposed to those who will choose to align themselves with the Devil – the Deceiver, in spite of all the love that Jesus would have shown and the good that He will have provided during His millennial reign as King.

Again, in the hearts of mortal mankind, those who will be alive at Jesus' Second Coming and those who will be born during His millennial reign, their hearts are yet or still tainted with evil: see Gen. 8:21; Ps. 51:5 and Prov. 22:15. According to Scripture, rebellion against God is for one to embrace or have been taken over by witchcraft: see 1 Sam. 15:23). **Verse 8 concludes:** In number, they – *God's enemies*, are like the sand on the seashore. **9** They marched across the breadth of the earth and surrounded the camp of God's people, the city he loves. But fire came down from heaven and devoured them. **10** And the devil, who deceived them, was thrown into the lake of burning sulfur, where the beast and the false prophet had been thrown. They will be tormented day and night forever and ever.

The Judgment of the Condemned Dead

11 Then I saw a great white throne (where evil will finally be judged and sentenced) and him – *the Triune God*, who was seated on it. The earth and the heavens fled from his presence (thereby making way for the new heaven and earth: see Rev. 21:1), and there was no place for them. **12**

And I saw the dead, great and small, standing before the throne (this is also the 1st resurrection but a separate resurrection of the damned dead as seen in verse 5), and books were opened. Then, another book was opened, which is the Book of Life. And the dead (those who were without glorified bodies who died during Jesus' millennial rule) were judged according to what they had done, as recorded in the books.

In the Bible, there are mentions of different books that largely record the activities, deeds, and even the words we speak, among other things. Regarding the life we live, everything about us is known to God. However, regarding the Book of Life, written therein will only be the names of all who accepted Jesus as their Lord and Savior. Now, God created man with eternity in our hearts: see Ecclesiastes 3:11. Therefore, Scripture suggests to me that at creation and even before humanity existed, all of mankind was written in God's Book of Life. In Exodus 32:32,33, Moses, interceding on behalf of his rebellious people, prayed to God for Him to blot Moses himself out of God's Book and not the people.

In Rev. 3:5, Jesus mentions those belonging to the Church of Sardis and says: "For those who are victorious having remained faithful to Him, that their names would be preserved in the Book of Life. The Psalmist laments as he expresses these words, "May they be blotted out of the Book of Life and not be listed with the righteous," Ps. 69:28. And John later records in Rev. 22:19, "And if anyone takes words away from this scroll of prophecy, God will take away from that person any share in the tree of life and in the Holy City, which are described in this scroll.

Regarding the questionable and greatly debatable doctrinal matters of "Election and/or Predestination" as offered by those embracing Reformed Theology or Calvinism. Unlike such ones, I understand Scripture as saying that God has chosen us all – He is our Creator, the Giver of life, who even knew us before we were formed in our mother's womb: see Ps. 139:13-16 and Eph. 1:4,5. Nevertheless, **all** have the free will as created free moral agents to reject God and this – their loving Creator. Or, after having been lovingly provoked by the Holy Spirit, one can choose to say "Yes" to Jesus. I arrived at this understanding from reading the Bible. However, I discovered as a result of my continuing extra-biblical studies that my view finds a place within the doctrine of Molinism rather than me having been influenced by this school of thought.

When one hears the saving message of Jesus, it is also the Holy Spirit that they hear...resulting from His message or invitation to become one with Jesus. As free will moral agents, one can reject the salvation offered by Jesus. Or one can respond, "Yes" to the love of God. Even so, it is the responsibility of the one who has accepted Jesus' invitation to remain in Him...And to lovingly remain faithful to Him until physical death brings one into His presence forever...It's a marriage with Jesus our Bridegroom that, as individuals and collectively the universal Church, we of our own volition enter into this union with the Triune God. Be it understood that Jesus will not, neither can He coerce one to unite with Him or to remain faithful or remain in a loving relationship with Him. That said, Scripture strongly presents to us that God has and will use certain individuals to bring about His will, purpose, or glorified end. However, it is God's desire that **all people** be saved and to come to the knowledge of the truth: see 1 Tim.2:3,4; 2 Pet. 3:9 and Ezek. 33:11. From Luke's gospel, Chapter 15:7, he provides the following, "There will be more joy in heaven over one sinner who repents than over ninety-nine righteous persons who need no repentance." Clearly, God's desire is, that all would receive His love and New Life offered through the Sanctifying Blood of Jesus.

Regarding the salvation of children: Whereas every child who dies before the age of accountability will be saved: see Deut. 1:39; 2 Sam. 12:23; Matt. 18:2-4 and Rom. 5:13. Everyone thereafter, their unique age of accountability known only to God, will have to choose God as He stirs their hearts toward His truth and love; even so, such ones who have not heard the Good News of Jesus, but are led by their conscious unto moral acceptance unto the Holiness or Righteousness approved of by God their Creator: see Romans 1:19,20 and 2:14,15.

I liken this proposal or invitation from the Holy Spirit to an individual who is irresistibly fond of some other. The pursuer may be the ideal person who possesses a righteous character and who lacks in no manner; just the same in putting their best foot forward, nevertheless, they are rejected by the person of their loving desire. This person of their affection exercising their free will has the right to choose to reject their invitation. Even so, if they do accept the proposal, nothing is keeping this person from exercising their free will yet again to reject this person who offered and presented nothing but good for the one they desired. Even so, God so loved the world – everyone in it that he sent His Unique - Eternally Son. That whosoever shall believe in Him shall not perish but have eternal life: see John 3:16. We must, as Scripture says, "Choose this day whom you will serve." (See Joshua 24:15; Deuteronomy 30:19,20; Matt. 7:13,14 and John 14:6).

God knows the heart of man; therefore, He knows what our final end will be, as well as the circumstances in our lives, whether they be good or evil, our lives being covered or directed by prayer or not, that will lead us to our end or final destiny based ultimately upon our exercise of free will. This...the activities of others and not the least of which our actions or choices will ultimately determine our outcome and final destiny, even that of others. Listen, nothing happens in a vacuum or by happenstance. We all, by the actions of others, notwithstanding our own actions to one degree or another, are affected or influenced by one another.

Likened to a masterful chess player, however, Greater; God knows our every move with or without His guidance and where we will end up. It is for this reason that we are to be prayerful people who are submitted to our Father's will even as we ask Him to lead and protect us. And so, through our prayers and faithfulness to God, He directs our path. Even so, the love we show toward others and our prayer to God for them, He will also, in His Omniscience and Divine Providence, move on our behalf, however, without violating the will of those who we are praying for that He may direct their path. Question. How well are you doing these things that God requires of His children? People need our love and prayers!

Yes, God has chosen us for eternity. Our names have been written in His Book of Life. Nevertheless, there are also forces at work in or against our lives that are often influenced by the unseen spiritual realm that wars against the best that God desires for us. No matter what this looks like or how it comes about, the greater one's disconnect from God, this includes the absence of prayer for Christians, the more likely this person or a people's destiny will end unfavorably in the sight of God. Even still, their names may be blotted out of the Book of Life as a result of such a one remaining one with this world or even one returning – here, a child of God back into the world; they, therefore, having chosen to reject the God who loves them: see 2 Pet. 2:22 and Proverb 26:11.

Be reminded Adam and Eve were without sin; heaven was one with earth; they, therefore communed with their God and Creator. Even so, during Jesus' millennial reign, Scripture seems to suggest that there will be some – mortal mankind who will die prematurely...we are not told how or why: see Isa. 65:20. After the 1000 years are completed, Satan is released from the Abyss, mortal man, yet again exercising their free will, reject Jesus as did Adam and Eve who rejected Yahweh, although they both – Father and Son met their every need and were nothing but good to them.

What we are to see here is this: Satan loosed or left unrestrained...as he currently is, and where sin's corruption still inhabits the bodies or souls of Sinners and Saints alike; as for the Christian or a child of God, if we don't remain prayerful, watchful and close to or in God, we can become as rebellious and sinful as those belonging to this present evil world. This I have seen...Christians, yes, Christians that I know who have committed unbelievable evil, including murder! As for their names being blotted out of The Book of Life, only God knows if their hearts are truly sorrowful and repentant of their wrong. If this is the case, such ones are yet one with Christ. Remember, Jesus came to restore and forgive even the most wicked of Sinners – I am in the number, and so are you; nonetheless, we who have repented and embraced Jesus as Lord and Savior are forgiven of our sins and restored to right fellowship with Christ our Lord.

> *My brothers and sisters in Christ, we must embrace and understand the nature of causality – cause and effect. And thereby, be willing to pray more and do more for the lost to this world and for one another as this age and our end draws nearer!*

Verse 13: The sea gave up the dead that were in it, and death and Hades gave up the dead that were in them, and each person – *the wicked dead* was judged according to what they had done. **14** Then death and Hades were thrown into the lake of fire. The lake of fire is the second death. **15** Anyone whose name was not found written in the Book of Life was thrown into the lake of fire.

Where are the Dead? Provided is the Common View:

In the Old Testament, we are provided with the word Sheol, which means the place of the dead. The word Sheol is often translated as the grave: see 1 Sam. 28:12-15. This location is where the dead are kept: see Gen 37:35. Isaiah 14:9-10 suggests that there is a consciousness of those who are there. However, this does not imply that they know our affairs here on earth, nor does the dead in Christ look after us or attend to our needs. And neither are our dead loved ones, angels. In the New Testament, we are provided with the word Hades as the place of the dead. Unfortunately, some Bible translations have Hades translated as Hell; Hades is not Hell. Hades is the Old Testament's equivalent of the place of the dead, otherwise known as the Sheol.

In Luke's gospel, Chapter 16:19-24, we have this story regarding the abode of the dead: **19** "There was a rich man who was dressed in purple and fine linen and lived in luxury every day. **20** At his gate was laid a beggar named Lazarus, covered with sores **21** and longing to eat what fell from the rich man's table. Even the dogs came and licked his sores. **22** "The time came when the beggar died, and the angels carried him to Abraham's side. The rich man also died and was buried. **23** In Hades, where he was in torment, he looked up and saw Abraham far away, with Lazarus by his side. **24** So he called to him, 'Father Abraham, have pity on me and send Lazarus to dip the tip of his finger in water and cool my tongue because I am in agony in this fire.'

In this place of the dead – Hades or Sheol, we see two distinct conditions and locations. Lazarus is at the side or bosom of Abraham, while the rich man is in a place of torment. In this place of the dead, there is a great chasm that separates these two: see verse 26. The place of the rich man is described by Jesus as a place of torment; however, this is not the Lake of Fire – the Gehenna, where Hades, Death, the wicked dead, and rebellious spirit beings will be thrown. In the Bible, this was a place for burning what was discarded and even where children were sacrificed to the gods or Satan: see 2 Chron. 28:3 and Mark 9: 43-48.

Ephesians 4:8,9 share with us another wonderous act of Jesus. The text reads as follows: "This is why it says: "When he – Jesus ascended on high, he took many captives (those in Abraham's bosom to paradise, the place of the righteous dead: see Luke 23:42,43; 2 Cor. 12:3 and Rev. 2:7) and *He – Jesus* gave gifts to his people (the Church)" **9** What does "he ascended" mean except that he also descended to the lower, earthly region?

2 Peter 2:4 provides for us the following location for fallen angels: **4** For if God did not spare angels when they sinned, but sent them to hell (better translated Tartarus or the Abyss, a worse place or prison within the Sheol or Hades), and putting them in chains of darkness to be held for judgment: also see Luke 8:29-31, *after which these rebellious angels will be cast into Hell Fire or the Gehenna pending their final judgment.*

1 Pet. 3:19,20 has this to say: **19** "After being made alive, He – *Jesus* went and made proclamation (declaring Victory!) to the imprisoned spirits— **20** to those who were disobedient long ago when God waited patiently in the days of Noah while the ark was being built. In it, only a few people, eight in all, were saved through water;" also see Gen. 6:2.

Lastly, we have **The Lake of Fire, Rev. 20:14,15 and Matt. 25:41**, which reads: "Then he will say to those on his left, 'Depart from me, you who are cursed, into the eternal fire prepared for the devil and his angels. This Lake of Fire is the final judgment and place that was prepared for the fallen heavenly host. However, all people who reject Jesus, having made themselves one with the Devil, will likewise spend eternity in unimaginable suffering. As already mentioned, Hades – the realm of the dead and Death and the Devil will also be in this place forever! Mark 9:48 tells us: "Where the worms that eat them do not die, and the fire is not quenched: additionally see Isa. 66:24.

God's Judgment By Fire:

2 Peter 3:6-13 reads: **6** By these waters also the world of that time was deluged and destroyed. **7** By the same word, the present heavens, and earth are reserved for fire, being kept for the day of judgment and destruction of the ungodly. **8** But do not forget this one thing, dear friends: With the Lord, a day is like a thousand years, and a thousand years are like a day. **9** The Lord is not slow in keeping his promise, as some understand slowness. Instead, he is patient with you, not wanting anyone to perish but everyone to come to repentance. **10** But the day of the Lord will come like a thief. The heavens will disappear with a roar; the elements will be destroyed by fire, and the earth and everything done in it will be laid bare.

11 Since everything will be destroyed in this way, what kind of people ought you to be? You ought to live holy and godly lives **12** as you look forward to the day of God and speed its coming. That day will bring about the destruction of the heavens by fire, and the elements will melt in the heat. **13** But in keeping with his promise, we are looking forward to a new heaven and a new earth, where righteousness dwells. **14** So then, dear friends, since you are looking forward to this, make every effort to be found spotless, blameless, and at peace with him. **15b.** Bear in mind that our Lord's patience means salvation..."

God's judgment by fire is sure! Jude has this to say in verses 6 and 7: "And the angels who did not keep their positions of authority but abandoned their proper dwelling—these he – *God* has kept in darkness, bound with everlasting chains for judgment on the Great Day. **7** In a similar way, Sodom and Gomorrah and the surrounding towns gave themselves up to sexual immorality and perversion. They serve as an example of those who suffer the punishment of eternal fire." (And so Scripture has spoken, God has made it plain, sexual perversion and extreme wickedness in the Bible signaled the imminent return or judgment of God. We are shown this with the flood of Noah's day, wherein the fallen angel's sexual perversion with women and, thereby, global wickedness arose resulting from these forbidden unions. And as well, with the gross sexual perversion of Sodom and Gomorrah, God, therefore, arose as Judge and sent forth His condemnation and sentencing upon these perverse and wicked people.

Just look at how things are in our world! The Day of the Lord is yet again drawing nearer! God is soon to say, "Enough is Enough!

Lastly, Matthew has these words to share in chapter 3:10-13, here quoting John the Baptist. **10** "The ax is already at the root of the trees (those who are wicked), and every tree that does not produce good fruit

213

will be cut down and thrown into the fire. **11** "I baptize you with water for repentance. But after me – *says John*, comes one who is more powerful than I, whose sandals I am not worthy to carry (this speaks of Jesus). He will baptize you with the Holy Spirit and fire. **12** His winnowing fork is in his hand, and he will clear his threshing floor, gathering his wheat into the barn and burning up the chaff with unquenchable fire." **13** "Then *he* – Jesus will say to those on his left, 'Depart from me, you who are cursed, into the eternal fire prepared for the devil and his angels.'" Also, see Matt. 25:41; people, rebellion against God must be dealt with!

CHAPTER 23

OUTLINE AND REVELATION CHAPTER 21

The New Heaven and the New Earth:

1. **Verse 1-4:** The New Heaven and the New Earth
   - Introduction: John sees a new heaven and a new earth, for the first heaven and the first earth had passed away, and the sea was no more.
   - The Holy City, New Jerusalem: And he sees the holy city, new Jerusalem, coming down out of heaven from God, prepared as a bride adorned for her husband.
   - God's Dwelling with His People: And he hears a loud voice from the throne saying, "Behold, the dwelling place of God is with man. He will dwell with them, and they will be his people, and God himself will be with them as their God.
   - The End of Suffering: He will wipe away every tear from their eyes, and death shall be no more, neither shall there be mourning, nor crying, nor pain anymore, for the former things have passed away."

2. **Verse 5-8:** The One on the Throne Makes All Things New
   - Introduction: John hears the one seated on the throne saying, "Behold, I am making all things new."

- The Words are Trustworthy: He says to John, "Write this down, for these words are trustworthy and true."

- The Beginning and the End: He declares, "It is done! I am the Alpha and the Omega, the beginning and the end. To the thirsty, I will give from the spring of the water of life without payment."

- The Inheritors and the Cowardly: "The one who conquers will have this heritage, and I will be his God, and he will be my son. But as for the cowardly, the faithless, the detestable, as for murderers, the sexually immoral, sorcerers, idolaters, and all liars, their portion will be in the lake that burns with fire and sulfur, which is the second death."

3. **Verse 9-21:** The New Jerusalem
   - Introduction: One of the seven angels who had the seven bowls full of the seven last plagues comes and speaks with John, saying, "Come, I will show you the Bride, the wife of the Lamb."

   - The City's Splendor: And he carries John away in the Spirit to a great, high mountain, and shows him the holy city Jerusalem coming down out of heaven from God, having the glory of God, its radiance like a most rare jewel, like a jasper, clear as crystal.

   - The Walls and Gates: It has a great, high wall, with twelve gates, and at the gates twelve angels, and on the gates, the names of the twelve tribes of the sons of Israel were inscribed.

   - The Foundation and Measurements: The wall of the city had twelve foundations, and on them were the twelve names of the twelve apostles of the Lamb. The city lies four square, its length the same as its width. And he measured the city with his rod, 12,000 stadia. Its length and, width, and height are equal.

   - The Wall's Material: He also measured its wall, 144 cubits by human measurement, which is also an angel's measurement.

   - The City's Appearance: The wall was built of jasper, while the city was pure gold, like clear glass.

- The Foundation Stones: The foundations of the wall of the city were adorned with every kind of jewel. The first was jasper, the second sapphire, the third agate, the fourth emerald, the fifth onyx, the sixth carnelian, the seventh chrysolite, the eighth beryl, the ninth topaz, the tenth chrysoprase, the eleventh jacinth, the twelfth amethyst.
- The Gates and Streets: And the twelve gates were twelve pearls, each of the gates made of a single pearl, and the street of the city was pure gold, transparent as glass.

4. **Verse 22-27:** The Glory and Inhabitants of the New Jerusalem
   - Introduction: And John sees no temple in the city, for its temple is the Lord God the Almighty and the Lamb.
   - The City's Light: And the city has no need of sun or moon to shine on it, for the glory of God gives it light, and its lamp is the Lamb.
   - The Nations' Entrance: By its light will the nations walk, and the kings of the earth will bring their glory into it.
   - The Gates' Openness: And its gates will never be shut by day— and there will be no night there.
   - The Inhabitants: They will bring into it the glory and the honor of the nations. But nothing unclean will ever enter it, nor anyone who does what is detestable or false, but only those who are written in the Lamb's book of life.

This chapter describes the vision of the new heaven and the new earth, the descent of the holy city, New Jerusalem, and its splendor. It portrays the complete restoration and renewal of all things by God, where there will be no more tears, pain, or death, and where God will dwell with His people for eternity.

Revelation Chapter 21

In these final two chapters, John will be describing an external view of the new existence and dimension of heaven and earth – its eternal state exceeding our current reality and his and our ability to comprehend. This current world – its geography, atmosphere, and life on Earth after the fall of Adam and Eve, was not as it was before sin entered the world; nevertheless, it was and is spectacular. Our new heaven and earth will likewise be something quite astonishing and beyond our comprehension. And so, in comparison, our new eternal home – heaven and earth will be far grander than what we can understand of heaven and earth before the Edenic fall. Even though we are limited in our ability to grasp the splendor of our new home, it is what God said He would do – restore Eden after the pattern of the former Eden, but amazingly unimaginable as it will be built for eternity. God's conclusion of the Book of Revelation is to be understood as His restoration of Eden, now that He has dealt with the rebellion of man and the rebellion of the Supernatural realm. In order to understand what is occurring in this book of Revelation, the story of Genesis must be understood – in that God is reversing the curse!

1 Then I saw "a new heaven and a new earth," for the first heaven and the first earth had passed away, and there was no longer any sea. (In ancient times, the sea represented a place of chaos, danger, and judgment. However, in the New Heaven and Earth, neither will there be Night nor the curse, a temple, the Sun or Moon, nor sinners, and rebellion will be no more. And neither will there be the tree of knowledge; however, there will be the tree of life). **2** I saw the Holy City, the new Jerusalem, coming down out of heaven from God, prepared as a bride beautifully dressed for her husband.

3 And I heard a loud voice from the throne saying, "Look! God's dwelling place is now among the people, and he will dwell with them. They will be his people, and God himself will be with them and be their God. **4** 'He will wipe every tear from their eyes. There will be no more death' or mourning or crying or pain, for the old order of things has passed away."

5 He, who was seated on the throne, said, "I am making everything new!" Then he said, "Write this down, for these words are trustworthy and true." (God's words are the essence of who He is. Therefore, they will accomplish what He has said or purposed). **6** He said to me: "It is done. I am the Alpha and the Omega, the Beginning and the End. To the thirsty, I will give water without cost from the spring of the water of life. **7** Those who are victorious will inherit all this (all that John is describing), and I will be their God, and they will be my children.

8 But the cowardly, the unbelieving, the vile, the murderers, the sexually immoral, those who practice magic arts (this involves mind-altering drugs, to include occult practices of whatever the sort), the idolaters (those who give priority to whatever by which to establish their identity or worth, or such things or people made to have preeminence over God), and all liars (such people who are manipulative or deceivers or who practice falsehood)—they will be consigned to the fiery lake of burning sulfur. This is the second death." (See Rev. 21:27 and 22:15; they emphasize by restating the matter of those who will not belong to God's kingdom. And so must the Church emphasize these prohibitions)!

The New Jerusalem, the Bride of the Lamb:

9 One of the seven angels who had the seven bowls full of the seven last plagues came and said to me, "Come, I will show you the bride (the Church), the wife of the Lamb." **10** And he carried me away in the Spirit to a mountain great and high, and showed me the Holy City, Jerusalem, coming down out of heaven from God. **11** It shone with the glory of God (here, the Church – the body of Believers in all her splendor, not the least of which, her outward adornment is to the glory of God, even as a husband's wife should be his glory from the inside out, modeling or reflecting the moral character and beauty of their God unto holiness. As for precious stones – so are Believers described; their beauty is not seen until light passes through them and reflects their radiant and reflective splendor. So must the Light and Life of Jesus be in and radiate from a child of God: see 1 Peter 3:3,4. Satan's kingdom also has stones. However, it does not possess Rubies because he – Satan does not have a proper bride: see Rev. 17:4 and verse **20** of this 21st chapter). *Verse **11** begins with the Holy City shone with the* glory of God and its brilliance – (now both the Holy City and the Bride are in view with their glory and splendor on display). A*nd they were* like that of a very precious jewel, like a jasper, clear as crystal. (In these descriptions, the Bride and New Jerusalem are pictured as one, even as they are now one with the Triune God).

12 It – *the Holy City and New Jerusalem* had a great, high wall with twelve gates and with twelve angels at the gates. (The number 12 is symbolic of God's governance and divine order...we see this operating in our calendar year, in the Lunar year of 360 days, in keeping time and elsewhere. It also represents perfection and completeness or fulfillment of God's purpose). *Verse **12** continues:* On the gates were written the names of the twelve tribes of Israel: see Gen. 49:28. (These names have significant meanings that spoke to the tribes. They also speak to us as entrance is granted into these gates. After entering the New Jerusalem, Christ's Bride – His Church will be rewarded for their ministry or service rendered when they dwelt on earth: see Matt. 6:4). **13** There were three gates on the east, three on the north, three on the south, and three on the west. **14** The wall of the city had twelve foundations, and on them were the names of the twelve apostles of the Lamb (whose new names, those received from Jesus, hold Biblical or spiritual significance – namely, the gift of God. These foundations – the teachings of the Twelve, are of God, and what He has stated through them as recorded in the Bible are truths essential to His kingdom's governance and for His people's adherence).

15 The angel who talked with me had a measuring rod of gold to measure the city, its gates, and its walls. **16** The city was laid out like a square, as long as it was wide. He measured the city with the rod and found it to be 12,000 stadia in length and as wide and high as it is long (thereby encompassing approximately a total landmass of 1,380 miles, over half the size of the United States). **17** The angel measured the wall using human measurement (or three-dimensional measurement or spatial measurement so that John and we readers may be able to make partial sense of this actual city that is being presented). John continued, *saying that the wall* was 144 cubits thick *or over 200 feet.*

18 The wall was made of jasper, and the city of pure gold, as pure as glass. **19** The foundations of the city walls were decorated with every kind of precious stone. The first foundation was jasper, the second sapphire, the third agate, the fourth emerald, **20** the fifth onyx, the sixth ruby (which is likened to a good wife but who is more precious than this jewel: see Prov. 3:15 & 31:10,11), the seventh *precious stone was* chrysolite, the eighth beryl, the ninth topaz, the tenth turquoise, the eleventh jacinth, and the twelfth amethyst. **21** The twelve gates were twelve pearls, each gate made of a single pearl. (Look. Not just anybody will be granted access through these gates. Those who will be granted access must have first gained access to Jesus, in so doing He having first entered us by His Holy Spirit. Jesus said it plainly, "I am the gate, John 19:7-9).

These gates are also pictures of authority. There are the gates of Hell and/or gates belonging to Babylon's system. However, these gates cannot hold us if we choose to enter Christ. In Christ, we are safe and secure unless one chooses to venture outside of Jesus' protection or His gates. Even so, one can choose to return to Babylon to dwell, thereby abandoning God or even divorcing themselves from Him. Marriage to Jesus and whomever you partner with in marriage is a choice; therefore, one can also choose to leave the love of another if they so desire. And so it is, wide is the gate, and broad is the road that leads to destruction. In Jesus, however, small and narrow is the gate that leads to life eternal: see Matt. 13:13,14). *Continuing with verse 21*, The great street of the city was of gold, as pure as transparent glass: see Ezek. 48:30-35. (A study of these jewels will show that each of them is significant as they hold specific meanings here on earth and in heaven).

22 I did not see a temple in the city because the Lord God Almighty and the Lamb are its temple. **23** The city does not need the sun or the moon to shine on it, for the glory of God gives it light, and the Lamb is its lamp (a contrast to Gen. 1:3,4, where the world is described as being governed by celestial lighting and darkness – this darkness perhaps being an unusual phenomenon). **24** The nations will walk by its light, and the kings of the earth will bring their splendor into it. **25** On no day will its gates ever be shut, for there will be no night there. **26** The glory and honor of the nations will be brought into it. **27** Nothing impure will ever enter it, nor will anyone who does what is shameful or deceitful, but only those whose names are written in the Lamb's Book of Life.

CHAPTER 24

OUTLINE AND REVELATION CHAPTER 22

The River of Life, the Tree of Life, and Jesus' Last Words:

1. **Verse 1-5:** The River of the Water of Life
   - Introduction: John sees the river of the water of life, bright as crystal, flowing from the throne of God and of the Lamb through the middle of the street of the city.
   - The Tree of Life: On either side of the river is the Tree of Life with its twelve kinds of fruit, yielding its fruit each month. The leaves of the tree were for the healing of the nations.
   - The Throne of God: No longer will there be anything accursed, but the throne of God and of the Lamb will be in it, and his servants will worship him.
   - The Sight of God's Face: They will see his face, and his name will be on their foreheads.
   - No More Night: And night will be no more. They will need no light of lamp or sun, for the Lord God will be their light, and they will reign forever and ever.
2. **Verse 6-7:** The Assurance and the Warning
   - Introduction: John hears the angel saying to him, "These words are trustworthy and true."

- The Blessedness: And he – Jesus says, "And behold, I am coming soon. Blessed is the one who keeps the words of the prophecy of this book."
- The Testimony: John adds, "I, John, am the one who heard and saw these things. And when I heard and saw them, I fell down to worship at the feet of the angel who showed them to me."

3. **Verse 8-9:** John's Reaction and the Angel's Response
   - Introduction: But the angel says to him, "You must not do that! I am a fellow servant with you and your brothers, the prophets, and with those who keep the words of this book. Worship God."
   - The Seal of Prophecy: And he adds, "And he said to me, 'Do not seal up the words of the prophecy of this book, for the time is near.'"

4. **Verse 10-11:** The Time is Near
   - Introduction: "Let the evildoer still do evil, and the filthy still be filthy, and the righteous still do right, and the holy still be holy."
   - The Announcement: "Behold, I am coming soon, bringing my recompense with me, to repay each one for what he has done."

5. **Verse 12-16:** Jesus' Testimony and Invitation
   - Introduction: "I am the Alpha and the Omega, the first and the last, the beginning and the end."
   - The Blessing: "Blessed are those who wash their robes, so that they may have the right to the tree of life and that they may enter the city by the gates."
   - The Outside: "Outside are the dogs and sorcerers and the sexually immoral and murderers and idolaters, and everyone who loves and practices falsehood."
   - Jesus' Authority: "I, Jesus, have sent my angel to testify to you about these things for the churches. I am the root and the descendant of David, the bright morning star."

6. **Verse 17-21:** The Invitation and Final Benediction
   - Introduction: "The Spirit and the Bride say, 'Come.' And let the one who hears say, 'Come.' And let the one who is thirsty come; let the one who desires take the water of life without price."
   - The Warning: "I warn everyone who hears the words of the prophecy of this book: if anyone adds to them, God will add to him the plagues described in this book, and if anyone takes away from the words of the book of this prophecy, God will take away his share in the tree of life and in the holy city, which are described in this book."
   - Jesus' Testimony: "He who testifies to these things says, 'Surely I am coming soon.' Amen. Come, Lord Jesus!"
   - The Benediction: "The grace of the Lord Jesus be with all. Amen."

This chapter concludes the book of Revelation with the vision of the river of the water of life and the tree of life, the final assurance and warning, the invitation from the Spirit and the Bride, and the final testimony and benediction from Jesus. It emphasizes the imminence of Christ's return and the importance of keeping the words of the prophecy of this book.

Revelation Chapter 22

In this final chapter, we have been granted access to the Holy City; inside, there is eternal life.

Eden Restored:

1 Then the angel showed me the river of the water of life (a representation of the Holy Spirit), as clear as crystal, flowing from the throne of God (the presence of the Father) and of the Lamb (who is Jesus. The Holy Trinity is here in view). And so, the river of life – *God the*

Holy Spirit was flowing, **2** down the middle of the great street of the city (the Holy Spirit or God's Truth should also be going forth or seen flowing from each of us – God's children and Christ's Bride). On each side of the river stood the Tree of Life (a picture of Jesus, who has brought eternal life, healing, and restoration of God the Father's people back to Him). *This tree was* bearing twelve crops of fruit, yielding its fruit every month. And the leaves of the tree are for the healing of the nations (a picture of Jesus' Bride – all who have received Christ as Lord and Savior, possessing through Him everything she will ever need) **3** No longer will there be any curse (there will only be blessedness and abundance. This tree evokes the thoughts of paradise lost in Eden, where mankind had access to the Tree of Life but instead chose the forbidden tree – hence, mankind's former inheritance was lost, and their new inheritance of the curse of sin and death now reign and rule over them. In the Holy City, the Tree of Life will forever be accessible, a reminder of God's promise of eternal life and the restoration of all things through our Redeemer and Bridegroom Jesus). *The remainder of verse 3:* The throne of God and of the Lamb will be in the city, and his servants will serve him.

4 They will see his face, and his name will be on their foreheads (meaning the people's covenant relationship with Jesus and He forever being foremost in their thoughts). **5** There will be no more night. They will not need the light of a lamp or the light of the sun, for the Lord God will give them light. And they will reign forever and ever. (In the creation story of Genesis, God provided the heaven containing day and night. These were His delegated authorities assigned to govern our seasons and other ways of life. However, in the Holy City, there will no longer be any need for such principles of governance; we will have Jesus, the True Light of His new world order.

A read of the creation story seems to reveal to many that there is something else of theological significance occurring with this matter of Darkness and Light, and not merely the sun coming up and going down to order the days of creation or life on earth. Perhaps you recall the

Genesis account of creation, in which darkness is mentioned before the creation of the sun and the night lights. What we are to also see is not just the work of the Triune God at creation or the work of Jesus that is done in the day (see John 9:4), but also the opposing work of Satan that is done or is pictured as occurring during the darkened hours or the night: see Ephesian 5:1-11.

Here is one such reference, in John 13:30, of this cosmic disruption or spiritual darkness embodied in the night hour: Judas' betrayal of Jesus during Passover occurred at night; this passage made explicit mention that it was night – hence Satan at work and working through his son Judas – "the son of perdition:" also see Luke 22:53 and John 17:12 KJV. When the Genesis account mentions that "darkness was over the face of the deep," one can presuppose, although debated, that this darkness was a result of angelic upheaval or rebellion occurring before the creation of Adam and Eve. However, Scripture doesn't present a clear chronology either for or against the position I've offered and others embrace.

With all of the evil and immorality that is upon us, we are currently experiencing tremendous and gross spiritual darkness; however, things are going to get even darker in this fallen and corrupt world: see 1 Tim. 4:1 and 2 Thess. 2:3 – which mentions the great falling away or apostasy before the return of Jesus for His Bride – the Church. This event – the rapture happening likened to a thief in the night: see 1 Thess. 5:2; will be the resurrection of the dead and the immediate rapture of the Church: see Matt. 25:6. However, some view this event as the Second Coming of Christ and not the rapture. Although this text is likewise debatable, I maintain the view that Jesus is not going to permit His Bride to experience His fury marked by great darkness...what kind of sense does this make that Jesus' Bride will experience his wrath? Revisit my notes in chapter 5, under the subtitle: **The Church Will Escape the Great Tribulation**. Throughout the Bible, we are provided other night rescues by God: see Gen. 19:15; Ex. 12:29-31; Ex.14:21,22; Joshua 2:1-7 and; Acts 16:25,26. Although Satan is associated with darkness, nevertheless, God reigns

Supreme; therefore, He also has governance over darkness or the work of Satan. But in the New Heaven and New Earth, there will be no night, darkness, or Satan to oppose God).

John and the Angel:

6 The angel said to me, "These words are trustworthy and true. The Lord, the God who inspires the prophets, sent his angel to show his servants – *the redeemed of the Lord* the things that must soon take place." **7** "Look, *Jesus declares*, I am coming soon! Blessed is the one who keeps the words of the prophecy written in this scroll." **8** I, John, am the one who heard and saw these things. And when I had heard and seen them, I fell down to worship at the feet of the angel who had been showing them to me.

9 But he said to me, "Don't do that! I am a fellow servant with you and with your fellow prophets and with all who keep the words of this scroll. Worship God!" **10** Then he told me, "Do not seal up the words of the prophecy of this scroll because the time is near. **11** Let the one who does wrong continue to do wrong; let the vile person continue to be vile (for this is what their hearts are set on); let the one who does right continue to do right; and let the holy person continue to be holy." (Until the return of Christ, whether by the rapture of the universal Church or the Second Coming of Christ, we who are the Redeemed of the Lord and children of God must faithfully persevere until Jesus returns).

Epilogue: Invitation and Warning:

12 "Look, I am coming soon! My reward is with me, and I will give to each person according to what they have done. **13** I am the Alpha and the Omega, the First and the Last, the Beginning and the End. **14** "Blessed are those who wash their robes, that they may have the right to the tree of life and may go through the gates into the city. **15** Outside are the dogs, those who practice magic arts, the sexually immoral, the murderers, the idolaters, and everyone who loves and practices falsehood.

16 "I, Jesus, have sent my angel to give you this testimony for the churches. I am the Root and the Offspring of David and the bright Morning Star."

17 The Spirit and the bride – *the true Church of God* say, "Come!" And let the one who hears say, "Come!" Let the one who is thirsty come, and let the one who wishes take the free gift of the water of life. (Clearly, the Spirit of God has been and currently is inviting everyone to come to Jesus. Nevertheless, there have been and will continue to be those who reject God's invitation into His kingdom). **18** I warn everyone who hears the words of the prophecy of this scroll: If anyone adds anything to them, God will add to that person the plagues described in this scroll. **19** And if anyone takes words away from this scroll of prophecy, God will take away from that person any share in the tree of life and in the Holy City, which are described in this scroll.

20 He who testifies to these things says, "Yes, I am coming soon." Amen. Come, Lord Jesus. **21** The grace of the Lord Jesus be with God's people. Amen.

CHAPTER 25

BIBLICAL PROPHECY: THE INFALLIBLE AND TIME-TESTED WORD OF GOD

Brief Summary of the Bible:

The Bible is about the *Only Loving God* – mankind's Creator, and for the redeemed of the Lord Jesus, He is God our Father to whose kingdom we have been restored. Yahweh or Jehovah God – these being his personal names created this earth so that mankind would represent Him or display His glory. He gave to Adam as his Bride, Eve, his complementary opposite, his ontological equal as a suitable helpmeet or life partner, in God's communal love for them. They were to love one another and to love their God. He told them to have babies who also were to be one with God in His kingdom or His family; the earth would belong to Adam and Eve to steward and rule over it. This family unity – Deity with humanity necessitated, in turn, that Adam and Eve were to be in loving subjection and obedience to their Father and God.

It must be understood that love cannot be forced or coerced. Instead, love operates freely through or from free will, for this was how our God and Father created us. One, therefore, chooses to love or reciprocate loving affections towards some other. However, the test of love is proven when it stands against that which threatens to violate the loving marital covenant or one's oath of faithfulness to a spouse or one belonging to God's kingdom." God is "Love;" therefore, mankind was created to imitate God in or through love...love for self, love for others, but first love for God.

Adam and Eve failed to remain faithful or in love with their God and Creator; even so, with one another, they failed in this matter of love. When Eve, in particular, was deceived by Satan, and they chose to eat the fruit from the forbidden tree, as decreed by God for them not to eat, a curse or death came upon them and their offspring; sin and Satan now had rule over them, all of humanity and the earth were now under this curse and Satan's rule. God's unholy creatures – all of fallen mankind, because of their/our inherent sinful disposition were now estranged from our loving Father; we now, therefore, struggle to love with godly love and compassion such that He possesses.

God was heartbroken due to mankind's unfaithfulness to Him. Nevertheless, He foreknew what would become of His helplessly lost, wayward, and spiritually broken children. Now, sadly and tragically, mankind will come to see and know the ugliness, suffering, and sorrow that becomes mankind's reality when the love of our God and Father is rejected. Yet, in God's foreknowledge and omniscience, He had predetermined a plan to save His lost and rebellious children from themselves and Satan. God knew before He formed the earth how He would restore humanity back to their loving and rightful place in His care and kingdom. It would be through the death or self-sacrifice of His Unique Son Jesus and His ultimate defeat of Death and evil, as we have seen in our study from the Book of Revelation: see Ephesians 1:4,5.

Man's payment for their sin came at a great cost...it was the shed blood of Jesus that ransoms lost and sinful mankind. Now, unto all who believe in Jesus as Lord and Savior...no matter who you are or what you may have done in your sinful past, we are all gathered back to the love of our God and Father through our belief in Jesus – hence, Biblical prophecy fulfilled: see Isaiah Chapter 53; John 3:16 also Genesis 3:15 where we have the first announcement of the Protoevangelium – the Good News of the world's Savior – Jesus the Son of God, prophesied. And so, we have been welcomed back into God's family, those who believe in the saving grace of Jesus; even so, His invitation to the lost and broken people of this world remains in place. However, only for a short time, it stands as an open invitation to become one with Him in His kingdom...Jesus is soon to return; don't wait until it's too late. The Word of God has been spoken! Biblical prophecy will be fulfilled; God's words will not return to Him void: see Isa. 55:11.

In the Old Testament, God selected ordinary men, otherwise known as prophets, who spoke God's Word to His lost and defiant children, both the Israelites and Gentile nations alike. Regarding the Jewish people, whom Yahweh chose to be His special nation unto Himself, even so, His Bride, they were to shine forth as God's glorious light and truth bearer to the other nations. As it is or should be in marriages, spouses do not hide or keep things from one another. Therefore, God communicates to Israel, His chosen people or Bride, throughout the Bible as shared here in Amos 3:7, with the prophet saying: "Surely the Sovereign LORD does nothing without revealing his plan to his servants the prophets" (who again were God's spokespersons, in particular for Israel, His Bride).

Jesus, the Son of God, furthering His Father's mission and utilizing similar verbiage, expresses the following here in John 15:15: "No longer do I call you servants, for a servant does not understand what his master is doing. But I have called you friends because everything I have learned from My Father I have made known to you." (What Jesus is asserting is that He is the Fulfillment and the Executioner of His Father's prophetic plans and promises. In this statement, He wants His friends, even so, the emerging Church – His Bride to know His mission and ministry during His sojourn while on earth. As well as that which will occur after He ascends back to heaven and that which will occur at His Second Coming.

As we take a look at a few of the prophecies concerning God the Father and His Son ~ Jesus, I pray that your faith is stirred towards Jesus, and for those of you who are already committed to faith in Christ, that your faith will be strengthened as a result of this concluding study on Biblical Prophecy.

A Look At Biblical Prophecy Concerning Jesus, the Messianic King and Son of God

Isaiah's prophetic words regarding Jehovah's coming Servant are seen fulfilled through the ministry and life of Jesus:

Isaiah 42:1 – Dated approx. 690 B.C., Isaiah's prophetic proclamation that God gave to him: Verse **1** "Behold! My Servant whom I uphold, My Elect One in whom My soul delights! I have put My Spirit upon Him; He will bring forth justice to the Gentiles. **2** He will not cry out, nor raise His voice, Nor cause His voice to be heard in the street. **3** A bruised reed He will not break, And smoking flax He will not quench; He will bring forth justice for truth. **4** He will not fail nor be discouraged, Till He has established justice in the earth; And the coastlands shall wait for His law."

5 Thus says God the Lord, Who created the heavens and stretched them out, Who spread forth the earth and that which comes from it, Who gives breath to the people on it, and spirit to those who walk on it: **6** "I, the Lord, have called You in righteousness, and will hold Your hand; I will keep You and give You as a **covenant to the people**, **a light to the Gentiles**, **7** To open blind eyes, To bring out prisoners from the prison, Those who sit in darkness from the prison house. **8** I am the Lord, that is My name; And My glory I will not give to another, Nor My praise to carved images. **9** Behold, the former things have come to pass, **"And new things I declare; Before they spring forth, I tell you of them."**

Isaiah 48:3 speaking on Yahweh's behalf, says, "I foretold the former things long ago; they came out of My mouth, and I proclaimed them. Suddenly, I acted, and they came to pass." *The previous prophecy of Isaiah chap. 42:1-9 has been fulfilled in God's Servant Son – Jesus, the Messianic King.*

Let's Continue to Hear God's Words to Isaiah:

Isaiah 48:6: "You have heard these things; look at them all. Will you not acknowledge them? From now on, I will tell you of new things, hidden things unknown to you."

In **Isaiah 41:21-23,** Jehovah God challenges the people and their gods to prophesy or foretell the future as He does with 100 % accuracy. Considering the wealth of prophetic information and declarations God has provided within His Holy Word, He has, therefore, proven Himself to be the One and Only Faithful God. Biblical prophecy I likened to God's final argument to silence all other gods (Elohim), critics or naysayers of His, or mere mankind who present themselves as a god or wise in their own understanding! He, therefore, says to such ones, "Prove yourselves, proclaim what will happen in the future!" Needless to say, they can't because He alone holds or knows the future; God is Omniscient; He alone reigns Supreme! No angelic being created in heaven nor mere man made from the dust of the earth remotely stands as God's equal...far from it!

Now hear what Isaiah, God's mouthpiece and prophet, proclaims on Yahweh's behalf: **Isaiah 41:21-23. Verse 21:** "Present your case," says the Lord. "Set forth your arguments," says Jacob's King. **22** "Tell us, you idols, what is going to happen. Tell us what the former things were, so that we may consider them and know their final outcome. Or declare to us the things to come, **23** tell us what the future holds, so we may know that you are gods. Do something, whether good or bad, so that we will be dismayed and filled with fear" – *or awe and wonder.*

Jehovah, the Creator of heaven and earth, and all that dwells therein, as our Creator, He exists outside of mankind's time restrictions and boundaries of celestial and terrestrial governance appointed by Him. He has established these boundaries: the sun and moon, day and night, that sets our time, containing therein man's unfolding history and our near and distant future that is to take shape upon the borders of the earth. Although we live as His free moral agents, God our Creator knows our beginning, our outcomes, and our final end. God even knows the plans of fallen angels; furthermore, He knows the innermost secrets of mankind's hearts and, thusly, where they will lead us under every conceivable circumstance that we may dream up or think of as we establish our own odysseys.

Although we may find it difficult to reconcile in our finite minds, our free will with God's Omniscience and Divine Providence with His Supremacy and control over everything. Nevertheless, we are not puppets on a string or robots; we have free will endowed to us by God, our loving Creator. And yet, everything on earth and in heaven occurs because He either permits or mandates it to bring about His ultimate purpose to reconcile mankind to Himself and His final judgment upon the wicked. Therefore, He is God over time – the clock established by the sun and the moon, the day and night, and everything occurring within its span or this time, until time as we know it, is no more...culminating and being terminated at God's appointed time as revealed to us in the Book of Revelation.

The Prophetic Proclamation of God from the Book of Deuteronomy:

The book Deuteronomy was written in approximately 1407 B.C., Moses is God's "Called" or chosen penman of this book and Yahweh's prophet. In the ensuing Scripture, Moses speaks prophetically God's inspired Words about future events that will be established by God.

Throughout the Holy and inspired Word of God, as you will see from this limited study of prophetic Scripture and from also other Biblical authors, some who possess the title of Prophet in the Old Testament, while others don't. Yet, these spokespersons were inspired by God to speak on His behalf about current events. Even so, to speak of or proclaim occurrences that were to come to pass that are yet to be fulfilled in the near or distant future – The End of Days.

A Prophet was one "Called" by God in the Old Testament era as His specific spokesperson to the people. In today's terms, such individuals are generally referred to as *Preachers, who preach or prophetically proclaim the cause and truth concerning Jesus, the Unique – Eternally Existing Son of God;* their message is primarily to lead mankind to salvation – this is *The Good News of Jesus* for those who preach or ***forth-tell*** the saving message and grace of Jesus to the lost souls of this world.

Foretelling, on the other hand, or speaking about future events about God and His work regarding our time or this Church age, concluded with the Book of Revelation, therein underscoring Jesus' ultimate victory over the Devil, death, and all evil powers and wickedness. This will be The End of this world's history and story. Contained within the Old Testament, it is complete with hundreds of prophetic, God-breathed announcements about this world's coming King, Savior, Deliverer, Redeemer, Healer, and even that Great Prophet, who will come in the likes of Moses, but who is Greater than Moses because He will be none other than Jesus – the Unique – Eternally Existing Son of God, the prophesied and Messianic King of kings.

The Greater Prophet than Moses:

Deuteronomy 18:18-22: *Here, Moses is speaking, he says.* **18 "God will raise up for them a Prophet** like me (Moses) from among their brethren, and God will put His words in His mouth, and **He (this Great Prophet) shall speak to them all that God commands Him to speak.**

19 And it shall be that whoever will not hear My (God's) words, which He (the Great Prophet) speaks in My name, I will require it of him. (In the New Testament, Jesus proclaims that He is this Great Prophet. He states that His authority is from God and that He speaks on God or His Father's behalf: see John 5:45-47; John 12:49,50 and Hebrews 3:3).

20 But the Prophet who presumes to speak a word in My (Jehovah God's) name, which I have not commanded him to speak, or who speaks in the name of other gods, that prophet shall die.'**21** And if you say in your heart, 'How shall we know the word which the Lord has not spoken?'

22 When a prophet speaks in the name of the LORD (Yahweh), if the thing does not happen or come to pass, that is the thing which the LORD (or Jehovah God) has not spoken; the prophet has spoken it presumptuously (or arrogantly); you shall not be afraid of him.

We will now look at Jesus' prophetic messages or teachings, which involve His foretelling about Himself, His Church's commencement, and other future or prophetic events found in the New Testament. Then, we will revisit the Old Testament to hear the prophetic voices from a few of God's true Prophets, who spoke about Jesus, the Messiah's birth, or His arrival to earth through the virgin birth of Mary. Moreover, these prophets proclaimed that God the Father and His Son Jesus will be renowned or celebrated and have true and faithful followers throughout the world; this has already taken place with God's gathering of all people-groups and nations to Himself, which was accomplished through Jesus establishing His Church and yet others who will unite with Jesus as His faithful followers. God the Father and Jesus have influenced the world unlike any mere man! Countless men, women, boys, and girls proclaim Jesus as Lord, with countless becoming martyrs for their unfailing faithfulness to Jesus...Jesus and His Father Jehovah's name is renowned and even greatly revered! People, this simple fact here is Biblical prophecy that has been fulfilled!

Now emphasizing! People of every nation, ethnicity, hue, and language make up the Church – God's kingdom with His faithful followers of Jesus; you can clearly see that this has already occurred historically throughout the world. But this gathering is not yet complete; nevertheless, it will be perfected when Jesus returns at His Second Coming! Now, I prayerfully encourage you to submit to the Word or Spirit of God so that He may begin to change your heart toward Him and anchor you in your faith in Jesus, the very Son of God.

Prophetic Words of Jesus, The Great Prophet – The Son of God

Matthew, Mark, and Luke's gospels were written between A.D. 55 – 65. And John's gospel was written around A.D. 85. Jesus' crucifixion is believed to have occurred between A.D. 30 – 33. Fifty days following Jesus' ascension or return to heaven, the Church was birthed: see Acts Chapter 2. However, according to Acts Chapter 11:26, Jesus' followers were first identified as Christians in the city of Antioch; this occurred between dates A.D. 40 and 50. Behold and be amazed at how the Christian Church has grown and persevered since then, even amongst great persecution and millions being martyred for their faith in Christ! Jesus said, "His Church would be established, and nothing would stop its existence and growth, not even the gates of Hell or Death!" (See Matthew 16:18 and Psalm 118:21-29).

Jesus Speaks:

Luke 24:44 Then He – *Jesus* said to them, "These are the words which I spoke to you while I was still with you, that all things must be fulfilled which were written in the Law of **Moses and the Prophets and the Psalms** concerning Me." (Jesus is acknowledging and affirming that the Old Testament Prophets spoke about His arrival, His mission, and His ministry. Even so, He affirms that He had been sent from heaven by His Father to fulfill Biblical prophecy. As the Great Prophet, whom Jesus claimed He was, nevertheless, even His prophetic Words, or Prophecies, would also have to be put to the test – to be proven as either true or false. Even so, to be able to stand against the winds of time and all evil who would attempt to prevail against Him and halt His teachings, His claims, and His universal Church).

As for references made of God the Father: He is to be understood as *The First Person of the Trinity* or tri-unity of the Triune God – God expressing Himself as Father, as acknowledged by Jesus, who Himself is the only Unique Son of the Father, existing eternally and *The Second Person of the Trinity*. Now abiding within all Believers – those who confess Jesus as Lord and Savior – God's Only Son, who clothed Himself in flesh, we now have God the Spirit abiding or dwelling in our imperfect bodies, and yet sanctified or holy temples, resulting from the regeneration of Believers by God the Holy Spirit – who is *The Third Person of the Trinity.*

Jesus' Parable of the Mustard Seed:

Matthew 13:31,32 He – *Jesus* put forth to them, saying: **31** "The kingdom of heaven is like a mustard seed, which a man took and sowed in his field, **32** which indeed is the **least (or smallest) of all the seeds**; but when it is grown, it is **greater than the herbs and becomes a tree** so that the birds of the air come and nest in its branches."

Regarding the birds: This is a representation of all gentile nations – non-Jewish people who have found shelter and rest in Jesus. As for The Kingdom of Heaven, likened to a seed: This is the very Word of God or Jesus – this *Seed*, taken on flesh, who, therefore, was likened to mere man, and yet God, but in His humility, also needed empowering by the Holy Spirit as does fallen man that we may perform the work or ministry God has assigned to us. No one has performed a greater work or ministry than the Man of God – Jesus! Just look at this One – the God-Man – the *woman's Seed* (see Gen. 3:15 KJV) and His impact and influence upon mankind! What a Mighty and Strong Tree Jesus has become for all who find hope and rest in Him!

Here is something that every Christian should understand: When the Word of God is received into one's hearing and heart. Even though questions and even doubt may certainly arise with new converts of Christ, even so with mature children of God. Nonetheless, rest assured that *The Holy Spirit* has taken up residence in all Born Again Believers... the *Seed* of God or the Holy Spirit Himself has, in fact, been implanted in the hearts of all who have received the Word of God concerning Jesus, the Son of God – the Savior of the world.

This *One Seed* – Jesus Himself, for a short time during His humility, thereby surrendering His power as He dwelt, walked, and worked among humanity, was considered as this least or the smallest *Seed*. However, this *Seed* – Jesus has become a Great Tree that birds of many kinds, and again, a representation of all people, who now find rest upon His branches – Jesus, the very Root and Shoot of King David: see Rev. 22:16; Ezek. 17:23 and Isaiah 11:1. We, as Christians, have found our eternal resting place and comfort in Jesus and the indwelling Holy Spirit. Therefore, we are to be branches or places of comfort, one toward another and, in particular, those lost to this world. This *Seed* – Jesus, was the *Seed* that also had to be planted in the earth – this was none other than His death and burial. But, on that 3rd day, He ascended or sprouted forth from the grave as the root of David, as prophesied by Isaiah: see Isa.11:10 and Rev 5:5.

Jesus, represented by this Mighty and Strong Tree, and also through the expansion of His Church, has become that Great tree He prophesied about over two thousand years ago. As the branches – all Gentiles who have been engrafted into Jesus, how marvelous and grand has this Tree or the Kingdom of God has become! (See Romans Chapter 11:17-24).

Keep this in mind: Jesus came to die for our sins. However, those Jews and others who rejected Jesus, who did not turn their ears to hear

Him and whose hearts were as stone and therefore unable to receive the *Seed of Life,* plotted to kill their Great Prophet and Messianic King, even as the Prophets of Old, declared they would: see Isaiah Chapter 53 and Psalms Chapter 2. And yet, Jesus is alive and well! Even so, He continues to speak to us through His enduring Holy Word, the Bible, and His everlasting Church – and His branches collectively!

The Parable of Leaven:

Matthew 13:33, another parable He – *Jesus* spoke to the people: "The kingdom of heaven is like leaven, which a woman took and hid in three measures of meal till it was all leavened." (Leaven causes rising, spreading, it permeates throughout the bread; it reshapes and affects the bread entirely. Looking into the future, Jesus was proclaiming that the kingdom of heaven, even so, His very Word – they are synonymous; therefore, the people of His kingdom led by His indwelling Word will produce the same effect as leaven as we expand and reshape many belonging to this world. The Word of God – Jesus' teachings, although assaulted, will not cease but rather permeate the world! All nations, both Jew and Gentile Believers, do and will make up this historically expanding Church of the Living God. Jesus' Word, being described as leaven, will and has had a life-changing and eternal effect upon all throughout the world who receive Jesus, who is likened unto leaven into their hearts as their Lord and Savior!

The Parable of the Net:

Matthew 13:47-50 *Jesus is speaking:* "Again, the kingdom of heaven is like a dragnet that was cast into the sea and **gathered some of every kind,** (the sea is a picture of all ethnicities or people dwelling therein. Jesus' Word or the Bible is the dragnet that through the power of the Holy Spirit catches fish, which is likened to people from all nations and languages) **48** which, when it – *their net* was full, they drew to shore, and they sat down and gathered the good into vessels, but threw the bad away. **49** So it will be at the end of the age. The angels will come forth, separate the wicked from among the just, **50** and cast them into the furnace of fire. There will be wailing and gnashing of teeth." (This parable speaks emphatically of God's final judgment, where the good fish or the faithful of God will remain with Him; however, the corrupt fish or the rebellious and wicked fish or people are seen as worthless and therefore discarded.

Matthew 16:15-19 reads: Another time, Jesus questions His disciples and asks them, "But who do you say that I am?" **16** Simon Peter answered and said, "You are **the Christ, the Son of the living God.**" **17** Jesus answered and said to him, "Blessed are you, Simon Bar-Jonah, for flesh and blood has not revealed this to you, but My Father who is in heaven. **18** And I also say to you that you are Peter, and on this rock (or solid truth regarding Peter proclaiming Jesus as the Christ, the Son of God), Jesus, therefore, decrees **I will build My Church, and the gates of Hades shall not prevail against it.**

I could very well stop right here with this lesson. Why? Well, JESUS' CHURCH HAS PREVAILED! Jesus' unfailing prophetic word regarding Him establishing His Church has come to pass! The gates of hell did not and cannot overcome Jesus, His Word, or the establishment of His kingdom in the hearts of mankind! At His Second Coming, Jesus' Church will be formally inaugurated upon the earth!

Continuing with **verse 19** And I will give you the keys of the kingdom of heaven, and whatever you bind on earth will be bound in heaven, and whatever you loose on earth will be loosed in heaven." (This speaks to the authority Jesus gives to the church to self-govern. Regarding Peter's response to Jesus, he had an ear to hear and a heart to receive Yahweh – the Father's Truth spoken by Jesus. But this spiritual Truth was not from Peter's own reasoning; God alone by the Holy Spirit reveals

His Truth to mankind, such ones who have a heart and an ear to hear and receive the Word of God. Even so, God's Truth must take root in our hearts. This planting of the *Seed or Word of God* and the deepening of one's root or faith occurs within many of us progressively as we remain faithful to God and as we study His Word or Truth, which is also described as *"Living Water."*

Matthew 21:42 *Jesus makes the following statement:* "Have you never read in the Scriptures: 'The stone which the builders rejected **Has become the chief cornerstone**. This was the LORD'S doing, And it is marvelous in our eyes:' see Ps. 118:22,23. (This Chief Cornerstone represents Jesus' eternal existence and His firm and unmovable spiritual foundational teaching, upon which His Church has been built and which has endured and will endure forever!

I will now point out a very significant matter: Jesus expressed Himself as God, the very Son of God, accordingly, one with His Father in essence or deity, therefore also eternally existing. "Blasphemy" were the claims against Jesus; this was why, but there also being other reasons the Jewish leaders and other Jews wanted to kill Him. While Jesus proclaimed His Father's message and did His Father's will, He was worshipped by some as God and recognized as the Jew's Messiah. He acknowledged the fact that He was their long-awaited Messianic King and their Chief Corner Stone, which was to be rejected by man. However, His Church – the bringing unto Himself **all people** continues and, as previously stated, will be fully accomplished at His 2nd Parousia. Today's existence of God's universal Church is indeed a Biblical prophecy that has been fulfilled! We indeed stand on this Sure Foundation and Chief Cornerstone – Jesus, upon which the Church is built, with every member or Believer thereby being identified as living stones of God's spiritual building and kingdom: see 1 Peter 2:5.

Matthew 24:14 *Jesus yet again speaks*, " And this gospel of the kingdom **will be preached in all the world as a witness to all the nations,** (the 70 nations identified according to the Bible: see Gen. 10:1-

243

32) and then the end will come. (It's a historical fact that Jesus was crucified. Evidence that He conquered death and rose from the dead is **demonstrated through the existence of His universal Church** that acknowledges Jesus as their risen Savior and the Unique Son of God. As Scripture tells us, over 500 people saw Jesus as having risen from the tomb, as one who was dead in body but now lives forever: see 1 Corinthians 15:6. This was why the Church spread like wildfire; many, in fact, saw their risen Savior and King and consequently witnessed to this fact even at the cost of their very lives. The Church of Jesus has been preached to all nations and continues to be preached to all people... Hence, Biblical prophecy has been fulfilled!

Matthew 26:12,13 *Jesus puts forth this observation* **12** "For in pouring this fragrant oil on My body, she did it for My burial. **13** Assuredly, I say to you, **wherever this gospel is preached in the whole world,** what this woman has done will also be told as a memorial to her." (Again, Jesus proclaims that the Good News about Him will be preached throughout the then-known world and its expansion – the world as we now know it. Furthermore, the act of this woman who anointed His body for burial, additionally her story will also be told...Both prophecies are fulfilled unto this very day).

Mark 11:17a *Jesus remarks,* "My house *or Church or assembly of people who corporately worship together*, will be called a house of prayer for **all nations**...See Isaiah 56:7 and Jeremiah 7:11. (This has been accomplished in the ingathering of the Gentiles through Jesus to His Father's house or kingdom. When we gather together to worship and hear from the Holy Scripture in God's house, there is unceasing prayer offered to God, our Father. And yet again, prophecy has been fulfilled... God is Great and greatly to be praised)!

Mark 13:10: *Here, we hear from Jesus the following,* "The gospel must first be published among **all nations**." (As seen, this prophecy has also been fulfilled.)

Mark 13:31, Matthew 24:35, and Luke 21:33: *In these scriptures, Jesus says the same thing,* "Heaven and earth shall pass away: but **my Word shall not pass away.** (The Church is still here. And so is the Bible – the Word of God. This is worth mentioning; the Bible has been translated into more languages than any other written manuscript).

Luke 20:16 *Jesus declares,* "He – *God the Father,* shall come and destroy these husbandmen (or the rebellious Jews) and shall give the vineyard to others." (This "others" being believing Gentiles of Christ, who now make up the Church and are hence one with God the Father, Son, and Holy Spirit. However, as seen in our study of the Book of Revelation, God is going to restore His chosen people, the believing Jews of Jesus, back to His vineyard or to Himself. Until that time, Christians are responsible for sharing God's Word or working in His vineyard as husbandmen to the lost souls of this world. This has been done and will continue to be done by the Church – we individually until Jesus raptures His Bride).

Luke 21:8 *Jesus states,* "Many will come claiming to be the Christ." (We have seen this throughout the Church age, those who falsely proclaim to be the Christ or God. Here are a few such delusional people of our era: Jim Jones, David Koresh, Marshall Applewhite, and Jose Luis de Jesus Miranda).

Luke 24:47 *Jesus is speaking, He says,* "And that repentance and remission of sin shall be preached in his (Jesus) name among **all nations**, beginning at Jerusalem." (Again, this has been accomplished as seen in The Book of Acts, and yet, the furtherance of the Gospel of Christ will continue to be the work of the Church until she, Christ's Bride is Raptured).

John 3:13,14 *Jesus proclaims,* **13** "And no man hath ascended up to Heaven, but he that came down from Heaven. (This is a reference to Christ Himself – the Unique Son of God and His eternal existence). **14** And as Moses lifted up the serpent in the wilderness, even so, must the son be lifted up. (Additionally this text foretells Jesus' manner of death, He being raised or lifted upon the cross. As a result of Jesus sacrificing Himself upon the cross – being lifted up, mankind has now received spiritual healing and eternal salvation for all who put their hope in Him).

John 3:17 *Jesus declares,* "For God did not send His Son (Jesus Himself) into the world to condemn the world, but to **save the world through Him.** (It has always been God the Father's purpose to bring lost or sinful mankind back to Himself. Those belonging to God's universal Church are numbered amongst the redeemed and Saved of the Lord; we are now restored to our Father as His sons and daughters).

John 4:34 *Jesus explained,* "My food is to do the will of Him who sent Me and to finish His work." (This fulfills the Word of God as provided in Genesis 3:15, that Jesus will defeat Satan and Death and restore His Father's kingdom on earth for a millennium with His Son reigning as King. Even so, Jesus was to make His Father's name great or known globally by sharing His Word as provided to us in the Holy Scripture and accomplishing or completing His Father's mission or work whereby offering salvation to mankind. Regarding prophecies about God the Father's name becoming great...well, it certainly is! The Saved and faithful dead in the Lord rejoices and rejoiced in God the Father, even while the wicked war and rebel against Him...In their rebellion, they bring attention or renown to Yahweh and His Son Jesus. Additional Scripture will also speak to this fact that God's name will become great or renowned; again, prophecy has already been fulfilled regarding this matter. Jehovah God has been and is revered and worshipped by countless individuals throughout the ages).

John 5:19 *So Jesus replied,* "Truly, truly, I tell you, the Son can do nothing by Himself unless He sees the Father doing it. For whatever the Father does, the Son also does." (Jesus is acknowledging that He came from heaven; therefore, He is God. And that His Father's will is that which He came to carry out on earth – which was and is to redeem man from sin and eternal destruction. And to ultimately defeat death and

Satan. Considering the prophetic accuracy and fulfillment of Jesus' words, reason alone dictates one should give Him an audience, if not their full devotion; this is His hope.

John 5:30 *Jesus says*, "I can do nothing by Myself; I judge only as I hear. And My judgment is just because I do not seek My own will, but the will of Him who sent Me." (And the will of the Father is to gather the lost souls of this world back to Himself. Jesus establishing the Church was and is His Father's will).

John 8:28 *Then said Jesus into them*. "When you have lifted up the son of man, then shall you know that I am He, and I do nothing of myself." (Then all that Jesus has said will come to pass. Know this and embrace the fact that Jesus' Prophetic Word has come to pass and will continue going forward. Jesus has proven that He is to be the trusted Son of God and even God Himself who clothed Himself in flesh or took on the form of man: see John 1:1-4; Philippians 2:7 and Hebrews 2:14).

John 10:16 *Jesus states,* "And **other sheep** (the lost Gentile nations) I have, which are not of this fold (this being the Jewish nation) **them also – *the Gentiles* must I bring**, and **they shall hear my voice;** And **there shall be one-fold (the universal Church or Bride of Christ)** and **one Shepherd**" (which is Jesus, the Bridegroom and the **Great Sheperd of His sheep:** see: Isa. 56:6-8; Acts 15:14-17; Romans 9:24-26 and Hebrews 13:20).

John 12:32,33 *Jesus proclaims,* **32** "And I, if I be lifted up from the earth, **will draw all men unto me, 33** this signifying what manner of death Jesus would suffer." (Thereby gathering all people groups and languages to Himself, represented through His Church, or assembly of people. The meaning of the word church is assembly. The gathering of all people was stirred because of Jesus' resurrection from the grave and the indwelling and empowerment by the Holy Spirit within Believers that they may proclaim Jesus and Salvation that comes through one's belief in Him as Lord and Savior).

John 15:26,27 *Jesus expresses the following*: **26** "When the Advocate – *or Holy Spirit* comes, whom I will send to you from the Father—the Spirit of truth who goes out from the Father—he will testify about me. **27** And you also must testify, for you have been with me from the beginning." (The witness of the Apostles and the witness of the early Church; and the Church's continuous witness of Jesus is prophecy being fulfilled. Even so, this is evidence of the Holy Spirit, who indwells all Believers and also enables or empowers Jesus' people to share the saving grace or Good News about Jesus. This ministry or work of God is not from man's contriving or work performed through mankind's efforts, but rather it is an empowering from God the Holy Spirit Himself)!

Acts 1:8 *Jesus announces*, "But you shall receive power after that the Holy Ghost has come upon you, and **you shall be witnesses unto me** both in Jerusalem, and in all Judea, and in Samaria, and the **uttermost part of the earth.**" (God's Word and the witness of the Church has and will continue to prevail. God, the Holy Spirit, will see to this personally until such time that His work for our Church age is complete. When He leaves this earth along with the rapture of the Universal Church, then Jesus will return to bring His judgment and wrath upon the wicked and rebellious ones of the world; neither will the fallen angelic being escape Jesus' wrath and condemnation! Jesus' words are true, enduring, and final! Will you heed His Voice and call for you to 'Come unto Him...' see Matt. 11:2)?

Quick References of Jesus' Prophetic Declarations:

1 JESUSE WILL BUILD HIS CHURCH – HIS ASSEMBLY OF ALL PEOPLE

2 ALL MEN OR ETHNICITIES WILL BE REPRESENTED IN JESUS' CHURCH

3 JESUS' TEACHING WILL GO THROUGHOUT THE EARTH

4   THE LAW AND COMMANDMENTS OF GOD WILL STAND FOREVER

5   JESUS' TEACHINGS – HIS WORDS WILL NOT BE OVERCOME

6   ALTHOUGH REJECTED, JESUS HAS BECOME THE HEAD OR CHIEF CORNERSTONE

7 DEATH, HADES, OR HELL WILL NOT PREVAIL AGAINST JESUS' CHURCH

8   GOD'S KINGDOM IS LIKENED TO A NET THAT GATHERS IN ALL NATIONS

9 THE MUSTARD SEED...BECOMING A GREAT TREE FOR ALL TO FIND REST THEREIN

10 GOD'S CHURCH OR WORD LIKE LEAVEN WILL HAVE A GLOBAL EFFECT

11 THE BIBLE DECLARES: ALL NATIONS WILL COME TO THE KNOWLEDGE AND GRACE OF GOD, WHO IN THE OLD TESTAMENT WAS KNOWN AS THE GOD OF ISRAEL. JESUS HAS REVEALED HIS FATHER TO THE WORLD. TODAY AND THROUGHOUT THE CHURCH AGE, GOD HAS BEEN WORSHIPPED GLOBALLY BY ALL NATIONS AND PEOPLE GROUPS. WE HAVE CLEARLY SEEN THUS FAR THAT BIBLICAL PROPHECY HAS BEEN FULFILLED!

OLD TESTAMENT PROPHECY CONCERNING GOD, THE FATHER, AND GOD THE SON

God Speaking Through His Prophets:

Zephaniah 2:11 – Date written approximately 625 B.C., "The LORD (Jehovah God) will be terrible – *or revered* unto them: for He will famish all the gods of the earth: **And men shall worship him, everyone from his place, even all the isles of the heathens *or gentiles.*"** (The

God of the Old Testament – Israel's God, will forever reign. Jesus' ministry and His message saw to this. Other false gods of old are no more. And today's false gods will soon come to nothing. But the God of the Judea-Christian Bible, He, and His Son Jesus, reigns and will eternally rule).

Genesis 10:5 – Date written approx. 1430 B.C., "By these, was the isles of the Gentiles divided into their lands; everyone after his tongue, after their families, in their nations." At that time in mankind's history, the Jewish nation had not been established by God. Then, in **Gen. chapter 11,** there was the Babylonian rebellion of these unified Gentiles who were under Nimrod's rule, and he was under the Devil's rule; subsequently, all these people were given different languages and were scattered by God throughout the then-known world. Because of their sinfulness and rebellion against God, these once unified people under Nimrod, this being in opposition to their God, and hence under Satan's rule, were, therefore, scattered and divided; they had chosen Satan and, therefore, were no longer in community with their Creator and God. However, God the Father has seen to it, through Jesus, that all nations, tongues or languages, and people groups who were God's lost children, in countless numbers, would be and have been, and will continue to be gathered back to the Father through Jesus. This worldwide regathering to God the Father began in **Acts Chapter 2** when the Holy Spirit descended on earth during the day of Pentecost. **Joel, in chapter 2:28-32,** prophesied about this great day of the outpouring of God the Holy Spirit.

Deuteronomy 32:43 – Date written approx. 1430 B.C., "Rejoice O ye **nations, with his people.** (God has called all people to rejoice with the Jews." (The universal Church is represented by all walks of life. Because of Jesus saving grace, we rejoice. And in the New Jerusalem, the Jewish people will have received Jesus as their King; together, we all will rejoice)!

Psalm 117:1,2 – Date written approx. 1410 – 1450 B.C., "O praise the LORD (Jehovah God or Yahweh) **all ye nations:** praise him **all ye people. 2** For his merciful kindness is great toward us (through Jesus): and the **truth** (or the Word) **of the LORD** *which* **endures forever.** Praise ye the LORD."

Malachi 1:11a, – Date written approx. 420 B.C., "For from the rising of the sun even unto the going down of the same my name **shall be great among the gentiles;"**

Zechariah 2:11a – Date written approx. 480 B.C. "And **many nations shall be joined to the LORD** in that day and **shall be my people:"**

Habakkuk 2:14 – Date written approx. 610 B.C., "For the earth, SHALL be **filled** with the **knowledge** of the glory **of** the **LORD**, as the waters cover the seas."

Hosea 2:23 – Date written approx. 730 B.C. **"**And I will sow her (the Jews) unto me in the earth, and I will have mercy upon her (all nations) that had not obtained mercy, and I will say to them (the Gentiles) which **were not my people, Thou art my people:** and they shall say **thou art my God."**

Ezekiel 36:24 – Date written approx. 580 B.C., "For I will take you (the Jews) from among the heathen and gather you out of **all countries and** bring you to your **own land."** (The Jews or Israel, after over 2000 years of dispersion, was reestablished as a nation on May 14th, 1948).

Ezekiel 38:23 says, **"Thus will I magnify myself**; and **will be known** in the eyes of **many nations,** and they shall know that I am the LORD."

Isaiah 2:2-4 – Date written, approx. 690 B.C., **2** "In the last days, the mountain of the Lord's temple will be established as the highest of the mountains; it will be exalted above the hills, and **all nations** will stream to it. **3** Many people will come and say, "Come, let us go up to the mountain of the Lord, to the temple of the God of Jacob. He will teach us his ways so that we may walk in his paths." The law will go out from Zion, the word of the Lord from Jerusalem. 4 He will judge between the nations." (This was fulfilled in part when Jesus taught and ministered while on the earth. However, at His 2nd Advent, His ministry will be completed and perfected).

Isaiah 55:5 says, "Surely you will **summon nations you know not, and nations you do not know will come running to you,** because of the LORD your God, the Holy One of Israel, for he has endowed you with splendor."

Isaiah 56:8 says, "The Sovereign LORD declares— he who gathers the exiles of Israel: **"I will gather still others to them besides those already gathered."**

Isaiah 65:1 says, "I am sought of them that ask not of me; I am found of them that sought me not: I said behold me behold me, **unto a nation (here the gentiles)** that was not called by my name."

Isaiah 66:8 says, "Who has ever heard of such things? Who has ever seen things like this? Can a country be born in a day, or a nation be brought forth in a moment? Yet no sooner is Zion in labor than she gives birth to her children. (See above, Ezek. 36:24).

Isaiah 66:19 says, "And I will set a sign among them (this Sign was Jesus), and I will send those that escape of them unto the **nations,** to Tarshish, Pul, and Lud, that draw the bow, to Tubal and Javan, to the isles afar off, that **have not heard of my fame, neither have seen my glory;** and they shall declare my glory **among the gentiles.** (The spread of the Good News of Jesus is recorded in the Book of Acts; at that time, the people or nations of the world heard the Good News of Jesus proclaimed, and many believed in Him and trusted Jesus as their Lord and Savior).

Joel 2: 28 – Date written approx. 820 B.C., "And afterward, I will pour out my Spirit on **all people.** Your sons and daughters will prophesy (or proclaim the saving grace of Jesus), your old men will dream dreams, your young men will see visions." (This is the ministry of the Holy Spirit, and His outpouring of Himself that all who would believe in Jesus would bear witness of Him, as He, the Holy Spirit inspires and/or empowers the universal Church – you and I, and all who will come to Christ, to continue the great work or ministry of Jesus to the saving of lost souls throughout the world).

RECAPPING AND CONCLUDING BIBLICAL PROPHETIC SUMMARY

Jesus emphatically acknowledged speaking the Words of God as given to Him by His Father ~ Jehovah, therefore, also making in His claim that He was one with or equal to His Father – hence God Himself. One who spoke as a prophet of God received validation as the words spoken by the prophet came to pass; however, in the case of Jesus, He was and is "The Great Prophet." Yahweh, aka LORD, and Jesus made many prophetic proclamations, of which many have come to pass with other prophecies yet to be fulfilled...But they will! As a result of this brief study, we have seen just a few prophetic statements spoken by the chosen or divinely "Called" prophets of God the Father and God the Son that have been fulfilled. From this evidence presented, we can conclude that God the Father and His Son are worthy of our trust and the hope that can become ours in the triune God – *The Father, The Son, and God The Holy Spirit,* resulting from Jesus' faithful labor of love that was ultimately manifested in His Self-sacrifice while He dwelled with mankind. Now, because of the Holy Spirit's ministry of comfort, teaching, and leading mankind as He indwells us, we can rest in the assurance that the Word of God – Jesus Himself, as being *Trustworthy*, *Sure*, and *Enduring Forever!*

Jesus' Prophecies Have and Will Continue to Come to Pass:

1. Jesus said, "If I be lifted up from the earth, I will draw all men unto me." **John 12:32**

2. Jesus said, "Heaven and earth will pass away, but my words will not pass away." **Matt. 24:35**

3. Jesus said, "The kingdom of heaven being a net that catches all people." **Matt. 13:47-50**

4. Jesus said, "The stone which was rejected has become the Chief Cornerstone." **Ps. 118:22,23**

5. Jesus said, "Many deceivers will claim to be the Christ." **Matt. 24:5**

6. Jesus said, To His apostles, "Follow me, and I will make you fishermen of men." **Matt. 4:19**

7. Jesus said, "Wherever this gospel shall be preached in the whole world, so shall what the woman has done by the anointing Him will be told as a memory of her." **Mark 14:3-9**

8. Jesus said, "The mustard seed, which is the smallest seed, will become a Great tree providing comfort to all people." **Matt. 13:31,32**

9. Jesus said, "The house of God being called a house of prayer for all nations." **Isa. 56:7 and Matt. 21:13**

10. Jesus said, "And the gospel must first be published among all nations." **Matt. 24:14**

11. Jesus said, "That repentance and remission of sin should be preached in his name among all nations beginning at Jerusalem." **Luke 24:26,27**

12. Jesus said, "But you will receive power when the Holy Spirit comes upon you, and ye shall be witnesses unto me both in Jerusalem and in all Judea and Samaria, and to the ends of the earth." **Act 1:8**

13. Lastly, God, through His Son Jesus, both have become renowned and great throughout the earth. For over 2000 years, Their Church and the Word of God, through the power of the Holy Spirit, has prevailed and will continue to stand! **John 17:26 and Malachi 1:11**

Bonus Prophetic Content:

The Jewish people had **Seven Prophetic Feasts** that they celebrated, which also pointed to and were pictures of the life of Jesus. These feasts are Jesus' *set times* and events occurring on the Biblical calendar, which the Jews were governed by and which will ultimately be completed during Christ's millennial reign.

Calendar Order and God's Set or Appointed Times or Feast to be Fulfilled in Jesus

1. Unleavened Bread – Jesus was the Unleavened Bread, the sinless and broken Bread. This festival lasted a week; 1 Cor. 5:6-8...**Prophecy Fulfilled!**

2. The Passover Feast was established the first month of the Jewish calendar – Jesus was the Passover Lamb; 1 Cor. 5:7...**Prophecy Fulfilled!**

3. First Fruits – Jesus was the First Fruits, the first to rise from the grave. He represented the New Harvest; 1 Cor. 15:17-20...**Prophecy Fulfilled!**

4. Pentecost, Harvest, or Feast of Weeks – Jesus' coming, the Holy Spirit's arrival; Acts 2:1; 2:2-4...**Prophecy Fulfilled!**

5. The Feast of Trumpets – Jesus' Second Coming is the blowing of trumpets; 1 Cor. 15:53; 1 Thes. 4:16,17...**To be accomplished at Jesus' 2nd Advent**.

6. Yom Kippur or Day of Atonement – Jesus is the Solemn Assembly; sin is atoned for Israel; Zec. 12:10-13:1...**To be accomplished at Jesus' 2nd Advent**

7. The Feast of Tabernacle – Jesus, the dwelling of God with man and His Second Coming...Fulfilled in part at His 1st Advent. **To be completed or perfected at Jesus' 2nd Advent**

8. The Feast of Dedication, John 10:22, resulting from the Maccabean Revolt...**To be accomplished at Jesus' 2nd Advent**

9. The final feast – The Feast of Purim; Ester, 9:28-30...**To be accomplished at Jesus' 2nd Advent**

As we reach the end of this journey through the book of Revelation and the prophetic fulfillments concerning the Triune God – God the Father, God the Son, and God the Holy Spirit, we are reminded of the unwavering faithfulness and sovereignty of our Lord. The prophecies that have come to pass and those that await fulfillment reassure us of God's perfect plan and His ultimate victory over darkness. Let us hold fast to the promise given in Revelation 22:12-13: "Behold, I am coming soon, bringing my recompense with me, to repay each one for what he has done. I am the Alpha and the Omega, the first and the last, the beginning and the end." With hearts filled with hope and eyes fixed on eternity, may we live in anticipation of His glorious return, steadfast in faith, and ready to proclaim His truth until the very end.